'This timely and provocative book shows
and some of the ways higher education (
developing education for practical pol

– Matthew Flinders FAcSS, FRSA; Chair,
Director, Sir Bernard Crick Centre for the Public Understanding of
Politics, University of Sheffield

'Titus Alexander has a long and distinguished record of promoting the
capabilities of citizens to affect outcomes in the state and in society. This
book helps to explain why citizens who do wish to contribute in this way
in democratic politics need to understand the dynamics of politics, and it
helps us to educate the young in ways that will enable them to do this.'

– Rt Hon Sir Oliver Letwin MP; Minister for Government Policy in the
Cabinet Office, 2010–16; Chancellor of the Duchy of Lancaster 2014–16;
Conservative MP for West Dorset from 1997

'Education and engagement are ... crucial to maintaining and renewing
the democratic fabric of our country. This book contributes to ... these
critical challenges.'

– Rt Hon David Blunkett, Professor of Politics in Practice, University of
Sheffield; Secretary of State for Education, Home Secretary, Secretary of
State for Work and Pensions, 1997–2005; MP for Sheffield Brightside and
Hillsborough, 1987–2015

'There are lots of books about political theory, ideas, policies and
personalities, but this is one of the few which introduces the reader to the
nuts and bolts of political life: a welcome contribution.'

– Rt Hon Vince Cable, Secretary of State for Business, Innovation and
Skills, 2010-15; MP for Twickenham, 1997–2015

'*Practical Politics* is a worthy successor to John Dewey's Democracy and
Education, and comes at a critically important time in our history ... I
would recommend this book to every school board and teacher at every
level of education, as well as to parents, to better and more clearly inspire
young people to take part in the democratic life of our country.'

—Dr Jane Bluestein, Author, The Win-Win Classroom and Creating
Emotionally Safe Schools

'There is some tremendously challenging and useful material here.'

– Professor Hugh Starkey, UCL Institute of Education, London

'This book is a must for those who know politics is far too important to be left to someone else and who want to get involved.'

– Ruth Spellman, Chief Executive, Workers Educational Association

'I'd definitely order copies for the library and recommend to my colleagues that teach both Year 1 British Politics, Politics of Protest and global politics.'

– Dr Joanie Willett, Lecturer in Environmental Politics, Environment and Sustainability Institute, Exeter University

'Every head of department and leader in higher education should read this timely book ... One day all education will include democratic politics. Practical Politics: lessons in power and democracy is a good place to start.'

– Dr Harold Goodwin, Professor of Responsible Tourism, Manchester Metropolitan University

'It is not only a stimulating read full of real-world examples for students of education and politics, it is an invaluable resource for anyone dedicated to strengthening our democracy.'

– Dr. Brenton Prosser, Australian National University

'Titus Alexander shows the diversity of politics in practice, from family relationships to global governance. Education in political skills is as important as business education, which has informed the cooperative movement from the start.'

– Ed Mayo, Secretary General, Co-operatives UK

'This book encourages educators everywhere to think critically about how they can help people learn political skills to act as global citizens and solve problems of poverty, war and unsustainable growth.'

– Professor Katarina Popovic, Secretary General, International Council for Adult Education (ICAE), Serbian Adult Education Society and University of Belgrade in Serbia

'Education in practical politics, as advocated by this book, will give campaigners a solid grounding. There is growing demand for political skills across all sectors, so learning practical politics will improve people's job prospects and go towards meeting the increasing demand for campaigning skills.'

– Jonathan Dearth, Director, The Right Ethos, Recruitment for Communications, Public Affairs, Campaigns, Policy PR, Press & Media | Programme Management

Practical Politics

For Orlando and the millennium generation –
who don't need to repeat our mistakes.

Practical Politics

Lessons in power and democracy
An introduction for students and teachers

Titus Alexander

 is an imprint of

First published in 2016 by the UCL Institute of Education Press, University College London, 20 Bedford Way, London WC1H 0AL

www.ucl-ioe-press.com

British Library Cataloguing in Publication Data:
A catalogue record for this publication is available from the British Library

ISBNs
978-1-85856-784-6 (paperback)
978-1-85856-785-3 (PDF eBook)
978-1-85856-786-0 (ePub eBook)
978-1-85856-787-7 (Kindle eBook)

Typeset by Quadrant Infotech (India) Pvt Ltd
Printed by CPI Group (UK) Ltd, Croydon, CR0 4YY

Contents

Part 1: Politics as a public good
This section asks what is politics, what is it good for and where it happens to show why we need education for practical politics.

Part 2: Lessons in power

This section looks at the way in which power is used, by whom and for what purposes.

Part 3: Learning for democracy

This section provides more detail on how people can learn practical
politics.

Acknowledgements

Above all I would like to thank Oona and Orlando, who have put up with my absence during holidays, evenings and weekends for over a year, as well as my in-laws and wider family without whom it would not have been possible.

I owe a very special thanks to George Efstathiou, who made Democracy Matters possible, created our website and was very generous with his time, skill and wisdom. Thanks also to Gillian Klein, Nicole Edmondson, Charles Searson, Sally Sigmund and the team at Trentham Books / UCL IOE Press who applied their professionalism with patient diligence, as well as the many people in the supply chain from forests and woodpulp to distribution and library shelves. We should never lose sight of the wealth created through networks of people working together across our interdependent world.

I would like to thank Theresa Wisniewski, Betty Kelly and my colleagues at UK Training & Development (UKTD) for being able to do some useful work while writing.

I would also like to thank the thousands of people I have learnt from, by working together on campaigns, in the community, classroom, conferences and offices, as well as the members of Democracy Matters, and the many campaigners I have studied or observed, who helped make this world a better place. This is an immense debt: we in the West take our relative freedoms and security too easily for granted.

Thanks also to BBC Radio 4, *The Guardian, Financial Times, The Telegraph* and other media that invest in journalism and critical analysis to help people like me understand what's happening, as well as Google Search, Wikipedia and people who share their knowledge online rather than hide behind a paywall.

I owe particular thanks to people who gave me frank feedback on early drafts, including Cordelia Bryan, Simon Burall, Diana Coyners, Ian Davies, Jonathan Ellis, John Field, Andrea Fischetti, Matthew Flinders, Harold Goodwin, Ted Harley, Tricia Hartley, David Hopson, Neil Jameson, Steve Kennedy, Brian Lamb, Jason Leman, Marjorie Mayo, David McGibney, Tony Giddens, Jol Miskin, Megan Poyiadzis, Breton Prosser, Matthew Scott, Hugh Stalker, Perry Walker, Joanie Willetts and Tom Woodin: only those who have written a book will know the value of feedback during the long and lonely struggle with words.

I would also like to thank everyone who contributed to the seminar series on education for practical politics, which informed my thinking for this book: Jonathan Dearth, Anita Howarth, Mardi McBrien, Chris Stalker, Director, Phyllis Starkey, Elaine Unterhalter, Sophie Stephens, Emma Taggart, Duncan Green, Jim Coe, Bev Douglas, Harmit Kambo and others who also read sections and are mentioned above.

I am grateful to the authors and publishers who gave permission to use their illustrations, particularly Simon Key for the cover, Pippa Norris for her general model of democratic deficits (Figure 3.1), John Murray for Charles Arnold-Baker's 'Power Petals' (Figure 7.2), John Gaventa and the Institute for Development Studies for the 'Power Cube' image (Figure 7.3), Chris Rose for Figure 11.2, and the originator of the concept for Figure 2.1 'equality does not mean justice', found on Imgur.

I am very conscious of the limitations of this text, but I hope it will inspire others to do better and create learning for democracy, particularly with people who have least power in society. So my biggest thanks is to readers, educators and institutions that have the courage to make education for practical politics accessible to all.

About the author

Titus Alexander

Titus Alexander is founder of Democracy Matters, the UK Alliance for Learning Practical Politics, and a Fellow of the Bernard Crick Centre for Understanding Politics at Sheffield University. He is a community educator, campaign coach and author of *Learning Power* (2007), *Family Learning: Foundation of effective education* (1997), *Citizenship Schools: A practical guide to education for citizenship and personal development* (2001) and *Unravelling Global Apartheid: An overview of world politics* (1996). He has created and facilitated many courses, including Find Your Focus, Inspiring Change, Campaign Strategy and Uniting Humanity, a one-year trainer of trainers programme in education for global citizenship.

He studied Maths, Physics and Intellectual History at Sussex University, and Philosophy of Language at Marburg, Germany. He then worked with grassroots communities in Brighton and London for ten years, and in 1986 was appointed Principal Lecturer in adult education at Islington Institute in the Inner London Education Authority (ILEA). Since then he has worked as Adviser for Community Education for a London borough, a schools inspector, head of education at two charities and freelance speaker, facilitator and campaign coach.

He has founded or worked on a wide range of campaigns. As a founding member of Parenting UK he initiated an influential campaign for family learning and parenting education. As Chair of Westminster United Nations Association, he initiated Charter 99 for Global Democracy to influence the Millennium Summit, which led to the One World Trust's Global Accountability Project.

Foreword

The focus on political education, and the need for it, seem to have an inverse – and perverse – relationship. The more urgent it becomes, the greater the reluctance to promote it. In the United Kingdom it has generally been an eggshells issue. Attempts to revive dull and dated 'civics' in schools have enjoyed only limited success. The last high-profile initiative was taken in 1998 during the early days of the New Labour Government when the new Secretary of State for Education, David Blunkett, asked Professor Bernard Crick to advise him on civic and political education. Crick duly reported, but his proposals tended to get crowded out of the school curriculum by supposedly more relevant subjects that contributed directly to improving skills and employability.

Elsewhere, there have been more sustained attempts. In France, teaching the lessons and values of the Republic (and, more controversially, *laïcité*) have always been key elements of education. In Germany, teaching students the lessons of the Nazi past is regarded as fundamental to the building of post-1945 democracy (with excellent results if Germany's openness to refugees fleeing oppression and hardship can, even in part, be attributed to the success of political education in German schools). In the United States also, democratic education has always been a keystone of the curriculum, not only in high schools but also in higher education. It is no accident that Thomas Jefferson, one of the authors of the Declaration of Independence, was also the founder of the University of Virginia. Authoritarian regimes, of course, take political education very seriously.

A justification for the low-key approach to political education in UK schools, and its effective absence in colleges and universities, may be that in the UK, liberal and democratic values have been so thoroughly internalized, and the institutions through which these values are realized are so solid and well established. In short, as long as politics are 'normal', political education, apart from understanding the nuts and bolts of government, is barely required. However, as Titus Alexander ably explains in this book, politics in the 21st century are very far from 'normal'. The list of disruptive factors is long – the challenge of fundamentalism (and not just of an Islamic variety), shading at its extremes into terror; the alleged 'hollowing out' of traditional political parties (and other established institutions, notably trade unions, although other civil society associations have also been caught in the chill wind); the erosion of older forms of solidarity and rise of new and more febrile identities; the still unresolved crisis of corporate governance exposed so sharply by the banking crisis of 2008 (but also in the collapse of Kid's Company); the challenge of new technologies, social media and cyber-worlds; even the shock waves of the UK's decision to leave the European Union. The need for political education has never been greater.

The strengths of this book are its breadth and its practicality. Alexander shows that politics are about much more than what happens in cabinets, parliaments and elections (even referenda that take existential decisions). He broadens this conventional definition of politics to much wider arenas – from the global, organizations like the IMF and corporations like Apple, to the personal (although some will resist his alignment of some parts of family life with 'politics'). He is right to insist on the broadest possible view because politics are everywhere – in authoritarian as well as democratic states, in hierarchical workplaces (even if the BBC's programme *The Office* had already primed us to recognize as well as ridicule 'office politics'!), as well as in more familiarly 'political' associations and campaigns. His account of politics is very far from the conventional and comforting world of Westminster and Whitehall.

The practicality of this book is equally important. Although hardly an activists' or agitators' cookbook, it offers a toolkit – not just for teaching politics, but for practising them as well. Most of the advice suggested by Alexander is common sense; its novelty lies rather in the wide territory over which it ranges. And he has largely avoided the trap of allowing the practice of politics to be dominated by ideology, the fear that has so often inhibited the development of political education. Not entirely, of course – there are some foundational elements that cannot really be avoided, such as tolerance, law, respect and equality (of persons not, of course, of property). But he recognizes that even when these elements are absent, there are still politics. It is a delicate line to walk. To reduce politics to the working out of 'British values', as proposed by Gordon Brown and his successors as British Prime Minister, in essence the – particular – political culture of the West, will not do. But to throw out values along with ideology also poses risks – both for educators and for citizens. Politics have always been, and always must be, about beliefs and passions. Alexander walks this line with skill and sensitivity.

Peter Scott
Professor of Higher Education Studies
UCL Institute of Education

Preface

This book is written for my son's generation, the billion-plus people born since 2000. If they get the politics right and are lucky, many will see a world of peace and prosperity by the twenty-second century. In the past century hundreds of millions of people were killed, imprisoned or forced to flee their homes as a result of politics. Our legacy of conflict, pollution and other problems could bring even greater suffering in the century ahead. But politics has also increased freedom and prosperity for billions of people. It has enabled nations to gain independence and govern themselves. Politics is not just about big issues. It is also about creating safer streets, better schools, healthcare and a cleaner environment. It is about solving problems and reconciling conflicts of interest at all levels.

My hope is that this book will enable educators to equip people to do politics better so that we can all can share this beautiful planet in peace. Politics is something anyone can learn.

I have been privileged to work with people at the grassroots, bringing about change from the bottom up. I have campaigned on national and global issues, lobbying governments as well as in international agencies. I have also worked in all phases of education, as a parent, adult educator, teacher, schools inspector and education officer in local government, and as a visiting lecturer in higher education. This has taught me a lot about education and practical politics.

My biggest lessons are:

1. Power is very unequal: there are vast gulfs between the refugee, citizen, government official, chief executive and prime minister, but skilful politics can narrow the gaps.

2. Most people don't know how to use what power they have. Many people in powerful positions are not very effective: they create waves, people get drenched, boats bob wildly up and down, but most things stay the same. This creates opportunities for people with relatively little power, if they know how to use it.

3. A few people with very little power can make a big difference, if they have clear aims, focus on what they *can* do and don't give up. Anyone can sail against the wind, if they know how. The world is better as a result.

Most people have more power than they realize, and can achieve more than they imagine, when they know how to use their power well. People can learn how to do politics, just as they can learn how to do business, engineering, sport or drama.

This book provides an introduction to learning and teaching practical politics: why it matters, what politics and power is and how teachers in schools, universities and other settings can help people learn how to do it. It includes examples of practical politics from the very local to global, showing the main skills, strategies and ideas. It also includes ethical guidelines and principles.

Practical politics is not an abstract subject. People can learn how to do it through case studies, practice and work alongside experienced practitioners. The core skills are critical thinking, communicating, organizing, influencing and deciding. It also needs knowledge about the world and the ability to use findings from anthropology, economics, history, management, politics, psychology, sociology, technology and any disciplines relevant to problems that people want to solve.

Every educator can teach practical politics by encouraging students to ask questions: What's really going on here? Who has power? How do they use it? How are decisions made? Who benefits? Who loses? What is the right thing to do? What should be done when and how?

Questions like these can arise in any subject and every education institution. They may be prompted by the news, a novel or film; by the Bible, Quran or other religious texts; or by economics, history, geography and other subjects. They can range from conduct in the classroom, free speech or student fees, to climate change, war and peace. At their heart is the question of democratic citizenship: if people think something is wrong or could be better, how can they learn to do something about it?

Why and how educators can explore questions like these is the subject of this book. It is a big subject, but students and teachers can start anywhere, with small steps, so that one day all citizens can learn how to take part in democratic politics and make a difference.

Practical political education in schools and colleges should not be partisan nor take sides on issues that divide society. Educators have a responsibility to encourage people to see the other's point of view and decide for themselves what is the right thing to do on any issue. But education for practical politics must be guided by core ethical principles of inclusive citizenship, the Universal Declaration of Human Rights (UDHR), pluralism and respect for evidence. Democratic politics is about the responsible use of power by and for the people. This book aims to show why, how and where people can learn to do it.

Learn more: a note for students, teachers and facilitators

Education for practical politics is not yet on the curriculum of many institutions, but students, educators and citizens can put it there. You don't need permission to learn or teach practical politics, at least not in democratic societies. Many countries have public commitments to education for democracy, such as the African Union's *Charter on Popular Participation* (1990), Europe's *Charter on Education for Democratic Citizenship* (2010) and India's National Curriculum Framework (NCF) (2005). Many universities are committed to serving their local communities and wider society, such as America's Campus Compact. These policy documents give educators a framework for education in practical politics, as discussed in Part Three.

Like medicine, law and other vocational subjects, practical politics requires both knowledge and skills. This means studying case studies, learning from practitioners and finding opportunities to practice. Each chapter starts with a case study and ends with suggestions for further reading or practice. The accompanying website and workbook will provide more suggestions and opportunities for students and teachers to share lessons.

The activities and case studies aim to explore the complexity of real-world situations. Education for practical politics is not about winning arguments without evidence nor advocacy for policies regardless of their merits. When you really go into an issue, you may find that your adversary is right, or part of their case is stronger than yours. Campaigners harm their cause by proposing solutions that don't deliver. Understanding an issue and knowing what is to be done about it is more important than winning a misjudged campaign. Sometimes it is better to admit your mistake, learn from it and do better next time.

Where practical politics is not on the curriculum, I encourage students to organize their own learning groups and practise the core skills of organization, leadership, teamwork and collective self-management.

We make the path by walking.

Who is this book for?

This book is for anyone who thinks people should be able to learn how to take part in politics. The main audience is students, teachers and leaders in education and political studies. People engaged in practical politics through civil society organizations, pressure groups, political parties, think tanks and the media will also find it useful.

It is written for an international audience, including students from authoritarian societies where practical politics can be dangerous. I hope they find lessons here they can safely use at home.

Titus Alexander
1 July 2016

Part One

Politics as a public good

1

This section addresses four questions:

1. Why do we need education for practical politics? (Chapter 1)
2. What is politics? (Chapter 2)
3. What is it good for? (Chapter 3)
4. Where does it take place? (Chapter 4)

Chapter 1

Introduction

Why we need education for practical politics

In this chapter you will learn:

- About the problems facing humanity
- About four levels of political activity: governing, challenging, supporting and submitting
- About the abuse of power
- How sharing and spreading power enables problem solving
- The meaning of democracy
- Six reasons why universities should teach practical politics
- Why ideology gets in the way of practical politics

Introduction

Humanity faces immense problems: conflict, crime, corruption, discrimination, disease, poverty, pollution and more. These are likely to get worse as our population grows by about a quarter within 40 years – another China and India. But we *can* learn how to solve problems better. Humanity has a great deal of knowledge about how to solve problems. Our planet has abundant resources, many of them untapped or used wastefully. We do not lack the knowledge or resources to solve the world's problems, just the political ability to use them wisely. Our main challenges are political. Conflicting interests, beliefs and values make it difficult to solve problems.

A hundred years ago H.G. Wells wrote, 'Human history becomes more and more a race between education and catastrophe' (Wells, 1920: 504). The following century was indeed scarred by catastrophe. On balance education is still winning, but only just. Storm clouds of economic crises, climate chaos, mass migration and conflict are looming.

Anyone can learn how to do politics, just as we can all learn to speak a foreign language. Practical politics is useful anywhere there are conflicts of interest or differences in power between people. The visible politics of parties, governments and pressure groups are a tiny fraction of all political activity. Most politics is out of sight, behind closed doors in offices, businesses and organizations everywhere. To take part in politics you need to know who is

2

deciding what, where and how in order to influence what's happening to get the outcome you want.

The internet creates new possibilities for politics and makes global citizenship possible, just as the printing press did at a national level. But cyber citizenship also needs political literacy to be democratic and effective. Violent, anti-democratic groups use the internet to outflank peaceful politics. Corporations use the internet to gather immense quantities of information about people, disrupt economies, avoid tax and change the balance of power between citizens and states. This may be good or bad, but in democracies citizens need to understand and influence what's happening.

Like learning a language, a few words and a positive attitude can go a long way in politics. But you can go much further with practice. It also pays to study the customs, culture and lie of the land. Making friends and allies will open doors and break down barriers. As you learn how to do politics, you will discover those small actions with most impact. You will learn how to make progress against any opposition, like sailors tacking against the wind. You will also discover the exhilaration of making a difference to solve problems you think are important, in your neighbourhood or on a larger scale. With every action you can improve the world, and learn how to do more in future. Good politics is more fun than the most exciting sport, but it's a long game and takes practice.

Many people want to make a difference but waste a lot of effort doing things that don't work, like flies buzzing against a window with an open door nearby. They could achieve more if they took time to learn how to find the right doors.

The scope of practical politics

There is an old saying that a few people make things happen, some people watch what happens and most people don't know what hit them. The ambition of this book is to make it possible for everyone to learn how to see what's coming and, at the very least, not get hit. The ultimate aim is that all citizens learn enough practical politics to make things happen and create a world where no one is hurt as a result of abuse of power. This is not as fanciful as it might seem. After centuries of war, Western Europe has been at peace since 1945 as a result of politics. Science, technology and trade have flourished worldwide as a result of politics. People live decades longer than in 1900 as a result of politics. Absolute poverty has fallen as a result of politics. But politics also creates problems. Political mistakes can make life worse for people or even lead to war. The more people learn how to do democratic politics, the more they can create a better world for everyone.

From my experience political activity can be roughly divided into four levels:

1. **Governing:** the politics of running a state, corporation or organization of any kind, large or small, and the actions of power-holders who make things happen, or stop things from happening.

2. **Challenging:** the politics of people who want to influence power-holders or take power from them; the actions of activists, lobbyists, opposition parties and pressure groups.

3. **Supporting** those in power or their challengers, as followers or employees who take directions from others. They are largely observers, but in representative democracies they decide who governs.

4. **Submitting** to people in power, by those who feel powerless to influence events. This includes most employees and many subjects in every country.

The first level is about exercising power and has the biggest impact on people's lives. **Governing** involves relatively few people who take decisions at the helm of states and organizations. Elites have been taught practical politics since ancient times. More than 4,000 years ago (*c.* 2100 BCE) the *Instructions for King Merikare* told a future king of Egypt how to stay in power: suppress rebels; be skilful in speech 'for it is stronger than fighting'; keep your underlings happy; make your officials great, so that they carry out your laws; protect your borders, and raise taxes (Faulkner, 1973). Confucius, Lao Tzu and Sun Tzu wrote leadership guides used by Chinese rulers for more than 2,000 years. Aristotle taught three future rulers, Alexander the Great, Ptolemy and Cassandra, from 343 BCE. Machiavelli's *The Prince* (1532) showed rulers how to use cunning and duplicity in statecraft.

Today all leading politicians employ advisers to coach them through turbulent political currents. Every corporate chief executive has consultants, lobbyists and public relations staff to help them create a favourable political climate. Most citizens, however, do not have the confidence, knowledge or support to have an effective voice. They do not have teachers, advisers or coaches to help them use their power.

Challenging involves many more people, competing to influence or replace those in power. Campaigning, lobbying and public affairs are well-developed professions, with specialist training and support available to a few.

These two levels of political activity dominate political news and commentary. But most people are engaged in the third and fourth levels, **following** or **submitting** to people with power. In the media they are shown as supporters of people engaged in the first two tiers, or as problems – refugees, rioters or victims. But people with the least power can also learn how to use what power they have to transform their situation. They can benefit most from learning practical politics, but have the least opportunities to do so. This book is above all about increasing opportunities for people who feel powerless to learn how to become influential citizens and exercise power.

Abuse of power

For more than 30 years young women in the United Kingdom told people in authority about sexual abuse by the television celebrity Jimmy Savile, but no one believed them. Savile was given unrestricted access to vulnerable young women in hospitals, schools and television studios, protected by his star status and lawyers. Inquiries by journalists and police were dropped. His behaviour was eventually exposed by a television documentary in 2012, a year after his death. Police investigations then identified 450 victims of alleged abuse by Saville, including children as young as eight (BBC, 2012). An internal BBC inquiry found that many people knew what was happening but were too afraid to speak out, so the abuse continued.

Journalists in America, Ireland, India, Southern Africa and elsewhere have exposed people who abused their power to sexually exploit young people and were protected from investigation. The film *Spotlight* dramatized the exposure of abuse within the Catholic Church in Boston. In case after case people in authority ignored, dismissed and denied appeals for help from people in vulnerable positions.

Each act was a criminal offence, but the scale of abuse, collusion and neglect by those in authority makes it political. It is now being addressed by the criminal justice system and political process, as well as by the agencies that let it happen.

Abuse of power, collusion and cover-up happen at all levels in every society over many issues: illegal land seizures and corruption in China; deaths of black people in police custody; the banking scandals of the past decade; illegal logging across the Amazon and Indonesia; false accounting in Enron, Worldcom and other companies; the Watergate scandal in 1972–4; the use of chemical weapons by Presidents Hussein of Iraq and Assad of Syria: the list is endless. Every day abuse of power takes place at work, in families, schools and neighbourhoods. Practical politics involves bringing abuse of power into the open and stopping it.

Democratic political systems aim to create fair, open and peaceful ways of dealing with problems. For democracy to be effective, several things are necessary. First, citizens need power to make laws that say what is a crime, because for centuries child abuse, domestic violence, slavery and other inhuman acts were not crimes. Second, everyone must be treated equally under the law and have an equal right to redress. Third, citizens must be able to expose wrongdoing without fear. And, finally, institutions must create systems that make wrongdoing less likely to happen again and stop it sooner if it does.

Democratic systems often don't work well. We can all think of times when people have not been treated equally or suffered for whistleblowing. But democratic politics gives citizens the power to continuously improve the system without fear of arbitrary imprisonment or death. Education for practical politics is about learning how to do it better.

> *The abuse of power, collusion and cover-up happen at all levels in every society. Politics is how societies deal with it.*

The use of power

No one is completely powerless and everyone can do something to make a difference. In December 1844 a group of 28 weavers and skilled tradesmen opened a store in Rochdale, England. It offered a meagre selection of butter, sugar, flour, oatmeal and candles, but it meant people like them could buy cheap, good quality produce, and it broke the company store monopoly.

Today they are remembered as the Rochdale Pioneers. Each paid £1 to create £28 of capital to start the venture. They had learned from failures of earlier co-operatives and worked out seven principles:

1. Open membership

2. Democratic control (one person, one vote)

3. Distribution of surplus in proportion to trade

4. Payment of limited interest on capital

5. Political and religious neutrality

6. Cash trading (no credit extended)

7. Promotion of education

Many followed their example. In 1852 the movement got a proper legal framework in the Industrial and Provident Societies Act. They established the Co-operative Wholesale Society in 1863. The movement spread globally through the International Co-operative Alliance, formed in 1895 to 'end the present deplorable warfare between capital and labour and to organize industrial peace, based on co-partnership of the worker … [and] self-governing workshops' (Birchall, 1997).

The enterprise was purely commercial, politically neutral and independent of government. But the Principles made it profoundly political. At the time only 14 per cent of men and no women could vote, most people were badly paid and were sold poor quality goods. The shop pioneered mutual societies, enabling millions of working people to build or buy their own homes and get affordable education, banking and insurance. The Rochdale Principles inspired a worldwide co-operative movement. By 2014 it had almost one billion members and more than 250 million employees in thousands of enterprises with a combined turnover above \$2.6 trillion worldwide (ICA, 2014, 2015). In some countries co-operators have formed parties and run for office.

The foundation of the movement is people organizing to pioneer the kind of society they want, based on equality, democratic control, sharing based on contribution, and education. Today the co-operative movement faces political challenges of self-government, engaging members and raising finance, like most democratic societies. But the pioneering principles continue to inspire.

> *Working people organized themselves to pioneer a society based on co-operation, equality, democratic control and education.*

Many people don't choose to get involved in politics, until something hits them. Sue Williams was 52 when a 38-tonne tanker with faulty brakes rolled down a hill and crushed her to death inside her car in 1992. The courts sentenced the driver to 200 hours community service and fined the owners of the truck £2,300. Sue's daughter Mary was shocked at the low penalty and the lack of support for the victim's relatives.

Mary Williams was a transport journalist with *Commercial Motor* magazine and three years later she formed Brake, a one-woman campaign to improve victim support and prevent road deaths. In 1997 her partner Richard Longworth was killed by an overtaking truck on a rural road.

Twenty years later the Huddersfield-based charity works across the United Kingdom, New Zealand and partner organizations around the world. It has about 35 staff and more than 1,000 volunteers, and is funded by individuals and some of the biggest names in transport. Williams said in 2009, 'Road crashes, and inadequate support of bereaved road crash victims, are among modern society's biggest social ills.' Every year in the region of 1.2 million people are killed on roads and about 50 million injured. It is the leading cause of death among young people aged 10–19. The World Health Organization (WHO) predicted that these figures will increase by 65 per cent by 2024 unless people take action (WHO, 2004, 2013).

Williams took action in response to a personal tragedy. She created an organization, supported others, raised awareness and campaigned for road safety. These are all political actions to influence drivers, governments, professionals, schools and communities. Brake's action-orientated website gives anyone something they can do to understand the issue and support the cause: www.brake.org.uk.

> *Creating an organization, raising awareness and campaigning for road safety are political actions.*

Politics is a necessary skill in any society. If authorities are deaf to child abuse it is because no one was able to make the issue a priority for those in power. If people are killed on the roads due to poor safety standards, political action can improve and enforce them. And if people want to pioneer social initiatives, they need political skills to organize themselves. Some people have the confidence to learn how to do it through experience, but education can help everyone to take part.

Political decisions shape people's life chances, whether they are aware of them or not. If people don't know how to influence decisions that affect them, they will almost certainly lose out to people who do. In authoritarian regimes political ability can be a matter of life or death. In representative democracies people can organize to promote their interests, campaign for or against decisions, have a say in who governs and run for office themselves. But they need to know how. And the reality is that most people do not know what decisions are likely to affect them, who makes them or how to influence them.

Practical political education can help with every level of politics: to govern well, challenge effectively, support wisely and, above all, enable people who feel powerless to develop power to influence events. Good governance is in everyone's interests. Modern societies cannot afford to waste anyone's talents. Those who currently feel powerless and excluded should be able to learn how to have an effective say about issues that concern them, and do something about them. Society will be better as a result.

Sharing power

Increasing the number of people who do politics well will solve more problems facing humanity. However, like upstart companies in a market economy, political action by citizens makes life difficult for established powers. People in the top tier of politics naturally prefer to decide things themselves, in their own interests. It is easier, they enjoy the benefits and they are less likely to be found out if things go wrong. But challenge is as important for public policy as for the economy. It drives innovation and improvement. Political action improves decision-making because it:

- ensures that people's needs and concerns are addressed
- provides early warnings about problems
- generates more solutions to problems
- reduces blunders by challenging authorities to think more deeply about decisions.

For 70 years the white minority in South Africa used its power to protect its interests and exclude the non-white majority from government. After a long political struggle, all adults won equal rights to vote for a government, regardless of colour, in 1994. The white minority lost many of its political privileges, but the country was able to address the needs of the majority better. The last white President, F.W. de Klerk, said, 'We too have been liberated.' De Klerk became a Vice President in a Government of National Unity under its first black president, Nelson Mandela, and a new political era began. Problems remain, but power is spread more widely and more people can take part in tackling those problems.

What is democracy?

Democracy means 'government of the people, by the people, for the people' in Abraham Lincoln's famous phrase, from his Gettysburg address at the end of the American civil war in 1863. What this means in practice is complicated, but its essence is simple: all citizens are equal, they have an equal say in how they are governed and they are governed by their equals. That is not how it is in practice. In the United Kingdom and United States millions of poorer, younger citizens are not even registered to vote. People on low incomes are also less likely to vote than the well-off. Meanwhile the political agenda is largely set by those with the money to fund parties and candidates, so that many poorer people don't see politics as relevant.

Democracy was not a gift from generous rulers to their people. Everywhere it has been a struggle, against kings, tyrants, occupying powers and entrenched elites. People fought for the right to elect and remove governments. Even today basic principles of equal citizenship, the rule of law and civil liberties are not available to more than half of the world's people (Freedom House, 2014). In many countries people who criticize their rulers are imprisoned, tortured or murdered.

For democracy to flourish, every citizen needs to be able to learn political skills, so that they can have some equality of influence. Practical politics is a basic skill in the modern world. But like literacy in the Middle Ages, only a small minority learn how to do it. It should be universal, through schools, colleges, community education and the media, so that everyone knows how the system works and how to influence decisions that affect their lives, as equals to the powerful. Democratic rights and freedoms without the skills and knowledge to use them are like owning a car without being able to drive.

Why teach practical politics at university?

Practical politics is a necessary and difficult subject, but it is not yet widely available in education. It can be learnt through life experience and specialist agencies that provide training in advocacy, campaigning, communications, leadership and lobbying for people in business, government and pressure groups. But ordinary citizens have few opportunities to learn it.

As the pinnacle of education systems, universities influence learning across society. They educate people who will take leadership roles in business, politics and public service. They train teachers for all areas of education. Most journalists and commentators develop their intellectual foundations at university. More than half (58 per cent) of all young adults in OECD countries are expected to enter university-level education (OECD, 2014). In many developing countries a quarter of young people could pursue advanced study in the next ten years (World Bank, 2000). This gives leaders in higher education a special responsibility for the education and welfare of humanity.

There are at least six reasons why students should learn practical politics at university. These range from the pragmatic – to improve job prospects, research impact and problem solving – to social aims of restoring trust in democracy, increasing equality of influence and developing self-confidence of citizens.

1. Increasing employability

The most pragmatic reason for learning practical politics is that a growing number of jobs in business, charities, the media and public service need political skills as well as professional knowledge. The ability to analyse problems and devise solutions is not enough. Organizations want impact by influencing others. Adding political skills to almost any course will increase job prospects for graduates.

Practical politics will also increase graduates' ability to create employment. Whenever people identify a need and mobilize resources to meet it, they create jobs. Co-operatives, road safety and child protection addressed political problems and created jobs in the process. As technology cuts drudgery and jobs in many areas, political action can create new sources of income and employment. Political ability can also help graduates navigate the office politics of institutions they join, to work in teams and take leadership roles to help organizations fulfil their mission.

Civic engagement also improves academic performance of young people (Morgan and Strebb, 2001; Yates and Youniss, 1996), so that a good programme in practical politics will increase people's ability to learn, find work and contribute to society.

2. Improving research impact

A second pragmatic reason is that political skills improve the ability of university departments to influence people who can use their research and increase impact. Funding for academic research increasingly requires universities to demonstrate impact. Most applied sciences have a well-developed pipeline from basic research to application, but even then political wrangles can reduce impact. In the human sciences the gap between research and impact is often greater. Even evidence-based disciplines like medicine have difficulty. Haines and Donald observed that 'reliance on the passive diffusion of information to keep health professionals up to date is doomed to failure in a global environment in which around two million articles on medical issues are published annually' (1998).

Getting research to practitioners and policymakers takes skill, knowledge of the system and persistence in any policy area. Smoking, obesity and climatology are just three examples of controversial subject areas where sophisticated political skills are essential to inform public policy. Universities have a responsibility to do it as well as they possibly can.

3. Social problem solving

A third pragmatic argument is that democratic politics is probably the best way to solve social problems in complex societies. Humanity faces many problems that are getting worse faster than our ability to solve them. Drug-resistant diseases, climate change, soil erosion, terrorism and about 20 critical issues threaten humanity (Rischard, 2002). Professor of geophysics

William McGuire published *A Guide to the End of the World* (2002). Britain's Astronomer Royal, Sir Martin Rees, wrote *Our Final Hour – A Scientist's Warning: How terror, error, and environmental disaster threaten humankind's future in this century – on earth and beyond.* He concluded, 'I think the odds are no better than fifty–fifty that our present civilisation on Earth will survive to the end of the present century' (2003: 8). What happens, he says, depends on the choices we make.

Humanity needs to get smarter at solving problems. Improvements in life expectancy, productivity and many other areas of life since 1900 show what is possible. With education, encouragement and opportunity every person on this planet can make life better for themselves and their neighbours. Humanity has the ability to solve most problems. If we don't know the answer, research and development can find solutions. Lack of knowledge is not the problem.

Politics is often difficult. There are often no easy solutions to entrenched differences. But political ability enables people to make things better faster. In the nineteenth century child labour was widespread in Europe and the United States, with many children working from the age of three. Campaigns led to Factory Acts, which cut working hours to 12 hours a day in 1819, then gradually raised the age from which children could be employed, reduced their hours and introduced universal education. Today millions of children worldwide are still forced to work, but numbers are coming down as a result of political action: approximately 168 million children aged 5–17 worked in 2013, about 78 million fewer than in 2000 (UNICEF, 2013b). Political action has given millions a childhood. Many problems could be reduced or solved if more people have the ability and confidence to tackle them effectively.

4. Restore trust in democracy

Solving problems better can make the political system more effective and help restore trust in democracy. This is not a trivial issue. In most Western democracies trust in politicians has fallen and people feel powerless to influence decisions that affect them. Colin Hay and other political scientists have shown that people feel real power is elsewhere, in unaccountable bureaucracies, corporations or financial markets (Hay, 2007; Galil, 2015; Stoker, 2006). International IDEA, an independent research institute on democracy, identified money as one of the greatest threats to democracy, concluding that 'the greater the influence of money on politics, the less influence the average citizen has.' (IDEA, 2015)

Practical political education can increase the influence of citizens and make politics work for them. Restoring trust is necessary for democratic societies to retain legitimacy with their own citizens in a world where authoritarian politics are gaining appeal.

However, increasing political competence of a minority will only increase the sense that real power is elsewhere if the average citizen does not gain a stronger voice as well.

5. Equality of influence

Democratic politics today is like elite sports, where a few teams have the best facilities and the winner takes all, while active participation plummets. The game on the pitch is decided by men with money who hire top managers, players and coaches from across the world. Spectators pay rising prices while public facilities are run down or sold off. The game is dominated by sponsors and media companies who control its governance and manipulate supporters to make money. Corruption scandals in Fédération Internationale de Football Association (FIFA) are matched by the scandalous lack of playing fields, coaches and opportunities for people in poor areas who want to play but lack opportunities.

When people feel powerless they can resort to authoritarian or anti-democratic solutions, as in Germany's Weimar Republic in 1933 and the rise of far-right parties in Europe today, or the spread of militant Islam in many parts of the world. In this context people need to be able to voice their grievances and find peaceful solutions through the political process.

This is not easy, but to deny people opportunities to learn how the system works and how to exercise power as citizens, is to deny democracy. Without universal practical political education there cannot be democracy.

Unequal opportunities can be changed. Britain's fortunes in the 2012 Olympics improved dramatically following the decision in 1994 by John Major's government to fund training and support for participation in sport through the National Lottery (Jefferys, 2012). Support for the Paralympics created new opportunities for people with disabilities. Political participation can also be nurtured with a combination of investment, inspiration and opportunities.

> *Political skills, like skills in sport, should not just be available to the elite, but every citizen.*

6. Citizen's self-confidence

Finally, good practical political education can raise people's self-confidence, self-worth and ability to get things done. Numerous studies have shown that people who have more control over their lives are more self-confident and have a greater sense of efficacy. This contributes to resilience and the ability to achieve positive outcomes in adverse conditions. (See, for example, Alkire, 2008; Bandura, 1997; Batty and Flint, 2010; Ginwright *et al.*, 2006; Mone *et al.*, 1995; Morgan and Strebb, 2001; Zimmerman *et al.*, 1992, 1999).

These arguments and the evidence are discussed more fully in chapter three.

> **Six reasons for learning practical politics:**
> 1. Increase employment opportunities.
> 2. Improve the impact of research.
> 3. Help solve problems to make the world a better place.
> 4. Restore trust in democracy.
> 5. Make democracy work better for all.
> 6. Raise self-confidence and resilience of citizens.

Academic foundations

The ultimate test of education for practical politics is not in the discourse of political education, but a better society, just as the ultimate test of medicine is better health, the test of business studies is successful enterprises and the test of drama school is better performances. Practical politics is an empirical discipline, which uses findings from many subjects to inform action. Theory and knowledge are useful, but not sufficient. It takes ability, confidence, contacts, knowledge and action to make things happen.

There is very little in this book about political ideologies for three main reasons:

1. Ideology and political labels are often flags of convenience for fear, greed, power lust, vanity, good intentions or principles that do not correspond neatly to a particular ideology. You need to understand the actual aims, allies and beliefs of people involved in any issue. Focusing on ideology rather than specific personalities and power dynamics often blinds people to political possibilities in particular situations.

2. Education for practical politics is about people making up their own mind about issues and learning how to influence decisions that concern them. The ideas, emotions and values that guide people's actions are usually more complex than any pre-conceptions about conservatism, nationalism, neoliberalism, socialism or whateverism. Political philosophies can have less influence on what people do than opportunism, institutional incentives, management doctrines and funding arrangements. It is more productive to start with diagnosis than prognosis.

3. There are many other books about political ideologies.

Beliefs, worldviews, conceptual frames, ideas and ideologies do matter in politics. Changing the way that people and institutions think is one of the most powerful ways of bringing about political change. But you need to start by understanding the actual power dynamics, systems and beliefs of the people involved in the moment, and develop your own ideas based on values and an empirical analysis of what is happening. The ancient Greek concept of *phronesis* (practical wisdom) may be more useful for doing politics than ideology.

Of course this book is informed by values, ideas and assumptions, including pragmatism, pluralism and the intrinsic equality of every person. Equality is an ideological concept, to which every member state of the United Nations (UN) has signed up. In reality no state gives people real political equality, but as an operating ideal 'faith in fundamental human rights, in the dignity and worth of the human person' provides an ethical foundation for education in practical politics that all nations accept under the UN Charter.

This book is also committed to democratic self-government, another ideological concept. Democracy takes many forms, and there is clearly room for improvement everywhere. The term is used very broadly for societies where people elect their government and representatives who make laws without fear for their lives. It is for people themselves to develop a political system for their time, place and priorities, within the framework of human rights.

Above all, this book is inspired by a belief that human beings can learn how to do things better, individually and collectively. It is a messy process, in which chance may matter more than diligence or intelligence. Progress is not inevitable, nor linear. Bad decisions can make life worse for decades or even centuries, which is why political education matters.

I suggest that practical politics is the applied science of the humanities and that institutions are collective theories or hypotheses about society.

In other words, institutions are the way in which societies understand themselves and harness social power to create their future, more powerfully than any ideology, but that's another subject (Alexander, 2016).

This book draws on the work of many authors. It owes a particular debt to the late Bernard Crick, with whom I discussed education for democracy. He always welcomed debate and encouraged my writing, so our conversation continues through this book.

It is impossible to acknowledge every influence, but the ultimate basis of these ideas is not in reading, but experience, informed by practitioner-writers such as Saul Alinsky, Aristotle, Albert Bandura, W.E. Deming, John Dewey, Paulo Freire, J.K. Galbraith, Duncan Green, John McKnight, Geoff Mulgan, Carl Rogers, Chris Rose, Amartya Sen, Peter Senge and many others mentioned in the text.

> *Practical politics is the applied science of the humanities.*

THREE KEYS TO PRACTICAL POLITICS

Any political movement or campaign embraces three key questions:

1. <u>What's happening?</u>

    Do you understand the issue you want to influence? Who has the power? What are the trends and influences?

2. What is the <u>result</u> you want?

3. What <u>action</u> can you take to influence those with power to bring about the result you want?

With imagination, knowledge, luck, contacts, passion and persistence you can succeed.

This book aims to help you apply these questions in any situation.

Chapter 2

What is politics, really?

In this chapter you will learn:

- How community organizing put the living wage on the political agenda
- That politics is about *Who Gets What, When and How?*
- That every organization is a 'unit of rule'
- Families are often fundamental in politics
- Many political battles are about what 'units of rule' should govern people's lives
- Rule-making is central to politics
- Politics is everywhere, but not everything is politics
- Most politics is not democratic
- Corporations are among the world's most powerful units of rule
- The nature of identity politics
- Why politics is the 'master science', above all other subjects
- And the purpose of politics is the common good.

Image inspired by Imgur. Redrawn by EMC.

Figure 2.1: Most countries have signed the Universal Declaration of Human Rights to recognize the dignity and equal rights of all as the 'foundation of freedom, justice and peace in the world'. However, people cannot use them equally without open institutions, education and support to use their freedoms.

Case study: Community organizing

Sir John Bond, chairman of HSBC bank, did not answer letters from the people who cleaned his building, so in 2003 Abdul Durrant attended the bank's annual meeting to confront Bond about cleaners' pay: 'I work in the same office as the board,' he said. 'I don't operate computers. My function is to operate a mop and bucket.' Sir John said he couldn't 'buck the market'. Cleaners' terms and conditions were not his responsibility. Durrant was a member of London Citizens, an alliance of community leaders, faith groups, schools and unions. They used imaginative tactics to spotlight low pay. Eventually Sir John met the cleaners and HSBC paid the living wage. By December 2015 more than 2,000 employers had the campaign's Living Wage Employer Mark, including Chelsea football club, British Gas and Oxford University. The Conservative Chancellor George Osborne used the trade union slogan 'Britain needs a pay rise' to raise the minimum wage from £6.50 an hour to £9 by 2020, calling it a 'living wage'. Although less than the current living wage, it promised a significant pay rise for millions.

London Citizens launched the Living Wage Campaign in 2001, after years of building relationships to create local democratic organizations. It was started by Neil Jameson, who trained people in Saul Alinsky's community organizing methods. The campaign was inspired by the living wage movement in the United States, launched in 1993 by the Baltimoreans United in Leadership Development (BUILD), another Alinsky organization. There are now living wage agreements across the United States (Luce, 2004), Asia (Asia Floor Wage campaign, 2009), New Zealand (2013), South Africa and elsewhere.

London Citizens have won many campaigns, from demands for litter bins to safe havens from gang violence, jobs for local people on construction sites, community land for housing and a 'living rent'. Community organizers start by listening. They ask people what makes them angry to find common themes, around which they organize and challenge people in power. Citizens UK is an alliance of 300 schools, faith communities, unions and voluntary sector organizations in five cities, reaching about half a million people, addressing issues identified by members. Before the general elections in 2010 and 2015 members of Citizens UK wrote their 'People's Manifesto'. It identified eight areas for action, setting out what Citizens UK will do and what they want the government to do. More than 2,000 people took part in an assembly with leaders of the three main parties, challenging them to support their manifesto.

Community organizing is about learning as much as politics. People in local communities learn about themselves, their neighbours, their needs, fears and hopes, as well as about power and influence. It also educates people in powerful positions about the impact of their decisions and their wider responsibilities to others. It inspires local people to believe that change is possible and learn how to take action. Some university departments in the United Kingdom have become members of Citizens UK, offering students opportunities to learn by working with their local community. Their current chair, Kaneez Shaid, first joined Citizens UK through her college.

Politics in practice

The Living Wage campaign is an example of citizens organizing for a political objective, for working people to earn enough to live decently. Citizens UK trains community leaders to influence people in power through creative demonstrations, public assemblies and dialogue. Their political activity involves one-to-one conversations and community meetings to build broad-based organizations that make power-holders address their concerns. Community organizers connect existing associations of local people, most of which are not overtly political, such as churches, mosques, schools and unions. This process echoes politics in the earliest democracies.

The democratic practice of self-governing assemblies can be traced back to late Bronze Age civilizations in Mycenae and the Peloponnese (*c.* 1500 BCE), at least 1,000 years before ancient Athens (Keane, 2009). The word 'politics' derives from the classical Greek πολιτικός (*politikos*), meaning 'affairs of the city' (from *polis*, city), described in Aristotle's treatise on government in 350 BCE. Aristotle called politics the 'master science' because it was how the *polis* decided priorities between everything else.

The American political scientist Harold Lasswell bluntly described politics as *Who Gets What, When, How* (Lasswell, 1936). 'The study of politics is the study of influence and the influential' (295). Historically, 'who got what' was based on power and position. Elites used their power to command the largest share of wealth, as Lasswell observed: 'The influential get the most of what there is to get.' Since his time democratic politics has spread influence and with it wealth. Politics is not simply about sharing out the spoils, but making rules that create more to share, including art, clean water, education, freedom, security and anything else that people value.

> *Politics is about* Who Gets What, When, How.
> *– Harold Lasswell (1936)*

What is a 'unit of rule'?

The British political philosopher Bernard Crick defined politics as 'the activity by which differing interests within a given unit of rule are conciliated' (Crick, 2000: 21). 'Units of rule' are building blocks of political organization, within which decisions are taken about who gets what.

I suggest that a 'unit of rule' includes *any* organization where decisions are made about 'Who Gets What', from household and workplace to global governance. The boards of HSBC and Citizens UK are both political bodies ('polities') that influence people's lives. Employers often have more command over people than governments. Big corporations exercise more power in small countries than any political party, particularly if it is the largest industry and main source of foreign currency.

At a global level there is no single ruling authority, but complex systems of governance that influence *who gets what* in every area of life through trade, tax and communications. The laws of the sea, accounting standards and trade agreements are rules drawn up by reconciling differing interests at international conferences. These rules are applied by many agencies, from global regulators and nation states to voluntary associations and corporate boardrooms. We may not be aware of them, but they regulate our lives in myriad ways. To exclude them from our understanding of politics is to ignore the world's most powerful units of rule.

Most 'units of rule' are not democratic. Even in representative democracies most citizens – the *demos* (people) – have a limited role. Every few years they can elect an assembly (parliament, congress or council) and chief executive (president or mayor) to govern. The chief appoints a board (cabinet or politburo) that directs the work of civil servants, the permanent government. Countries differ in how far elected governments can change civil servants. A few countries have a tradition of town meetings, referenda and direct democracy, but in most countries the majority of decisions are taken by officials with little public involvement. However, the fact that decision-making is not democratic does not mean it is not political. Indeed, most collective decision-making is political and takes place in all kinds of units of rule, including families and firms.

The rule of family politics

Crick argued that politics is about the state, not activities within groups such as the office, families or between states (Crick, 2000: 30). This is to ignore reality. Many of the world's oldest political units were once families. Europe's constitutional monarchies still have a subtle but vital role in their political systems. In many states the 'unit of rule' still revolves around families, whether the kingdoms of Arabia, the dynastic dictatorship of North Korea or political families of the Americas. Political families have shaped politics for generations: think of Gandhi/Nehru (India), Bhutto (Pakistan), Bush, Clinton (US), Lee (Singapore) or Benn, Cecil, Churchill and Johnson (UK). Parliaments are full of prominent political families. In India, 27 families were represented in the Lok Sabha in 2009 (Karri, 2009). Political families are often even more influential in local government.

Families are also polities in their own right. Power dynamics within families directly affect people's life chances, particularly between women and men. In many countries decisions about sending a daughter to school, whom she should marry or whether women can work, earn outside the home or drive a car, are purely political, not personal, matters. Questioning this kind of family politics takes courage, risking banishment, torture or death. Conflicts of interest between men and women can be conciliated within families, but gender issues usually need to be tackled at a wider level.

Politics within aristocratic and wealthy families also has a direct influence on public politics. Wealthy families like Arnault, Bush, Du Pont, Howard, Koch, Mars, Murdoch, Oppenheimer, Porsche, Rothschild, Rupert, Tata or Walton can dominate industries and sway public policy. Family wealth enables them to fund candidates, pressure groups, think tanks, research, charities and other activities to influence policy. Some, like the Murdochs, control media channels. They influence who gets what and how on a scale greater than many governments. The world's 12 million or so super-rich families have a direct line to cash-strapped politicians if they choose to use it, and many do.

The world's most powerful criminal organizations, such as the Camorra, 'Ndrangheta and Triads, are also family based. These ruthless 'units of rule' have their own systems of governance and enforcement, running a shadow political economy of arms, contraband, drugs, people trafficking and racketeering. Occasionally they buy, extort or threaten their way into public politics. Ending their influence is a major issue for democratic politics.

Not everything that happens in families is political, far from it, but some activities in families are profoundly political, and the politics of families can shake the state. Family politics also enter the public domain through campaigns about domestic violence, female genital mutilation and forced marriage or abortion, childcare, women's right to work, equal pay, maternity leave or gay rights.

Families are the largest influence on the political behaviour of their members (Wasby, 1966). Family traditions nurture young people in a conservative, democrat, liberal, republican, socialist or apolitical direction. Political affiliation can be like a family or tribe for some people, who expect familial loyalty in their political battles, or even call each other brother or sister. People make political assumptions based on their own family experiences. Some rebel against authority as a reaction to their family, or expect people in organizations to behave like their family and can't cope when they don't. For these reasons, practical political education may need to make time and space for people to reflect on the influence of their own family background and culture on their political views and abilities.

Families have a profound influence in practical politics, from the power inequalities between family members, particularly men and women, to the rich, royal or ruthless families that wield power in many realms. The UN Year of the Family in 1994 was about 'Building the smallest democracy at the heart of society'. Its logo was a heart sheltered by a roof, symbolizing life, love and the home as a place where 'one finds warmth, caring, security, togetherness, tolerance and acceptance'. UN Assembly President 'Rudy' Insanally of Guyana said, 'If we want better people to make a better world, we should begin where people are made – in the family.'

What are our units of rule?

Practical politics involves many units of rules, nested within each other or pulling in different directions. For most people, most of the time, what matters are units nearest home. Every school, college, church, mosque, community group and work place is a 'unit of rule' where politics takes place, resolving differences and deciding who gets what in its area of responsibility. Some schools give young people opportunities to develop confidence, skills and knowledge to do politics, usually under the name of leadership, teamwork, drama, debating or history. Some people develop their abilities through student societies, community groups or non-profits, and then use these skills within party politics and government. Civil society, self-governing associations and institutions of all kinds are vital for the political development of any country.

Perhaps the oldest continuing 'unit of rule' is the Catholic Church, founded in the first century CE. The Vatican has been recognized as a sovereign state since the Lateran Treaty in 1274. Its global network of parishes, orders and missions, as well as the Pope, still have influence beyond the Church. Other denominations and faiths, both older and newer, also have influence, but none has the reach or assets of the Church.

In much of the world the very existence of a 'unit of rule' cannot be taken for granted. Poland ceased to exist between 1795 and 1918. The Soviet Bloc and Czechoslovakia seemed secure until 1989, then rapidly unravelled. Many conflicts are about the boundaries or existence of a 'unit of rule', such as Russia's boundaries with Ukraine, Georgia and Moldova; the division of Ireland and campaign for Scottish independence in the United Kingdom; over the statehood of Israel and Palestine; or struggles for statehood by Biafrans, Kurds, Kashmiri, Saharawi, Tamils and many others. Battles over the powers of units of rule cast long shadows into modern politics, such as the American civil war (1861–5), partition of India and Pakistan (1948) and Bangladesh from Pakistan (1971–8), or the breakup of the former Yugoslavia (1991–2001).

Politics is also about creating a 'unit of rule', not just resolving conflicts within existing ones. The transformation of ruling royal families into modern states was a complex political process that took centuries in Europe, and still continues. Seven absolute monarchies have barely begun this journey. Significant political struggles to create units of rule include the United Kingdom in 1707, the United States from 1776 to 1779, the Republic of Ireland from 1874 to 1949, the United Nations after 1944 or the North Atlantic Treaty Organization (NATO) and the European Union through a succession of treaties since 1950.

At an international level there has been a rapid growth in units of rule since the 1980s, rising from fewer than a hundred intergovernmental organizations in 1979 to more than 7,000 in 2009 (UIA: *Yearbook of International Organizations*). Multinational agencies and treaties govern many aspects of our lives, from air travel, disease control, medicines and trade to wildlife conservation and zoos. Some of these are run by governments, such as UN agencies, the International Monetary Fund (IMF) and World Trade Organization (WTO), but many are international non-governmental organizations (INGOs). These have grown from 10,000 in 1979 to more than 64,000 in 2009 (UIA). Many non-governmental organizations also run vital areas of global governance, such as the Bank of International Settlements (BIS), the Marine Stewardship Council, the International Chamber of Commerce (ICC) or ICANN, the non-profit organization responsible for internet domain names (Pattberg, 2004). Most societies could not function without these units governing part of our lives. Each of these agencies is a political arena, where important political battles are fought unseen over the rules of trade, travel, finance and war.

Many political conflicts are between local populations and remote units of rule, such as national independence movements or the campaign for Britain to leave the European Union. But some people campaign for new forms of pan-national rule, such as a caliphate uniting the Islamic faith or Ummah, the Baha'i vision for 'unification of the human race in a single social order whose boundaries are those of the planet' (Baha'I, 1985: 2) and the World Federalist Movement. These political struggles have a direct impact on people's lives.

Local government is the political unit closest to citizens, which is often overlooked. It aims to address local needs, reconcile conflicting interests and resolve external pressures within an area. How countries distribute power and resources to the local level varies widely, and has a huge influence on the competence of the state. Many cities today have bigger budgets, more staff and wider responsibilities than most nation states had in 1900, but they often have little power to decide policy or raise revenue. In England control over local services is fragmented between different state agencies, with very weak powers of local co-ordination. Local government is a vital area of practical politics, with huge potential for citizen engagement and democratic renewal, as discussed in chapter ten.

Community organizing is a bottom-up process to create 'units of association' below local government. Together with community associations, development trusts, faith communities, tenants associations, transition towns and other voluntary bodies, they are part of a patchwork of organizations that help citizens develop power in their neighbourhoods. Power struggles and intrigue can be as rife at this level as at any other, so that practical political education and support can make a significant difference at every level.

Rule-making for freedom and responsibility

Making rules is a key task for every 'unit of rule'. Rules create conditions for what people can or cannot do within their area of authority, depending on their power to enforce them. Rule-making is central to politics, whether HSBC's rules governing pay for cleaners, financial regulations that govern the bank or religious rules and family traditions governing whether or not a woman can work.

The rules of every 'unit of rule' interact to create possibilities or close them down, so that practical politics needs to pay attention to the interaction between levels of government. Deregulation of global financial markets made it possible for banks like HSBC to grow and serve millions of customers worldwide, transferring money instantaneously across continents to meet demand. National rules on migration made it possible for Abdul Durrant and his family to settle and work in England, while labour laws influenced his pay and conditions. Rules governing the movement of money, people and goods influence who gets what, how and where.

Making rules does not necessarily mean those rules are obeyed. Illegal trade in drugs, arms, people and other services is worth at least one or 2 per cent of global income. Many clever people are employed to find legal ways round rules of tax, trade and tariffs to boost the incomes of their employers, while governments try to devise the best rules for their nation.

Making and interpreting rules is the everyday business of practical politics. How they are enforced influences what is possible: in some countries it would be difficult or even impossible to start a private enterprise, organize workers or challenge the board of a bank. These actions may be illegal, stifled by bureaucracy, or threatened by thugs. Rules create the freedoms and responsibilities that shape our lives.

Companies as units of rule

When Bill Gates, Steve Jobs or Narayan Murthy started Microsoft, Apple and Infosys respectively, they were not engaged in politics, but politics made it possible for them to start companies. As their business grew, each faced organizational challenges, which required political skills. In 1985 Steve Jobs lost an internal political battle and was ousted from the company he founded, before returning in 1996. Even more important than internal politics, these three companies changed the world. They now run computer operating systems, mobile communications and management information for billions of people. They have a direct impact on people's productivity, working lives and well-being, including their social lives through communication, music, films, apps and games. They connect all regions of the world through supply chains, electronic data streams and markets. They have a huge impact on their places of origin, in Bangalore, Cupertino and Seattle. Their income has made many people very rich. They financed the Gates and Infosys Foundations to provide healthcare, education and development for some of the world's poorest people. They also have conflicts with governments and regulatory authorities, spending millions on lobbying and political donations to promote their interests.

Microsoft, Apple, Infosys and other major companies are units of rule with more influence than most governments. Their top executives have more power than many ministers, particularly in smaller countries. Their standards of employment and production, contracts and conduct affect more people than most government regulations. In many parts of the world, corporations effectively set the rules.

There is a profound relationship between the development of nation states and corporations. Companies like Sweden's Stora, the British East India Company, Hudson Bay Company and banks financed, conquered, populated and sometimes ruled large parts of the world (Robins, 2006; Rothkopf, 2012; Wilks, 2013). Corporations were licensed by European states to trade and take territory. They brought goods, wealth, opportunity and power to their home countries. The dynamic relationship between corporations and states is a central issue in politics. Not to recognize the governance of corporations as units of rule is to overlook our most powerful political arenas.

In *The New Machiavelli*, British businessman and Conservative political operator Alistair McAlpine wrote 'there is a striking similarity between the city states of fifteenth-century Italy and the great corporations' (McAlpine, 2000: xiii). Companies are the main *polis* for their staff, subcontractors, suppliers and other stakeholders. Office politics affect their lives more than politicians. Where and how banks and big businesses invest, employ people or pay taxes have more impact on affairs of state than most party politics. For big businesses and media empires like News Corporation, governments are just one among many actors in their office politics. They need a favourable environment for their business, as well as good relations with other corporate princes and regulators.

Corporate assessments of a country's prospects inform decisions about investment, exports, imports and development that affect ordinary people's lives through pay, local spending and tax receipts. Decisions within finance companies can have a dramatic impact on countries, such as the billion dollar bet against sterling by George Soros's Quantum Fund in September 1992, the 1997 Asian financial crisis after the Thai baht was attacked by speculators or the prolonged global financial crisis since 2007. Rare but dramatic examples of interventions by businesses and foreign governments to override national democracies include the *coups d'état* in Iran in 1953 (de Bellaigue, 2012; Gasiorowski and Byrne, 2004), Guatemala in 1954, and Chile in 1973 (Kornbluh, 1973; Goodman and Gonzalez, 2013). In each case external intervention was a response to internal political decisions, but decisive power was exercised by businesses based on their commercial and political priorities.

Corporations pay more attention than citizens to the internal politics of global institutions like the IMF, World Bank, World Trade Organization and specialist agencies such as CODEX Alimentarius that governs global food standards. These agencies can intervene in national politics more powerfully than local organizations, such as the IMF's Structural Adjustment

Programmes (Konadu-Agyemang, 2001; Abouharb and Cingranelli, 2007), the Investor-State Dispute Settlement (ISDS) procedures in international trade agreements, or measures to control carbon emissions through UN treaties on climate change.

These are just a few examples where national 'units of rule' are subject to global politics by wider 'units of rule', whether state, corporation or international agency. The nature of office politics is explored more fully in chapter six.

Defining politics: Who gets what, when and how

Politics may be hidden, dictatorial, open or democratic, but who gets what, when and how is the result of a political process somewhere. Politics takes place among town hall officials and in cabinets of elected governments, between courtiers of an absolute monarch and in the inner circles of dictators, in corporate boardrooms and gatherings of citizens. Most of it is out of sight. The politics of palaces and corporations are not public; dictators wield power through coercion not consent. But many people in democracies experience their state as bullying and secretive. Most elected governments also do politics behind closed doors and use pressure to get their way. Nevertheless, politics in representative democracies are much more accessible, responsive and safer than in closed political systems. Redress is often easier than people realize. Dissenters do not risk being 'disappeared', imprisoned or killed. People can organize to replace rulers through elections.

Bernard Crick's definition of politics identified three critical points:

- It is the activity of reconciling different interests (deciding who gets what, when and how).
- It is about the exercise of power.
- It concerns 'the welfare and the survival of the whole community'.

Power struggles between different interests mean that some win and others lose. The welfare of the community may rise or fall as a result. Competing interests may not care about the common good or have radically different ideas about what it is, but the outcome always affects the common good. Corrupt rulers use political skill and force to amass fortunes, impoverishing their countries. A benign ruler may pursue well-intentioned policies, aimed at benefiting everyone, which are misguided and bankrupt the country. Good politics means taking decisions that benefit the whole community.

Crick's 'welfare of the whole community', with its notion of a common good, is contentious. It is also unavoidable. Every 'unit of rule' has a purpose or mission, with survival at its core. Its purpose may be narrow ('make money') or as broad and diverse as a nation. Its common good may include a commitment to open competition in which there are winners and losers, as in sport, politics and markets, but they require rules to protect losers from being slaughtered or starved. The politics of an institution, neighbourhood or family envision a common good bigger than sectional interests. Individuals may be better or worse off as a result of internal politics, but the outcome always affects the common good. Most people who do politics are motivated by some idea of a greater good, of the country, party, city, firm or simply their family, even if their motivation is misguided or largely self-interested. Even the belief that 'greed is good' for free markets is based on the idea that self-interest and creative destruction are ultimately better for society (Schumpeter, 1942).

In my view the definition of democratic politics should also include the principle that differences are resolved by peaceful means. *Realpolitick* involves coercion and sometimes violence, but violence is a failure of democratic politics. It is equivalent to corruption, fraud and extortion in commerce. They are illegal, but inescapable when doing business in some countries. Many people still see violence as a legitimate part of politics. States are allowed to use force in certain circumstances. But democratic politics should aim to reduce and eventually eliminate the use of force to resolve differences. This value judgement is discussed later, but it is worth noting that the rise in democratic politics has been accompanied by a fall in political violence, despite the huge rise in global population (Pinker, 2011).

This leads to my working definition of politics as 'the activity by which differing interests are resolved and power is exercised by peaceful means for a common good'. The second part, about peaceful means and a common good, is aspirational, a statement of what democratic politics should be. Crick called this an 'operative ideal' (1982 [1962]: 162).

> *Politics is the activity by which different interests are resolved by peaceful means and power is used for a common good.*

The purpose of politics

For Aristotle the purpose of politics was the good of humanity, the city-state or nation. He said that politics aims at 'the highest of all goods achievable by action' (*Nicomachean Ethics*, 1,094–5). There are widely differing opinions about 'the highest achievable good', but politics is about reaching a working agreement of what it is at a particular time and place.

When advocating education for practical politics, I propose a discipline that is about the peaceful pursuit of a common good. Actual politics involves conflict between competing interests and different visions of the common good, by people motivated by self-interest, who use coercion, dirty tricks and lies to get their way. Learning how to do politics means being able to deal with bad practice without succumbing to it. The 'operative ideal' of a good political system is one where self-interests can be aligned with the common good; where good argument, evidence and organization can create better outcomes; and where everyone feels they belong and can have a fair say, even if they don't always get their way.

Politics is above all a practical activity, about making and carrying out decisions about collective affairs. This includes judgements about: What is the common good? How do we achieve it? What forms of governance serve us best? And how do people learn how to take part? This last question is the central concern of this book.

The nature of politics varies dramatically according to the institutions, time and place where decisions are made, but its existence is inescapable. In a dictatorship most people are excluded from politics, but survival may depend on political skill and connections. Living under dictatorship takes different political skills from life in a democracy, but getting rid of a bullying chief officer can be as difficult as removing a tyrannical ruler. Politics in democratic societies is less dangerous than under dictatorships, but vulnerable or powerless people may see little difference in practice.

The failure of democratic politics can lead to dictatorship, as in the catastrophic collapse of Europe's nascent democracies in the 1930s, the Greek military junta of 1967–74 (Mazower, 1998), Latin America during the 1950s and 1960s or the military coups in Thailand and Egypt in 2014.

We should not underestimate the importance of investing in skills for democracy, so that people are able to solve problems by peaceful means and avert violent, undemocratic alternatives.

What is <u>not</u> politics?

To recognize politics in everything does not mean that everything is politics. Most human activity has a political dimension, but the politics only becomes explicit when an individual or group asserts a cause or interest, or challenges another's interests, to create a conflict that needs to be resolved.

The decision to resolve a conflict by force is politics, but the exercise of force itself is not politics. It is policing, military action, terrorism, bullying or crime, depending on the circumstances. Once an army has a mandate to fight, the military command makes operational decisions and orders troops into battle, which is not politics. However, military leaders may pursue local political deals with the enemy or others in the field of battle to support their operations. They may engage in national politics to get more resources or new weapons systems. They organize parades and displays to get public support. Politics is about policy, judgement and decision-making, while operations are about carrying out policy. However, if you defy orders on grounds of conscience, your action becomes political, even if it is treated as disobedience and a disciplinary matter. Most struggles for national independence and democratic self-government began as disobedience and defiance.

Many conflicts of interest are not political. They may be economic, cultural, personal, professional or social. Whether they become political depends on the circumstances and purpose. For example, companies compete in the market and may knock out the competition, just as Apple, Samsung and others toppled Nokia and Blackberry as market leaders for mobile phones. This is purely economic, but it becomes political if Nokia or Blackberry seeks state aid, tariff barriers or other measures to fight back. Advertising campaigns to promote products or criticize the competition are not political, but calling for a boycott or ban of rival products to protect national interests is political, because it asks people to act on claims for a common interest rather than a commercial or personal preference. This is not an abstract distinction. Many political battles are about economic threats. There are often political choices to be made about which economic decisions should be left to market forces and what constraints or rules should be imposed on commercial decisions.

For example, do you permit goods produced by prison labour or children? What about workers paid a pittance for 12-hour days in conditions that would not be allowed in your own country? Should all goods sold in your economy be produced according to the same minimum working conditions? After all, we expect goods to have the same standards of safety and consumer protection. What about environmental standards of production: Do we permit goods to be imported that pollute water, destroy habitats and poison the air where they are made, in faraway countries? Or should the same environmental standards apply to imports as to goods produced in our own country? What about the use of antibiotics, steroids and genetically modified organisms in food production? Or animal welfare? These are all political decisions about commercial matters. A great deal of politics at an international level is about resolving differences between countries and companies that have different standards.

SLAVERY: BUSINESS OR POLITICS?

For centuries human beings were legitimate spoils of war or commodities to be traded. Slavery was recognized as legal in the code of Hammurabi in 1750 BCE. From the 1700s entrepreneurs transported millions of people from Africa to the Americas, enriching European plantation owners, stockholders and their economies. The trade was politicized by the Religious Society of Friends (Quakers) and evangelicals like William Wilberforce. The campaign to end slavery was clearly political, as was the campaign for the trade to remain as non-political business. Britain made a political decision to use diplomacy and navy warships to stop other countries trading slaves. In the United States the issue of slavery triggered a Civil War (1861–5) between Northern (Union) and Southern (slave-owning Confederate states), a political act. Although slavery may have been seen as 'natural' for millennia, and largely commercial for centuries, its human impact meant that it was a political power relationship from the beginning, and its abolition was a political struggle that continues to this day.

Identity politics and difference

Politics takes place anywhere there are differences of interest and power – in families, offices and sport as well as governance. Although most of what people do is not politics, everything has a political dimension. This becomes visible when people challenge power relationships or interests clash. Thus, second-generation feminists declared the 'personal is political' to highlight unequal relationships between women and men in the home, workplace and party politics (Hanisch, 1969).

Identity politics arise when people define their interests in terms of gender, caste, class, colour, race, religion, sexuality, disability, language, nationality or other category in opposition to other identities. In some Western contexts it is to 'prototypically male, property-owning or labor-selling heads of household' (Calhoun, 1994: 3). Elsewhere the main conflict is between Catholic and Protestant. In the Middle East the conflicting identities are between Shia and Sunni or Arab and Jew. Identity politics are almost always about issues of injustice arising from differences in power.

Interests and power are constantly shifting, often slowly, sometimes suddenly, as a result of changes in technology, economics, behaviour or politics. Tribalism and nationalism are among the oldest forms of identity politics, where people define themselves as a nation, often in response to a perceived threat. The politics of class were clear when income from production was divided between wages or profit (Marx and Engels, 1848), but they become diffused when income is also distributed through tax, pensions, welfare and shorter working hours. In countries where the state redistributes more than 40 per cent of national income, new divisions emerge between workers with secure employment, pensions and welfare rights, and contract workers, immigrants or the invisible workforces overseas.

Practical politics is the art of using or influencing power, whether it is about who does the housework, who gets to live in an area, who decides where to build homes or whose incomes are taxed. Politics takes place wherever there is a contest between different interests. Political labels (black, British, catholic, communist, conservative, feminist, gay, gun owner, liberal, Muslim, white, working class and so on) are one of many ways in which people define their interests and their adversaries to mobilize for their cause. But society is more complex than most political labels. Differences of power and interest between groups can change. Homosexuality was illegal in Britain and seen as a security risk, but in 2013 a Conservative prime minister legalized same-sex marriage and in 2016 the secret service was recognized as the most gay-friendly employer by Stonewall. Effective politics means being alert to shifts in power in order to bring about a desirable outcome.

What matters is how, where and by whom power is used for what purpose. Abuse of power, bullying and tyranny can happen at any level of society, among those who are marginalized and oppressed, and within elites. The key distinctions, described in the introduction, are between submitting or following, challenging and governing. These political activities also happen at all levels. There are self-governing organizations of people who are relatively powerless in society – like BUILD, Citizens UK and many co-operatives – who also challenge those more powerful. Throughout society there are 'units of rule' nesting inside bigger units like Russian dolls, others alongside them, as rivals or allies.

Summary: What is politics?

Politics take place wherever there are different interests, where decisions are made and power is used. Not all decisions are politics: they may be primarily administrative, cultural, economic, military or social. But most decision-making has a political dimension, which may be latent until challenged. Public politics concerns affairs of state. Party politics is the competition for power within and between parties. Office politics takes place within any organization, including political parties, government departments, churches and corporations.

Politics is how different interests are resolved by peaceful means for a common good within or about a 'unit of rule'. A 'unit of rule' is any social entity with a governing structure, such as a firm, voluntary association or family, as well as political structures from parish councils to nation states and global governance. Corporations such as Apple, Microsoft or Shell are more powerful 'units of rule' than many national governments, although they are ultimately governed by rules laid down by states. In democracies the priorities and policies of states are, in theory, decided by the people for the people. Practical political education aims to make this a reality.

Learn more about community organizing

Community organizing has been used across the political spectrum. The former Republican house majority leader Dick Armey and conservative FreedomWorks organization give Alinsky's *Rules for Radicals* to Tea Party leaders and a 14-page *Rules for Patriots* to members (Kibbe, 2013; Williamson, 2012). Talk show host Steve Deace has also published *10 Commandments of Political Warfare*, adapting Alinsky's rules for a conservative revolution (Deace, 2014).

Barack Obama and Hilary Rodham (now Clinton) both trained as Alinsky organizers. Clinton wrote a thesis on it in 1969.

To learn more you can:

1. Train as a community organizer and work with a local organization.

2. Read about community organizing and community action at http://comm-org.wisc.edu/

3. Find training materials and course outlines at http://comm-org.wisc.edu/node/23

Chapter 3

Politics as social problem solving

In this chapter you will learn about:

- Female genital mutilation (FGM) as a political issue
- The power of knowledge and innovation to improve society
- The scale of problems facing humanity
- What is good governance and why it matters
- That social capital can account for about 90 per cent of income
- Three democratic deficits and what to do about them
- How to improve governance

Case study: School students act on female genital mutilation

On 6 February 2014 a group of 17-year-old Bristol schoolgirls of Somali origin launched an online petition to ask the Secretary of State for Education to write to all head teachers about tackling female genital mutilation (FGM). The students had done a two-year project about eradicating FGM with a charity called Integrate Bristol and made a film called *Silent Scream*. Parents and professionals wanted to stop the film being screened because they were worried about the girls' safety, but the school principal Gill Kelly supported their right to show it and to campaign on the issue. *The Guardian* newspaper backed their campaign and within a few weeks their petition had been signed by more than 230,000 people and was supported by UN Secretary General, Ban Ki-moon. The Secretary of State met the young women and agreed to send guidance on FGM to schools. In Atlanta, Georgia, Jaha Dukereh, a young FGM survivor, was inspired to start a petition with Change.org that gained more than 250,000 signatures and support from more than 50 congressmen. Together they helped to get more than $1 million for media campaigns in Africa.

It is estimated that there are 66,000 victims of FGM in the United Kingdom and more than 24,000 girls under the age of 15 at risk. More than 500,000 women in the United States are estimated to be at risk of or have been subjected to the practice (*The Guardian*, 2015). The UN estimates that at least three million girls are at risk of genital mutilation every year (UNICEF, 2013a).

Confronting social problems

Many young people want to do something about issues that concern them, but rarely get support. Fahma Mohamed and her friends were lucky to have a supportive community group and school principal, as well as backing from *The Guardian*, Change.org and 234,375 signatories. As a result they achieved a victory in the wider campaign to protect young women from mutilation.

Concern about FGM was raised at least 100 years ago by the Egyptian Doctors' Society and protestant missionaries in Kenya (UNICEF, 2013a: 10). The issue was ignored and hundreds of millions of women have suffered since. However, campaigners repeatedly raised the issue, building support over decades, and in 2007 the UN launched a major programme to reduce FGM (UNFPA-UNICEF, 2013). In March 2013 the UK government committed £35 million to 'back the African-led movement to break the taboo on FGM' and reduce the practice by 30 per cent in at least ten countries in five years (DfID, 2013). Female genital mutilation continues due to deep cultural and social traditions. Ending it requires determined action in communities where it is practised, with their governments, and by international agencies. Young people can learn from the century-long campaign and maintain political momentum until it is stopped. In the process they will develop confidence and skills to tackle other issues.

Female genital mutilation is one of many problems crying out for action. Child abuse, rape and violence against women occur everywhere. Approximately a third of women worldwide (35 per cent) have experienced sexual violence according to the World Health Organization (WHO, 2013). In Asia more than 100 million girls and women are missing due to abortion or murder at birth (*The Economist*, 2010, 2015; Ebenstein, 2010; Warren, 1985). On the other hand, one estimate suggests that gender equality could increase annual global prosperity by a quarter by 2025, or $28 trillion, compared with business as usual (Woetzel *et al.*, 2015). Effective political action is needed to both reduce harm and unlock benefits for humanity.

The great global transformation

Many problems are well understood, but they are low priorities or their remedies are disputed. Knowledge about the harm caused by FGM was not enough to stop it. Political action alerts societies to what matters to people and which problems to tackle. This is how societies learn and develop.

The ability to learn, discover and invent better ways of doing things makes human beings unique. In genetic terms there is less than two per cent difference between humans and great apes. This tiny genetic difference does not explain the vast difference between them and us. The development of tools, fire, language and social organization enabled humanity to transform the planet. The ability to use knowledge is cumulative, so that measurement, money, writing and other pre-historic inventions are still essential today. But the growth of knowledge is not linear or certain. At different periods societies in Africa, China, the Middle East, India, Europe and the Americas have led the world in solving problems and improving people's lives. Small differences in technology gave some groups advantages over others, leading to conquest, exploitation or genocide (Diamond, 1992, 1997). Throughout history civilizations have been wiped out or marginalized by others, their knowledge lost or diffused. But despite our ever-growing numbers, humanity is becoming better at co-existence, due to politics.

Over the past 150 years humanity has created global institutions ('units of rule') to trade, share knowledge and resolve conflicts. Institutions like the Red Cross and Red Crescent, laws of war, human rights and United Nations, however imperfect, provide political mechanisms across state boundaries.

During the last 35 years humanity has begun a new stage of development, in which globalization and the internet connect people in new ways. It is no longer sensible to speak of separate civilizations (if it ever was), since we are all connected by communications, rules and institutions. Campaigns against FGM and for or against a caliphate, birth control or homosexuality, are some of the many clashes of traditions and values. This is an inevitable part of creating a new global civilization in which many traditions coexist.

There have been many times when traditions have clashed and people created a new political settlement. In 622 CE (or 1 AH) the prophet Muhammad established the 'Constitution of Medina' to end a century of fighting between rival tribes to create peace between Jews, Muslims and other faiths within one community (Ummah), with a shared code of conduct and process for conflict resolution. Western democracies created a new global settlement after centuries of brutal conflicts between Barons and Kings, Catholics and Protestants, slave states and free states, and two world wars. Today's violent conflicts are part of a long struggle to create peaceful means of resolving differences through politics and the rule of law instead of war.

New political settlements can take centuries to establish and may never be accepted by everyone. They also emerge through the actions of many people solving specific problems, and may be defined by a symbolic moment. Often we only see them when looking back, their milestones mythologized, like the Magna Carta, American Independence and birth of the UN.

The premise of this book is that pluralism, diversity and the rule of laws made through due process, accountable to everyone, offer the best means of solving problems facing humanity. This is not to say that existing democratic processes are good enough, far from it, but people can use democracy to make them better.

We are part of a great global transformation, driven by technology and trade more than politics. Internet services like Alibaba, Airbnb, Amazon, eBay, Google, Uber and Zynga spread more rapidly than ever in human history, creating new connections between people and new forms of economic activity. Innovations like smart phones, drones, agile robots, nanotechnology and big data will drive change in unpredictable ways.

As the 'master science', politics has a central role in deciding how this transformation will evolve, whether humanity will flourish, crash or muddle through. Ideologies like capitalism, consumerism, environmentalism, Christian evangelism and Islamic fundamentalism compete to influence how people respond to change. Education in democratic practical politics can equip citizens to steer change in more peaceful, sustainable ways.

Knowledge and action

Knowledge and innovation account for three-quarters of the difference in income per head between countries (Bounfour, 2000; Helpman and Grossman, 1991; Helpman, 2004). Ricardo Hausmann and colleagues studied paths to prosperity in 128 countries. They observe:

> *to make use of it, this knowledge has to be put back together through organizations and markets. Thus, individual specialization begets diversity at the national and global level. Our most prosperous modern societies are wiser, not because their citizens are individually brilliant, but because these societies hold a diversity of knowhow and because they are able to recombine it to create a larger variety of smarter and better products.*
>
> (Hausmann *et al.*, 2014)

Knowledge is growing exponentially, doubling in less than three years (Leydesdorff, 2006), or even every few days, depending on how it is measured (Schmidt and Cohen, 2013). The ability to find and use relevant knowledge is often more important than the ability to create it. Knowledge has little value if it cannot be used. The publicist, promoter, prize-giver and investor make the difference between obscurity and utility. Entrepreneurs, venture capitalists, large corporations, philanthropists and government departments decide what research is developed and applied. Prize-giving committees such as Nobel and Lister as well as bodies such as the US Defence Advanced Research Projects Agency (DARPA), Japan's Ministry of Economy, Trade, and Industry (METI) or NESTA in the United Kingdom, are part of a political process to sift and select innovations for development. This filtering process is also being democratized by peer platforms like Kiva, Kickstarter or Open Review; online feedback mechanisms and search engines. This creates a new global knowledge ecology.

Smart products are pointless if people can't find them, or can't use them because their country's media, distribution networks, financial system and security don't work well. As Hausmann noted, the ability to use knowledge depends on a country's institutions, infrastructure and social networks, which are the result of political decisions.

How much a society invests in eliminating FGM, curing malaria, creating low carbon energy, inventing new weapons systems, producing virtual reality, exploring space, devising new tourist destinations or other projects, are political decisions. Our political system determines the extent to which these decisions are taken by market forces (based on consumer spending power), by state agencies (based on political power), by non-profits or by research bodies (based on a mix of objectives).

Innovation clusters such as Bangalore, Cambridge and Silicon Valley are magnates for ideas and money, rapidly assessing, rejecting or developing new products and processes. Most fail but successes spread fast. Some people predict a new industrial revolution in which super smart robots, expert systems and big data will displace many professional and skilled jobs, making much of humanity redundant (Ford, 2015; Mindell, 2015; Schwab, 2015).

Most innovation clusters are the result of political decisions. Their ability to attract investment, skilled people and entrepreneurs are also the result of politics. The concept of a Fourth Industrial Revolution was promoted by the German government's high-tech strategy to promote research, innovation, training and industrial development (Platform Industrie 4.0).

The ability to create better institutions is therefore as important as the ability to make better products, because institutions help societies use innovation better. The people of Somalia have the abilities to solve their problems no less than the people of China, Germany or Malaysia. The question is whether their social and political systems enable them to do so.

Knowledge also creates problems

We cannot assume that greater knowledge and culture will create a better society. A century ago Germany was one of the most 'advanced' societies in the world, with a highly educated population, democratic institutions, sophisticated culture and leading research centres. Yet within a decade Germany established a totalitarian political system and factories for mass murder. The German state used knowledge for terrible ends.

Knowledge of any kind can have negative consequences. The motor car gives freedom of movement, but has killed more than 60 million in road accidents (McCandless, 2013). Coal and oil create cheap energy, but also dangerous climate change. Professor Sir Martin Rees has calculated that 'human-induced pressures on the global environment' mean 'humanity is more at risk than at any earlier phase in its history' (2003). A former vice president of the World Bank described 20 critical global issues that were getting worse faster than our ability to solve them (Rischard, 2002). Ten years later most are still getting worse. Many problems are unintended consequences of our knowledge and technical abilities, but there are no shortages of warnings about what is wrong, nor advice on what needs to be done. The real challenge is whether we have the political ability to act on them in time.

For every big issue there are hundreds of local conflicts over community safety, corruption, disabled access, housing, planning, transport and other problems. Some are picked up through complaints mechanisms and political representation, but many are not heard. Local issues often reveal systemic problems. Adulterated milk in China in 2008 poisoned hundreds of thousands of people, killing several children. It raised issues about food safety and corruption, leading to improvements in inspection and production methods, as well as punishment of the perpetrators. The neglect of patients at North Staffordshire Hospital in the United Kingdom put the spotlight on shortcomings in many other hospitals. Groundwater pollution at Hinkley, California, portrayed by Julia Roberts in the film *Erin Brockovitch,* addressed corporate behaviour and environmental safety.

It is easy to be overwhelmed by the scale of problems, but they should be a spur to creating more and better ways of helping people learn how to solve them.

Social problems are political

Many problems can be tackled by self-help, charity or private enterprise, but the choice is always political. Slavery could have been made more bearable by charity and benign slave owners, but only political action could end it. Smallpox could be treated by people with access to markets in medicine, but only concerted political action could eradicate it. Nature reserves have been created by wealthy philanthropists, but only political action and the law can permanently protect nature. FGM may decline as a cultural tradition but only political action can stop it.

Whether you decide to tackle a problem by self-help, charity, private enterprise or government action depends on what is most effective in the circumstances. There are times when the state is the least effective institution to solve a problem, and others where it is the best. But whether you believe that the state should be large or small, a well-functioning state and the rule of law are central to any effective political system.

Governance as political problem solving

The way in which societies deal with problems is a question of governance. This is wider than the state and public politics. It refers to 'all processes of governing, whether undertaken by a government, market or network, whether over a family, tribe, formal or informal organization or territory and whether through laws, norms, power or language' (Bevir, 2013). But the state, particularly central government, has overall responsibility for governance within a nation and, jointly with other states, for global governance.

Different systems of governance create big differences in outcomes. The contrast between North and South Korea, or East and West Germany before 1989, are extreme examples of the difference politics makes. Wide variations in child mortality, murder rates, employment, traffic accidents and other aspects of life reflect political decisions over centuries, sometimes outside the control of countries themselves.

Governance is the 'top tier' of political activity, where people have power to make decisions. It takes place at all levels, from global to local, within companies, public services and non-profits. The most fundamental political decisions of any society are about the distribution of problems and power between different kinds of institution – state, markets, non-profit (third sector) or personal (family sector). Domestic violence, FGM and many personal issues were traditionally handled within the family sphere, but as a result of political action they are now dealt with by international agencies, governments, local schools, hospitals and police. In Soviet societies almost all economic and cultural matters were dealt with by state agencies, while the United States leaves these to businesses, families and non-profits. The balances between them are political choices.

'Good governance' enables people to solve problems, through effective institutions. Every institution is a way of processing information to deal with different problems. Systems of governance are like computer operating systems that enable 'applications' such as families, farms, firms, public services, voluntary associations, organized crime and other institutions to function (or not, as the case may be). The operating system is the collective product of rulers, officials and the public interacting to solve problems. It is not quite open source, but nor is it a proprietary regime. In most societies the state and non-profit sector have grown to deal with failures in other sectors. Since the 1980s many states have contracted private companies to provide public services. In every case the decision about where and how problems are dealt with is political.

Many problems mentioned in this chapter could be solved by more inclusive governance. In *Why Nations Fail* Professors Acemoglu and Robinson (2012) showed that inclusive institutions create 'virtuous circles of innovation, economic expansion and more widely-held wealth'. Institutions that enable people to choose and remove their political leaders create different economic incentives and services from undemocratic regimes. Low levels of accountability result in greater corruption, incompetence and inefficiency. These institutional differences are the main reason why economic prosperity differs between countries. Officials in authoritarian regimes with rapid economic growth, like China, gauge public opinion in order to deal with grievances without reducing the power of the ruling group. But China also has accumulating problems of corruption, environmental degradation and conflict with local authorities. Professor Antonio Fatás and Ilian Mihov describe the structural reforms needed to overcome institutional problems as a 'Great Wall' that authoritarian regimes struggle to break through. They argue that this lack of institutional capacity prevents them achieving greater prosperity (Fatás and Mihov, 2009a, 2009b).

Research by Elhanan Helpman and others showed the importance of institutions such as property rights, legal systems, customs and political systems, for economic growth (Helpman, 2004, 2008). In *The Mystery of Capital* (2003) Peruvian economist Hernando de Soto contrasted the intricate network of laws that enables people in the West to unlock productive potential with the legal quagmire that prevents poor people in developing countries from making the most of their assets.

Herbert Simon, a Nobel-prize winning economist, observed that the differences between average incomes in rich nations and the Third World:

> *are not simply a matter of acres of land or tons of coal or iron ore, but, more important, differences in social capital that takes primarily the form of stored knowledge (e.g. technology, and especially organizational and governmental skills) ... When we compare the poorest with the richest nations, it is hard to conclude that social capital can produce less than about 90 per cent of income in wealthy societies.*
>
> (Simon, 2000; see also Van Parijs, 2000)

In other words, people in the West are more productive and earn more because they have the social, political, legal and other institutions that make it possible. These institutions are the product of centuries of political struggles between competing interests. The ancient civilizations of Egypt, Greece, Rome, China and the Middle East show that political struggles, stagnation and poor governance can also finish them.

The governance of many countries, including the poorest, enables small minorities to syphon off enormous wealth while preventing the majority from flourishing. In *The March of Folly: From Troy to Vietnam,* Barbara Tuchman described how governments through the ages have pursued a 'policy contrary to the self-interest of the constituency or state involved' (Tuchman, 1997: 3). Folly, in her view, was the result of self-deception and 'assessing a situation in terms of preconceived fixed notions while ignoring or rejecting any contrary signs' (Tuchman, 1997: 6).

Democratic systems are more open to challenge, but this has not prevented governments from folly. In Britain the cross-party Public Administration Select Committee (2012) highlighted 'failures of strategic leadership' by government that have led to:

> *mistakes which are becoming evident in such areas as the Strategic Defence and Security Review (carrier policy), airport policy, energy (electricity generation, nuclear new-build programme and renewables) and climate change, and child poverty targets (which may not be achieved), welfare spending and economic policy (lower economic growth than forecast).*

In a controversial study of *The Blunders of our Governments* (2013), Professors Anthony King and Ivor Crewe catalogued gross mistakes that have wasted billions of taxpayers' money. Sir David Normington, a senior civil servant who 'watched many of these blunders unfold' and was directly involved in two of them, admitted that 'this book is not just a chance for people like me to have a painful walk down memory lane. It is very much a text for today with lessons for all politicians and civil servants. It is a "must read" for anyone coming new to Government' (Normington, 2014). At a larger level the catastrophic failure of the global banking system in 2008 cost governments more than a trillion dollars and British citizens more than 15 per cent in lost output. Recent wars in Iraq, Afghanistan and Pakistan cost the United States alone more than four trillion dollars (CBO, 2007; Stiglitz and Bilmes, 2008) and more than 350,000 lives, not counting indirect deaths (Crawford *et al.*, 2015). Failures on this scale show that representative democracies also need to improve their systems of governance to deal with social problems better.

Problems with democracy

Many citizens in countries with a long tradition of democratic institutions do not feel that the system works for them. Voter turnout in parliamentary elections across the world has fallen below 70 per cent in many countries including the United Kingdom (66 per cent), United States (68 per cent) France (55 per cent), India (66 per cent), Mexico (62 per cent) and Poland (49 per cent) (IDEA, 2015). In Britain the Hansard Society Audit of Political Engagement (2013) showed that satisfaction with the system of governing was less than a third (27 per cent), although almost half (42 per cent) said they were interested in politics. A more recent survey showed that 77 per cent were dissatisfied with British democracy, with little variation across the United Kingdom (Eichhorn *et al.*, 2015). In the United States a national survey reported that more than two-thirds (64 per cent) thought members of Congress did not listen to and care about what people like me think, and cited the two main influences on members of Congress as personal self-interest (40 per cent) and special interests (37 per cent). However, 73 per cent agreed that the work of Congress has 'some' or 'a great deal' of impact on their life (Center on Congress, 2015).

There is a lot of research evidence about people's disenchantment with politics, why we should be concerned and what could be done about it, such as *Why Politics Matters: Making democracy work* (Stoker, 2006), *Why We Hate Politics* (Hay, 2007), *Democratic Deficit* (Norris, 2011) *Political Trust and Disenchantment with Politics* (Galil, 2015). Professor Norris analysed factors contributing to political disenchantment to suggest a general model, summarized in figure 3.1. She identified three democratic deficits:

1. **demand side,** which is the main focus of practical political education, and also an issue for political parties, civil society and anyone concerned about good governance

2. **intermediate,** as a result of negative media coverage, which provides highly distorted and misleading forms of political education

3. **supply side,** due to government failures to deliver and the lack of governance abilities, which concerns both the institutions of governance and practical political education of governing.

This creates a gulf between what people want and what they see their government doing. She concludes that *'the democratic deficit has important consequences – including for political activism, for allegiant forms of political behaviour and the rule of law, and ultimately for processes of democratization'* (Norris, 2011: 6, 8, italics in original).

Figure 3.1: Norris's general model of democratic deficits

Declining trust and political participation puts democratic systems at a risk, particularly where people turn to authoritarian, anti-democratic solutions. The Freedom House Index found an overall drop in democratic freedoms for the ninth consecutive year, with increased state surveillance, restrictions on internet communications, curbs on personal autonomy and more aggressive tactics by authoritarian regimes (Freedom House, 2015).

Citizens who are ignored, excluded or disaffected express themselves in ways that affect the whole of society. Exclusive politics, as in apartheid South Africa, Northern Ireland before the 1998 peace process or Israel-Palestine and Syria today, has global consequences. British politics was shaken by inner-city riots in 1981, poll tax riots in 1990 and fuel protests in 2000. Recurrent demonstrations in response to heavy-handed policing towards African Americans in the United States raise questions about the country's ability to create inclusive governance. However, most disaffection is expressed in subtle ways, such as anti-social behaviour, non-co-operation with authorities, non-payment of tax or even self-harm.

Political systems are often slow to respond to disaffection, first ignoring it, and then dismissing it and responding only when threatened at the ballot box or on the streets. Creating more responsive, inclusive systems of governance at all levels is therefore necessary to deal with the rapid growth of knowledge and innovation shaping global society today.

Tackling these three democratic deficits requires political action at a local, institutional and national level. It also requires practical political education to help people take part in politics (demand side) and govern (supply side). As an exercise to develop political skills, I suggest that students should not only study democratic deficits, but develop projects to address them, as proposed by Professor Gerry Stoker. He suggested that political scientists should experiment with 'political science design solutions' to 'deliver the core purposes of engaging citizens, resolving conflicts and responding to the challenges of our interdependent world' (Stoker, 2010). In other words, experiments in practical politics to improve the democratic system.

Improving governance

Campaigns by the Bristol schoolgirls, Citizen UK, Brake and victims of sexual abuse are calls for better governance, by institutions such as the BBC, schools, road safety bodies, employers and the state. People want 'units of rule' to be run well and solve problems better. This is the supply side of politics, what I call the top tier of political action, involving leaders and decision-makers at any level. Improving governance and the ability of political decision-making to respond better to citizens will also encourage people to take part, the demand side of politics, because better governance creates hope that they can make a difference.

LEARN MORE ABOUT THE POLITICS OF GOOD GOVERNANCE

Improving the ability of government to solve problems is one of the most challenging areas of practical politics. The following activities can develop insights into the issues:

- Attend open lectures at institutes and schools of government near you or online.
- Get experience of local or national government, by getting a job, placement, internship or work shadowing.
- Get involved in the Open Government Partnership between civil society and governments to increase transparency, accountability and citizen engagement (www.opengovpartnership.org/about/get-involved).

Read:

- Geoff Mulgan on *The Art of Public Strategy: Mobilizing power and knowledge for the public good* (2009)
- David Osborne and Ted Gaebler on *Reinventing Government: How the entrepreneurial spirit is transforming the public sector* (1993)

Learn about systems thinking:

- Donella Meadows, *Thinking in Systems: A primer* (2009)
- John Seddon, *Systems Thinking in the Public Sector* (2008)
- Peter Scholtes, *The Leader's Handbook* (1998); start with the 'Onion Patch Strategy' on p.390

Chapter 4

Political arenas

Where politics happens

In this chapter you will learn about:

- The origin, politics and power of national income accounts
- Six different types of political arena, including:
  - Realms 'above politics' that govern the system (and how to influence them)
  - The central role of party politics for government
  - The politics of elections, parliaments and governing
  - Why the politics of association and relationships matter
  - The practice of revolutionary politics
  - Cyber politics as a new sphere of political action

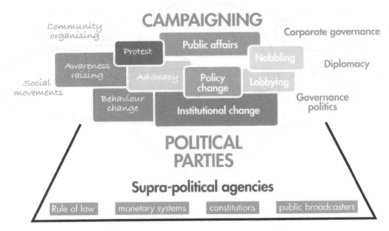

Figure 4.1: Alexander's political mosaic: advocacy, campaigning and practical politics

Case study: Gross deceptive product

After the Wall Street crash in October 1929, at the start of America's Great Depression, the US Department of Commerce asked Simon Kuznets to develop the first national economic accounts. From 1942 President Roosevelt used the annual estimates of national income, called gross national product (GNP), to manage the economy, plan for World War II and fund the Marshall Plan to rebuild Europe and Japan after the war. In their influential economics textbook, Paul Samuelson and William Nordhaus wrote that national income accounts and GDP (gross domestic product) 'are truly among the great inventions of the twentieth century'. (GNP and GDP are related measures of national income.)

Measurement of GDP involves many assumptions and estimates of market values for non-traded goods such as public services, DIY home maintenance and housework. Since the economy is constantly changing, charts of GDP growth over time do not represent the same thing. Alan Greenspan, chairman of the US Federal Reserve bank, pointed out that, as a 'measure of market value of goods and services, it is not necessarily a measure of welfare or even a significant measure of standards of living'. For example, southern states 'use a huge amount of air conditioning in the summer and that appears as output in the GDP. The wonderful breezes you get up in northern Vermont during the summer, which eliminates the requirement for air conditioning, doesn't show up in the GDP.' So 'GDP will be less in Vermont than it will be in the South'. Similarly, a homemaker produces 'goods that are not included in the GDP. But if you go out and you hire somebody to do it, obviously it's a market transaction and the value of the GDP goes up. It's hard to say that there's been a significant change in standards of living' (BEA, 1999). It's as if a tonne of weeds equals a tonne of wheat.

The politics of GDP

GDP was developed to tackle political problems of economic depression and war. It helped politicians justify spending on World War II, post-war reconstruction and other projects. It became a powerful economic indicator for every country through the internationally agreed System of National Accounts (1993). These are produced by representatives of the IMF, European Union, Organization for Economic Co-operation and Development, United Nations and World Bank (referred to as SNA93). Changes in GDP are reported monthly and inform decisions on interest rates, foreign exchange, public spending and economic policy, all of which affect people's lives.

Marilyn Waring, a New Zealand feminist, Member of Parliament from 1975–84 and chair of its Public Expenditure Committee, questioned its influence. In *If Women Counted* she showed that GDP ignored women's unpaid work and omitted up to half the productive activity of many countries, with wide-ranging consequences for policy (1989).

The biggest criticisms of GDP are that it counts everything as 'growth', including car crashes, oil spills and white elephants; it takes no account of depreciation in capital stock, infrastructure and natural resources; nor potential liabilities, such as pensions, pollution risks such as asbestos and nuclear waste; nor intangible assets such as knowledge, reputation, love and beauty. Its inventor Kutznets said, 'Distinctions must be kept in mind between quantity and quality of growth, between costs and returns, and between the short and long run. Goals for more growth should specify more growth of what and for what' (Kuznets, 1962). Free market economist Frank Shostak wrote:

> *the GDP framework is an empty abstraction devoid of any link to the real world. [But it] is in big demand by governments and central bank officials since it provides justification for their interference with businesses. It also provides an illusory frame of reference to assess the performance of government officials.*
>
> (Shostak, 2001; see also Shostak, 2014)

Many alternative indicators have been developed, including UN Human Development Indicators (since 1990), the Organization for Economic Co-operation and Development (OECD) *OECD Better Life Index* (2011) *oecdbetterlifeindex.org*, and the UN World Happiness Report (2011). China produced a 'green GDP index' in 2006. The US government's State of the USA project aims to create a 'key national indicator system'. In 2008 French President Nicholas Sarkozy commissioned leading economists to devise an alternative to GDP, on the grounds, 'We will not change our behaviour unless we change the ways we measure our economic performance' (Stiglitz *et al.*, 2010: vii). Their report, *Mis-measuring Our Lives*, showed how 'metrics shape our beliefs and inferences'. They proposed a dashboard of measures including well-being and sustainable development. However, the 21-member commission had only one woman (Professor Bina Agarwal) and showed little recognition of women's economic contribution.

None of these initiatives had the political status or impact of GDP, which continues to guide government policies worldwide. Why it continues is hard to say. Politicians don't have easy measures of performance, so perhaps its longevity is 'profit envy', an equivalent to the corporate bottom line. Perhaps it is a useful diversion from volatile and politically difficult figures such as tax revenues, budget deficits, balance of payments, changes in personal income or mental health, which are more relevant indicators of economic management. GDP has symbolic value for governments, who can point to rising growth as proof that things are getting better or use it to justify changes to economic policy, public spending or taxes when things are going badly. But as Stiglitz *et al.* say in *Mis-measuring Our Lives*, 'If we have the wrong metrics, we will strive for the wrong things. In the quest to increase GDP, we may end up with a society in which citizens are worse off' (xvii). And in their note to president Sarkozy they say, 'One of the reasons that most people may perceive themselves as being worse off even although average GDP is increasing is *because they are indeed worse off*' (xi).

GDP is an enduring example of the power of an idea to govern people's lives, even after it has outlived its utility.

Political arenas

Gross domestic product is 'above politics' in the sense that it is rarely questioned in public politics yet informs countless political decisions. GDP is one of many domains above the politics of parties, press and pressure groups, such as the civil service, military, monarchy, money supply, rule of law, secret services, universities and global governance. They are part of the deep constitution, which govern the ground rules and system conditions for everyday politics, business and personal life. In democratic states these domains are ultimately accountable to citizens through elected assemblies, but some provide checks against abuse of power by elected governments. Their actions are governed by rules that may have been laid down by a constitution, parliament, international agreement or pre-democratic times. Lifting certain matters above the political fray is meant to ensure that they are dealt with impartially, in the public interest, but sometimes they simply protect private privileges.

Politics can be described as taking place in at least seven distinct arenas, each of which has different rules:

- **Supra-politics**, such as the rule of law, civil service, GDP and transnational institutions that govern society from day to day, like automatic processes to secure the essential framework of society.
- **Public politics**, including political parties, elections and pressure groups where most visible politics takes place in representative democracies, at a local, state and national or continental level.
- **Institutional or office politics**, which take place in every organization and may be the biggest arena of all.

- **Markets** and the political economy can be the most powerful and dynamic arena of all, providing most goods and services and deciding who gets what and how independently of public politics.
- **Politics of association**, groups and relationships, which are more concerned with belonging, loyalty and identity than narrowly defined interests, sometimes called 'sub-politics'.
- **Revolutionary politics** arise when the political system is threatened and a new political settlement is possible.
- **Cyber politics** describes the emerging sphere of political action through the internet that cuts across all five levels and creates new possibilities for democratic development worldwide, but could also amplify existing inequalities.

These are like different levels of a multi-dimensional game, which are connected but distinct. Anyone doing practical politics needs to know which domains affect their issues, who runs them, how they work and how to influence them. For many issues it is best to work outside or across party politics, such as using the law to enforce environmental standards (supra-politics) or community organizing (sub-politics), while other issues are best addressed by bringing them into the party political realm. Skilled political operators know when and how to move between political levels to bring about the outcome they want.

The politics of supra-politics

One astute political strategy for governments is to lift an issue 'above politics', so that it is dealt with according to rules that are not subject to everyday party political bargaining. This does not mean they are outside politics, but they have a supra-political role, setting system conditions that govern society. Supra-political systems include the rule of law, markets, international diplomacy, national security, public service broadcasting, government agencies, Quasi-Autonomous Non-Governmental Organizations (quangos) and what J.K. Galbraith called the 'autonomous processes of government' (1983: 146). Every country has supra-political agencies, usually in alliance with the government but sometimes in opposition to it. They include central banks, the Church of England and the supreme leader of Iran. God and divine guidance are the ultimate supra-political powers, but science, markets and finance have supra-political status in much of the world.

The **rule of law** is an independent realm above politics, wrested from the personal rule of monarchs through the *Magna Carta*, judicial independence, parliaments, written constitutions, the press and protest. Treaties between nations establish international law and global governance. Following the horrors of the holocaust and Nazi Germany human rights conventions set international norms and some constraints on governments. Law can protect people against arbitrary government and defend the weak against the strong, or it can shield established powers against challengers.

Law enshrines a political settlement for a time and authorizes the state and other agencies to enforce it. The fundamental principle of representative democracy is that law is made through deliberation by elected representatives of the people, who are sovereign. The law is then administered by politically neutral, non-partisan police, prosecutors and judiciary. But law has its own politics, parallel to public politics and 'judicial activism' can modify the law, as recognized by the philosophy of legal realism. Its legitimacy rests on shared values and powers of enforcement, which change. Lawyers present themselves as 'neutral and objective social agents, ... as if they have no self-interest or values and are merely promoting what the law requires', but in many countries there are strong incentives for law to side with the rich and powerful (Kairys, 1998: 2–3, 15).

Litigation is a core strategy in practical politics. Activists use it to redress the balance of power in favour of the poor and disenfranchised, through judicial review, innocence initiatives and legal cases. Erin Brockovich, the American legal clerk, used law to win a case against the Pacific Gas and Electric Company in Hinkley from 1993 to 1996, as celebrated in film. Companies use litigation to protect their interests, including controversial measures such as investor-state dispute settlement tribunals. Jimmy Saville used the threat of litigation to stop allegations of child abuse. Authoritarian governments protect themselves by intimidating or imprisoning lawyers who attempt to challenge them in the courts.

The **civil service** aims to provide politically neutral delivery of objectives set by elected politicians, but they have their own internal politics, as dramatized in the television series *Yes Minister*. Civil servants are the permanent automatic processes of government, which Galbraith described as serving 'the highest civilized purposes – protection of the people from hardship, exploitation, and abuse ... support for industrial achievement and education; advancement of knowledge; encouragement of the arts; preservation of natural resources; and hundreds of other functions' (1983: 146–64). Much practical politics is easier and more effective when working directly with civil servants responsible for policy or delivery than with overstretched politicians.

Funding formulae are used to distribute money between rich and poor regions, states, services or families, and have a huge impact on people's lives. Arguments over farm subsidies, welfare benefits, local government grants or contributions to the European Union occasionally bring them into the public realm, but most are considered technical matters, negotiated between officials and influenced by lobbyists.

Large areas of government are run by **quangos**, semi-independent unelected government agencies. They account for between five and 25 per cent of public spending in the United Kingdom, depending on what you count. They include public watchdogs like the Ombudsman, Health and Safety Executive or Food Safety Agency; public services like the BBC and National Health Service; funding bodies like the Housing Corporation, Skills Funding Agency and Arts Council; and advisory agencies and regulators of all kinds. Democratic Audit pioneered research into quangos and produced recommendations to make them more accountable, open and effective (Democratic Audit, 2015; Flinders and Smith, 1998).

Regulators have a decisive role in most industries as well as public services from education to food safety, health and prisons. Some regulators are statutory while many are run by professional associations, such as the Law Society. Changing the rules, powers or membership of a regulator can be the best way to influence some policy areas. The global crash of 2007–8 was largely a result of financial deregulation. The UK phone hacking scandal from 2002 to 2014 showed failures in press regulation. Many areas of regulation are scarcely scrutinized by the public.

Constitutional monarchs of European countries, Bhutan, Japan, Thailand and 15 of Britain's former colonies are figureheads above party politics who provide stability, continuity and a national focus as head of state while governments change (Bogdanor, 1995; Bagehot, 1867). In most other countries a written constitution and the courts have the supra-political role of protecting the political system from elected politicians exceeding their powers.

In Britain the **Speaker** or chair of parliament also promotes democracy through strategic Commissions on issues such as Digital Democracy (2015) and Citizenship (1990) as well as education and outreach.

The **management of money** is a core function for any government, which rulers love to manipulate at the risk of debasing the currency, stoking inflation and undermining the economy, as dramatically illustrated by hyperinflation in Weimar Germany (1921–24) and Argentina (1989–90).

Making the central bank independent and above party politics is therefore seen as essential for financial credibility, although its policies for inflation, money supply, unemployment or other variables are set by governments. Money is a complex, powerful social mechanism that depends on credibility, productivity and robust institutions, created by financial institutions through credit. Interest rates, exchange rates and the supply of money influence the distribution of income and wealth through inflation, asset values and buying power. People with power in government, business and finance can manipulate money to enrich themselves, buy patronage or pursue other social purposes. Central banks can loosen or tighten the money supply through interest rates, Quantitative Easing (QE) (creating money electronically) and other measures. Factions within the system, such as members of the Monetary Policy Committee in the United Kingdom, may be identified as 'hawks' (for tightening the money supply) or 'doves' (for loosening it). The Bank of International Settlements (BIS) is a private arrangement between central bankers to regulate the world's money 'completely removed from any governmental or political control' to maintain monetary stability among the great powers (LeBor, 2013: 42). Understanding how the money works is a foundation of practical politics in any setting, whether a charity, local government or international affairs.

The **BBC,** Britain's public service broadcaster, has political independence written into its charter. This sets out its public purposes, including sustaining citizenship and civil society. Tensions between politicians and broadcasters occasionally erupt in high-profile conflicts, such the sacking of the Director General Alistair Milne under Prime Minister Margaret Thatcher in 1987 or the resignation of Director General Greg Dyke over a story about evidence on the case for war on Iraq in 2004. The BBC's rules on impartiality enable robust questioning of politicians, in-depth investigations into controversial issues and informed public debate. Like any institution, the BBC is rife with internal politics about priorities, policies and personalities that influence how issues are handled and what is broadcast (Higgins, 2014, 2015; Moore, 2015; Mosey, 2015).

Academic freedom, science and **universities** are above the party political fray and among the most skilful institutions at protecting their interests. The supra-political role of universities varies between societies and periods of history, providing intellectual justification for authoritarian regimes in some circumstances and '"protected space" in which critique and opposition could ferment' in others (Brennan *et al.*, 2004: 56; Bourdieu, 1988, 1996; Castells, 2001).

Transnational institutions such as NATO, the Bank of International Settlements, UN Security Council and thousands of international agencies are now the most important political arenas for the security and prosperity of most people. The ability of states to cooperate, resolve conflicts and maintain effective rules governing the world will determine the fate of humanity this century. The evolution of the European Union as a transnational arena of public politics, with an elected governing body (the Council of Ministers) and Parliament under the rule of law, highlights the challenges of bringing supra-politics into the public sphere.

Complexity and supra-politics

Each of these examples shows the benefits of taking matters out of party politics into a realm governed by people who are non-partisan and faithful to rules rather than a party. However, supra-political domains can be unaccountable, paternalistic, complacent, corrupt or even dangerous if they lack supervision. They can support citizens holding power to account or protect unaccountable power against the citizen.

The growth of the supra-political realm reflects both the complexity of society and distrust of politicians. Modern societies need specialist agencies to manage highly technical activities. Lord Falconer, Secretary of State for Constitutional Affairs in Tony Blair's government, went as far as to say in 2003, 'This depoliticising of key decision-making is a vital element in bringing power closer to the people' (quoted in Flinders and Buller, 2004, 2006). Flinders and Buller describe how successive governments have 'depoliticised' areas of decision-making while sometimes exercising informal influence ('government by luncheon'). They describe it as a process of 'arena shifting' and 'the transfer of power to new, but no less political, arenas'.

Because people don't trust politicians, they accept large areas of public policy run by officials with relatively little public oversight. This raises many issues for practical politics:

- How do you influence domains that affect your issue? The answer is, mainly through professional and private networks, discreet lobbying and whistleblowing when necessary.
- What kind of political oversight and accountability would make each domain serve people better? Directly elected police commissioners in the United Kingdom or sheriffs in the United States, elected school boards and public scrutiny of new supreme court judges are examples of existing models.

- How can the wider public understand and influence the priorities and policies of institutions run in their name, from their taxes? The answer is more openness, information and political education.

All political settlements reflect a particular balance of power and interest. The selection of officials, interpretation of rules and exercise of impartial authority are all part of a subtle (and sometimes not so subtle) 'supra-politics' that is harder to challenge than the jousting of party politics. In stable, mature societies change takes place gradually, through ambiguity, co-option and tactical concessions, while more rigid societies are subject to sudden shocks when authorities are overthrown and a new settlement is imposed.

Influencing supra-politics

One sign that an arena is 'above politics' is that its members conduct their politics with discretion and do not take a party political stand. A supra-political domain entrenches a political settlement and creates stability around certain issues so that everyday politics can concentrate on other problems. Many areas of supra-politics are older than representative democracy, such as the monarchy, military, rule of law, church and universities, so their practitioners are adept at survival.

Like most areas of human life, each supra-political arena has its 'units of rule' and factions that organize to promote or oppose particular policies and interests within it. Many are governed internationally by state agencies (such as the definition of GDP, aviation, postal services, NATO or human rights law) or by private bodies (such as accounting standards, central banking or the internet).

Often the best way to change a supra-political domain is from within, with support from public politics at critical moments. The more that supra-political change is presented as technical evolution, through dialogue, reviews and research within the domain, the more likely it is to stick. Changing the law, if necessary, is often the final keystone for a new settlement.

The most dramatic examples of this was the 'Big Bang' financial deregulation in the Stock Exchange on 27 October 1986, promoted by the financial sector. Another high-profile example was press regulation in the United Kingdom, where advocates of change represented by the pressure group Hacked Off were less successful. Other examples include corporate governance, environmental accounting and standards for medicines or food. Since relatively small regulatory changes within a supra-political domain can have big consequences, they need careful scrutiny.

Sometimes the best way to influence a supra-political domain is to show what's happening and put it onto the public agenda, such as revelations of surveillance by Edward Snowden, former Central Intelligence Agency (CIA) contractor (Greenwald, 2015; Harding, 2014), infiltration of protest groups by UK police officers (Fijnaut, 1995; Marx, 1989; Evans, 2013), or the campaign about the Transatlantic Trade and Investment Partnership (TTIP) trade agreement between the EU and the United States. The UK's referendum on EU membership shows how persistent campaigners can put a supra-political domain into the public arena for decision.

SUMMARY: SUPRA-POLITICAL ARENAS

A 'supra-political arena' is an area of public life that:

- is accepted by most competing interests as being 'above politics'
- has a key role in setting system conditions for society, such as governing the political system, economy or public service broadcasting
- is largely self-governing and subject to light-touch regulation or arms-length accountability by elected politicians
- is rarely questioned or examined in public, except by specialists, and is usually referred to with deference and respect
- sees major changes being often led from within, working closely with allies in party politics.

Sometimes, however, a particular settlement is challenged by significant groups in society to create a crisis to be addressed in public politics.

The drama of public politics

Public politics is what most people see – politicians, parties and pressure groups. Often they are a performance, a public show of power, while the real politics takes place elsewhere. This is particularly true in authoritarian societies, where public displays of loyalty sustain the legitimacy and power of leaders (as well as the survival of rivals and minions). Parties in representative democracies also use performance to show unity, determination and decisiveness while unruly reality rumbles behind the scenes. Oppositions and pressure groups likewise use stunts, slogans and stories to promote their case. Understanding how this public drama directs the institutions of state is vital in practical politics.

Party politics

Political parties are the main means of reconciling priorities and exercising state power in any regime. They provide political training and career routes for people ambitious to gain power. In authoritarian regimes like China, Russia or Vietnam, power is controlled through one party, so that politics are more like the internal politics of a corporation. But even one-party states have competing centres of power, in the army, industries, ministries and local authorities, where practical politics is more subtle and savage. Authoritarian regimes use patronage, privilege, pomp and fear to maintain party discipline and run the state, occasionally resorting to threats, prison, torture or even murder as political tools.

In democratic systems political parties are voluntary organizations dedicated to winning, holding and using power. They rely on peaceful persuasion rather than force, but also use patronage, privilege, pomp and more subtle coercion to get their way. Although membership and support for traditional political parties has fallen in mature democracies, their role in selecting political leaders, creating a programme for government and carrying it out is central to every political system.

Party politics are increasingly dominated by money rather than citizens. In *The Audacity of Hope*, Barack Obama wrote that 'politics today is a business and not a mission, and what passes for debate is little more than spectacle' (2007: 24). In *Ruling the Void: The hollowing of Western democracy*, Peter Mair (2013) described how parties have become disconnected from wider society so that the people, 'the ordinary citizenry, are becoming effectively non-sovereign' (p.2). As a result, he claims, 'The age of party democracy has passed' (p.1). Mainstream parties are no longer the grassroots organizations representing citizens' views to the state, but centralized, professional administrations, funded by special interests, that mobilize members as foot soldiers in a competition for state power. Policies are decided by small groups at the centre, and then sold to members and the wider public, not the other way round.

In this void challenger parties are growing to give voice to citizens – the Scottish National Party and UKIP in Britain; Syriza and Golden Dawn in Greece; Beppe Grillo's Five Star Movement in Italy; Podemos, Cuidanos and regional parties in Spain, and the National Front in France. The election of Jeremy Corbyn as Labour leader in the United Kingdom and support for Bernie Sanders or Donald Trump in the United States show that party politics is not dead but changing. However, most established parties have deep reserves of political experience, loyalty and connections to guide (and finance) their pursuit of power even when membership is down.

Party politics is an intense and specialized area of practical politics that is vital for good governance. People should be encouraged to understand and take part in party politics from an early age. The hollowing out of parties has many causes, but the widespread taboo on discussing party politics in education means that many young people never learn how to take part in governing their country.

Electoral politics

The ultimate test of party politics is the ability to win power in elections and then use it effectively in government. Election victories are often determined years before the vote, as a result of the voting system, population factors and skilful preparation and framing of issues by party strategists. Good planning, organization and communication are critical. Successful parties develop a sophisticated organization to win elections, including 'attack units' to research weaknesses and misdemeanours by opponents, 'rebuttal units' to counter attacks, a media grid to manage communications, private polling, campaign training, support for local party organizations and strategic networks within professions and key interest groups. The professionalization of electoral politics may be essential for victory at the polls, but they can drain politics of conviction, passion and spontaneity, widening the gulf between politicians and people. This in turn creates opportunities for new entrants to change the terms of debate.

The run-up to elections, before manifestos are written, are also the time when politicians listen intently and are most receptive to ideas, particularly those supported by key constituencies. This creates opportunities for citizens and pressure groups to push their priorities up the political agenda.

Elections are pivotal moments when the public choose between competing teams, priorities and policies. Issues are honed into a simple choice over a few months or even weeks. However good the preparation, the outcome is uncertain. It can be influenced by an unguarded remark, a chance event or rousing speech. Then at a stroke, the electorate propels one group into power and dashes the hopes of all others. It is a bruising, exhausting process. But compared with beheadings, exile or slaughter accompanying regime change throughout history, elections are marvels of modern politics.

Parliamentary politics

Democratic politics are most intense around the elected chamber, where representatives confront each other. Although largely a ritual spectacle while the hard politics takes place outside the chamber within the ruling party, the legislature is still an arena for power struggles. Elected representatives need to learn how to use their position effectively to have influence, whether in a national parliament or local council.

Elected chambers are a sophisticated information-processing centre to gauge the political temperature of the nation. Members sense what matters to constituents. It may be filtered by people who write, lobby or meet them, and distorted by their personal lens, but successful politicians develop sensitive antennae. They can read the mood of people they represent, put issues onto the political agenda and dramatize them through a human story.

Every country is different, so it is not easy to transfer lessons between different systems. Lord Hailsham famously popularized the phrase 'elective dictatorship' to describe the dominance of the executive over the British parliament, where ministers' wield considerable powers (Hailsham, 1976). The US Congress has much greater powers in relation to the President and frequently frustrates or blocks action by the executive (Davidson and Oleszek, 2013).

Practical politics in parliament is a discipline of its own, studied more by lobbyists than the public or even parliamentarians, but anyone who wants to influence legislation, government spending or priorities needs to learn how it works. Skilful use of parliament can enhance any campaign, even those not aimed at changing the law or government policy.

The politics of governing

Finally in this section I'd like to mention the politics of governing. This demands the ability to rodeo ride a 24-hour news cycle while steering ocean tankers of state, to mix metaphors. The politics of governing any organization are difficult, but democratic government of complex modern states verges on the impossible. In my view this can only be solved by increasing self-government at all levels, devolving power to neighbourhoods and local services, cities and regions, so that national governments can focus on creating the best system conditions for self-government internally and on improving global governance externally. Distributed leadership and devolution also enables more people to develop political skills, so that an effective political system is also a vehicle for practical political education.

Institutional politics

Most political activity takes places within institutions, described more fully in chapter 6. Almost every act of public politics by parties or pressure groups is first fought and won within an organization. Winning elections is crucial in party politics, where votes are the currency of power, but most elections are lost or won in the office politics of the party before they are tested in public. Once in government, the office politics of leading a department and the party in parliament become more important. Likewise, the internal politics of pressure groups are decisive for successful campaigns. The ability to win internal battles is the foundation of practical politics in any sphere.

Markets and the political economy

All societies decide what may be traded through markets; what should be provided by the state, other agencies or the personal sphere; and what is prohibited. Soviet societies attempted to bring the entire economy into the political sphere, while some economists argue that most decisions should be taken through the market, outside the political domain entirely. Where and how the lines are drawn is the central battle ground of politics, because they influence the productivity, cohesion and security of society. The ability of people to innovate, create enterprises and compete for custom has made some societies materially wealthier than others, while the ability of the state, families and voluntary associations to protect people and the environment is the foundation of civilisation. At an international level, the ability of powerful states to impose immigration controls, tariffs and other restraints on trade by other countries, to control key resources like oil or to manage the supply of credit, is central to global politics. Some understanding of political economy is essential for effective politics at any level.

Politics of association

A less tangible yet powerful political arena is that of personal relationships and associations below the radar of public politics. Associations form at all levels, among marginalized communities, within institutions, between executives that control giant corporations and among elites that meet at the World Economic Forum. Informal associations make practical politics work in any context. Ignore them and you may be mysteriously frozen out.

Associations are particularly important at a local level. People in disadvantaged communities can gain power in their neighbourhoods by building relationships and mutual support. This process has many names and practitioners, most of whom are anonymous and undocumented, but there are extensive published resources, case studies and research about grassroots community politics, such as:

- Asset Based Community Development (ABCD), developed by John McKight, John Kretzmann and associates at North Western University, Chicago
- community organizing described in chapter 2
- Judith Snow's Circles of Support, created to support people with disabilities like herself in Canada and now a worldwide movement (Pearpoint, 1990)
- *The Community Tool Box: Tools to change the world* at the University of Kansas http://ctb.ku.edu/en
- neighbourhood power in Seattle, described by Jim Diers (2004)
- The Manavodaya Institute of Participatory Development in India, described by Varun Vidyarthi and Patricia Wilson in *Development from Within* (2008).

The policy implications of association is rarely recognized by mainstream politics, despite rhetoric about the Big Society, communitarianism or localism, but political parties are also voluntary associations and the relational dimensions of politics may be more important than ideology or policy. The following three points illustrate the importance of association in public politics.

First, emotional attachment to a party affects people's political behaviour. People support their party (or faction within a party) more strongly than particular policy positions or values, and are willing to accept measures from their own party that they would utterly reject from another, such as the opening to China under President Nixon, financial deregulation from Democrats under Clinton or gay marriage by UK Conservatives (Petersen *et al.*, 2015; Goren 2005; Green, Palmquist and Schickler 2002).

Second, politicians form friendships across party lines, enabling bi-partisan agreement or even alliances over issues. This is probably more common in specialist policy areas and at a senior level, where political co-operation and compromise are practical necessities. The unlikely friendship between Northern Ireland's deputy First Minister Martin McGuinness, the Sinn Fein Irish Republican, and his former opponent, Ulster Unionist leader Dr Ian Paisley, is a striking example of this.

Third, political leaders associate with wealthy donors, press barons, chief executives, heads of government and other powerful people. Many form bonds that have political implications. Some even become godparents, like former Prime Minister Tony Blair for Rupert Murdoch's daughter.

Understanding the unseen associations and relationships across neighbourhoods, cities, parties, interests, faith communities and nations is a vital but neglected dimension of practical politics.

Revolutionary politics

The opposite of supra-politics is when the entire political system is challenged. Most nations are the result of revolution, in which one constitutional settlement was replaced by another. The American Declaration of Independence recognized that when a government becomes despotic 'it is the Right of the People to alter or to abolish it, and to institute new Government' (1776). More recently the people of Tunisia (2011), Egypt (2011, 2013) and Ukraine (2014) overthrew their governments and established new constitutions.

At times of economic or political turbulence, revolutionary movements are likely to grow and challenge the prevailing settlement, calling for the establishment to be swept away and replaced by a new order. Revolutionary movements take many forms, from the street violence of the anti-Semitic, anti-capitalist German Nazi party in the 1920s, the tactical sabotage of the South African National Congress or guerrilla warfare and outright war in Vietnam (1959–75), to non-violent resistance for Indian independence (1920–42), the 'velvet revolutions' of Eastern Europe (1989) or the anti-establishment rhetoric of the referendum on membership of the European Union in the UK (2016).

The arts of provoking, seizing, riding, leading or resisting revolutionary movements are a specialist branch of practical politics particularly important for people living under regimes that cannot be voted out. For guidance see Gene Sharp's *From Dictatorship to Democracy: A conceptual framework for liberation* (2010 [1993]).

Why Civil Resistance Works, a study of 323 resistance campaigns between 1900 and 2006, concluded that non-violence was twice as successful as violence (Chenoweth and Stephan, 2011: 213–15). The study gives a detailed analysis of factors that enable campaigns to succeed or fail. Non-violent campaigns are easier for people to support, have higher levels of participation, are more difficult to suppress and better able to attract support from within the establishment. More than half of successful non-violent campaigns are likely to be democratic five years later, compared with less than six per cent of successful violent campaigns.

Chenoweth and Stephan looked at politically motivated campaigns, not the spontaneous riots that Martin Luther King called 'the language of the unheard'. In the United States there have been almost a hundred race riots since 1900, usually triggered by discrimination and heavy-handed policing. Since the 1960s campaigners have won greater civil liberties, affirmative action and other measures to tackle discrimination, but the killing of an unarmed black teenager by a white police officer in Ferguson, Missouri, in 2014 and other deaths sparked street protests and the Black Lives Matter Campaign. These clashes show that problems persist and citizens lack confidence in democratic means of solving them. In areas like these, among the unheard and marginalized, associations like the Organization for Black Struggle, United Way and Baltimoreans United in Leadership Development (BUILD) enable communities to have a voice.

Democratic systems need to make it easier for people to change their political settlement without upheaval, so that fundamental change can occur peacefully. Over the past century all Western European nations have created universal social security and healthcare systems through the democratic process, redistributing almost half of national income through the state. In *The Great Transformation* (1944) Karl Polanyi described how politicians developed modern democratic states and social protection in response to the massive social dislocation following the expansion of market mechanisms. Authoritarian regimes have also learned to respond to citizens' concerns. The People's Republic of China has rewritten its constitution four times, most recently by Deng Xiaoping in 1982, to liberalize the economy, permit private enterprise and encourage foreign investment. These are very different examples of constitutional changes through party politics rather than violent revolution.

Cyber politics

The internet creates a new dimension for politics, used by challengers, governments and underdogs across all five levels. It can be fast moving, sometimes cruel, often illusory and a distraction. It has the potential to transform politics by giving established powers the ability to conduct mass surveillance and personalized communication, or by empowering citizens to challenge authority, or both. Citizens, the state and companies are actively testing ways of using the the internet to influence events.

In *The New Digital Age* Google's Chief Executive Eric Schmidt and Director of Ideas Jared Cohen called the internet 'the largest experiment involving anarchy in history', 'an online world that is not truly bound by terrestrial laws' and 'the world's largest ungoverned space' (2014: 3). The internet may not have the top-down control Schmidt and Cohen associate with government, but it is governed – by technical codes and protocols; by bodies like the International Telecommunication Union (ITU), ICANN, Internet Society and Internet Governance Forum (IGF); and by national laws. Authoritarian countries like China, Russia and Iran control the internet within their boundaries. The European Union, United States and other major powers try to regulate it through laws on competition, copyright, data collection, privacy and taxation. Companies like Amazon, Google and Microsoft clearly recognize this when spending millions on lobbyists, political donations and sponsorship to protect their interests (see www.opensecrets.org; *The Washington Post*, 2014; Reuters, 2015). They also arrange their business to minimize taxes, as if they were not 'bound by terrestrial laws' (Mail Online, 2013; *Financial Times*, 2014; Ethical Consumer, 2014).

In *The People's Platform* Astra Taylor (2014) described how the organization of the internet widens inequalities by enabling a relatively small group of companies to capture the monetary value of the network while most people provide content for free, as 'digital sharecroppers'. In *Who Owns the Future?*, Jaron Lanier calls the likes of Facebook, Amazon and Google 'siren servers', which harvest data and sell access to people. He warns of the concentration of money and power in the hands of small elites, and the destruction of opportunities for paid employment, pointing out that Google was worth $300 billion on the stock market, almost seven times General Motors, but employed only 53,000 people compared to 202,000 at the flagging GM (Lanier, 2013).

Yet Schmidt and Cohen have a point: 'Never before in history have so many people, from so many places, had so much power at their fingertips' (2013: 4). Their afterword concluded by noting the importance of interdisciplinary education to produce 'skilled problem solvers' and better 'leadership development, as students access the best practices for creating change in an organization, a community, or a country' (280). Their final remark was that 'statecraft is the art of troubleshooting the world's challenges, and we believe that technology is among the most important tools for doing so' (281). Leadership, social problem solving and statecraft are key elements of practical politics.

LEARN MORE ABOUT POLITICAL ARENAS

Devise activities to give you experience of politics of different arenas, such as:

- Take an issue that concerns you and identify every agency that influences, including 'deep structures', institutions and practices outside everyday politics, and then try to assess the influence of each one and decide which could be most effective in bringing about changes you want in relation to that issue.
- Follow the passage of a bill through an elected assembly, noting carefully which interest groups are engaged and what they do (the most effective are often the least visible).
- Explore the political economy of an issue such as alcoholism, betting, drugs, fossil fuels, pharmaceuticals, smoking or wages by volunteering with a pressure group, think tank or union.
- Volunteer for a political party you can support, ideally during an election campaign.
- Take part in a community association or affinity group and read some of the resources mentioned under the politics of association above.
- Compare the use of social media by two political parties and two campaign groups.

Part Two
Lessons in power

2

This section addresses three questions:

1. How do powerful people learn to do politics (and what can you learn from them)?

2. Why (almost) all politics is office politics.

3. What is power, and how can citizens use it?

Daniel Lovejoy

Chapter 5

Political education of the powerful

In this chapter you will learn:

- How professional political consultants help parties to win
- How powerful people in politics and business get political education
- Six ways government politics affect businesses
- Why business needs to be in politics (and is so good at it)
- How corporations have become institutions of global governance
- That the influence industry is 100 times bigger than political parties
- Why US citizens have little influence compared with business
- Ten reasons why people trust business more than politics
- Why citizens need to learn how to be equal with the most powerful
- The media as political education

Case study: Campaign consulting

Sir Lynton Crosby is a political consultant from rural South Australia who masterminded successful election campaigns for Australian Prime Minister John Howard (1996 to 2004); London Mayor Boris Johnson (2008); New Zealand's Joy Key, and the UK Conservative Party (2015), for which he was knighted. He also worked on unsuccessful campaigns for the UK Conservative Party in 2005 and the London mayoral elections in 2016, as well as running unsuccessfully against Labor in the 1982 South Australian election, when he turned a marginal Labor seat into a safe Labor seat. The Crosby Textor Group of campaign specialists claims to have run several hundred research projects and campaigns in almost 60 countries for corporate clients, industry associations, investors and governments.

Crosby is famous for his focus, discipline, blunt style and ability to motivate campaign teams (Grimson, 2012). He works behind the scenes, but is open about his strategy and tactics (see his website and Master Class for the Patchwork Foundation on YouTube). 'Mr Lynton places a very strong emphasis on a disciplined, consistent message,' ex-premier John Howard testified. 'He also understood for centre-right parties to win in Australia or the United Kingdom they need to harvest their base vote but also get votes from what I would loosely call blue collar conservative voters' (*Financial Times*, 2015). Tim Montgomerie, conservative activist who founded the Conservative Home website and The Good Right, has criticized Crosby's 'reduction of politics to a few simplified messages' (Montgomerie, 2015).

Crosby Textor use market research tools to find out what voters think and their underlying motivation in order to create 'behaviour changing communication'. The CT Group asked me not to publish its six 'strategic lessons of politics' or information from its website, but they can be read at www.crosbytextor.com/campaigns/ (or cached versions).

Crosby Textor is one of several thousand political consultancies that provide strategic support for companies, charities, trade unions, politicians and public services. Their role in politics is often overlooked and underestimated, but they are the elite of practical political education. The International Association of Political Consultants (IAPC) was founded in 1968 and has some 180 active members, most of whom it claims 'have played significant roles in electing the heads of state in the world's democracies' (2016). The largest regional association is in the United States, with several thousand members and the strapline 'Connect, Learn, Change the World'. The industry journal *Campaigns and Elections* promotes itself as the 'preeminent "how-to" journal of politics, focused on the tools, tactics and techniques of the political consulting profession'.

The political education of politicians

Every country has its political premier league inside the Beltway, Westminster Village, Brussels bubble or Kremlin. Like elite athletes, politicians who compete at the top hire the best coaches. They employ pollsters and market research to understand public perceptions, test their messages and pitch policies to the public. They plan for the short term and years ahead. They prepare intensely for set-piece confrontations like question time, speeches, media appearances and elections. They anticipate their opponents, create political traps and seek to set the agenda.

George W. Bush employed Karl Rove as political strategist to win the US presidential elections in 2000 and 2004. Senator Obama employed David Axelrod to help him defeat Hilary Clinton in the primaries and then his Republican opponents to become President in 2008 and 2012. In India Narendra Modi won power in 2014 with a high-powered team including professors and investment fund managers (Chakrabarti, 2014).

Campaign consultants are political educators, as much part of party politics as coaches are of sport. US Democrats and Republicans run their own campaign training schools. Some colleges offer professional courses for aspiring politicians and political consultants. In politics, as in sport, the best training is available to elite teams. But outside challengers, like the Williams sisters or Andy Murray in tennis, can also train to reach the top.

The politics of governing a modern state is many times more complicated than sport. It is more like multi-dimensional chess on parallel boards, each with its own rules, teams and moving goalposts. Dozens of different games are playing simultaneously – within your own party in Parliament, Europe, local government and constituencies; between parties and states, in the press and social media; across the civil service, public agencies and professionals including the military, medics and university professors; with lobbyists, regulators and the judiciary; between nations, through international institutions, and above all, with the free-booting financial markets that can crash your country's credit rating on a rumour. Team colours are deceptive. People change shirts during the game. New players or teams storm the pitch. And at any time a jail break, bombing, beheading or belligerent interest group can blow you off course.

To win elections and stay in power, parties need focus, discipline and the ability to perform with apparent ease for different audiences across all media. They need to keep their core supporters happy while contending with challengers like the Tea Party in the United States, UKIP in England or SNP in Scotland. Challengers also need skill and stamina to survive the ruthless response of dominant players. One unguarded remark or gesture can blow up through an unforgiving media. In this context politicians need the best possible advisers, speech writers and strategists to both win and use power.

The pedagogy of power

Learning politics starts young. Like language, music and sport, learning about power begins at the home. Family background is the biggest influence on political participation, closely linked to education, the second major influence (Verba *et al.*, 2003, 2005). It is no accident that many leading politicians come from political families. Conversations at mealtimes and frantic activity during elections makes politics commonplace. It exposes young people to the rollercoaster of political fortunes, preparing them for inevitable attacks and setbacks. They see the scaffolding and sticky tape behind the stage, the preparation behind the presentation and the post-mortem afterwards.

Children of leaders in politics and business are more likely to go to elite schools that prepare pupils for leadership. These schools aim to develop character, confidence and skills of debating, taking initiative and organizing, as well as academic training. Most leading politicians in the West have attended top universities like Cambridge, Harvard, London School of Economics and Political Science (LSE), Oxford or Les Grandes Écoles in France, and have studied law, economics, history or politics.

This may make politicians more competent to win power and govern, but it makes them unrepresentative of the people they represent. In Britain one-third (32 per cent) of the 650 MPs elected in 2015 and nearly half (48 per cent) of the governing Conservative Party went to fee-paying schools, compared with seven per cent of the population. Most MPs (89 per cent) were graduates, compared with 38 per cent of the working population; a quarter (26 per cent) went to Oxford or Cambridge (compared with 0.8 per cent of the population) and 28 per cent went to other Russell Group universities (compared with 11.4 per cent). In this they have more in common with other elites – senior judges, military commanders and members of the House of Lords – than with the public (SMCPC, 2014).

Most successful politicians also had mentors and patrons within the system to give them a hand up. They served apprenticeships in student, trade union or pressure group politics. They developed experience, skills and contacts as special advisers, policy researchers or local councillors. And, above all, they gained resilience on the campaign trail.

Yet parties do not have the pitch to themselves. They must contend with what US President Theodore Roosevelt called 'an invisible government owing no allegiance and acknowledging no responsibility to the people' (Roosevelt, 1926) – namely big business. Alan Greenspan, head of the US Federal Reserve bank from 1987 to 2006, memorably said, 'It hardly matters who will be the next president. The world is governed by market forces' (Greenspan, 2007).

Politics and business

Political parties are not the only organizations that employ professional campaigners. Businesses success often depends on government decisions about economic policy, regulation, tax, trade and public spending. Small changes in policy can have a big impact on companies. When the UK Chancellor announced in March 2014 that pension savers no longer had to buy an annuity, shares in annuity providers fell by up to 55 per cent (*The Guardian*, 2014). Planning permission dramatically changes land values overnight. Anti-trust laws can force companies to break up or pay large fines. In 1911 the Supreme Court broke Standard Oil into three dozen separate companies. In 1982 the Reagan administration split telecoms giant AT&T into eight 'Baby Bells'. Hundreds of US executives have been sent to prison for illegal price-fixing. Companies like Apple, Amazon, Google and Microsoft have spent hundreds of millions fighting anti-trust suits in the European Union and United States.

Industry fortunes rise and fall in response to government policies. Trade in alcohol, arms, energy, farming, housing, pharmaceuticals, transport, tobacco and indeed most products is governed by legislation that directly affects its viability. A study of 466 elections across 79 countries between 1980 and 2006 showed how political uncertainty during election years influences corporate behaviour and investment decisions (Durnev, 2010). It is not surprising that business people pay careful attention to politics.

Business is affected by politics in at least six ways:

1. **Infrastructure:** national security, the rule of law, effective institutions, transport, education and healthcare provide a stable, safe and sound environment to do business.

2. **Regulation:** good regulation makes it easy to do business, creates a level playing field for competition and protects third parties from harm, while poor regulation can increase costs, stifle legitimate business and make illegal trade attractive (World Bank, 2016).

3. **Tariffs and trade policy** influence what can be produced where.

4. **Taxation** affects incentives (and disincentives) for investment, purchasing power, jobs and almost every aspect of business.

5. **Subsidies and business support:** Businesses benefit from government support through grants, price support, tax reliefs, credit guarantees, trade missions and funding for training, research and development. According to one estimate businesses enjoyed direct subsidies of more than US$300 billion a year worldwide in the mid-2000s (Steenblik, 2008; WTO, 2006). The International Energy Agency (IEA) estimated that fossil fuels received US$548 billion in subsidies in 2013.

6. **Purchasing power:** government agencies are the biggest customers in many markets. The UK public sector spends about £187 billion on goods and services a year, from computers and healthcare to prisons (NAO Memorandum, 2013). This is about ten per cent of national income and the biggest outsourcing market outside the United States, according to the Holmes Report (2012).

Large companies and industry associations employ political consultants like Crosby Textor or Dodds to monitor and influence policies that affect them. Businesses are represented on government bodies for their industry. They second staff to help civil servants write policies for their sector. Occasionally they campaign openly for public support, but most of their effort is targeted at the few people with power over their industry.

Like political consultants, lobbyists are both players and coaches in this multi-dimensional contest. They act directly for their employers, but they are also educators, teaching executives about strategies, tactics, skills and contacts to influence decisions over the long term. Lord Tom McNally, former Labour MP, Head of Public Affairs at Shandwick Consultants, member of parliament in the unelected Upper House and a Liberal Democrat Minister of Justice in the 2010–15 coalition government, described public affairs as 'an operational necessity in the boardroom' (Harris and Fleisher, 2005: xxvi).

Businesses recruit former ministers and government officials for their skills, knowledge, kudos and, above all, contacts, as reflected in their market price. Bill and Hilary Clinton could command $200,000–750,000 for a single speech (Ghosh, 2013; Yoon, 2013). Former Prime Minister Tony Blair generated £10–20 million a year from business (Office of Tony Blair, 2013; This is Money, 2 July 2012). The revolving door of politics and business ensures those at the top understand each other.

Corporate power

In *Power Inc.*, David Rothkopf (2012) traced the rise of corporate power since 1288, describing the intimate relationships and struggles between business and government. Few countries are immune to its influence. A third of China's private entrepreneurs have joined the Communist party since 2001, when membership was opened (Lardy, 2014). In most democratic states elections depend on funding from business and wealthy individuals.

Stephen Wilks showed how international corporations have become institutions of global governance that constrain national governments in *The Political Power of the Business Corporation* (2013). The United Kingdom 'has moved to a significant level of "government by corporation", most obviously in the swathe of services now delivered by privatized corporations' (Wilks, 2013: 257) so that 'their political power is exerted on an everyday basis as part of our political system' (41) through a managerial elite that 'works in conjunction with political elites to create corporate strategies which favour their own and wider elite interests' (35).

When Alan Greenspan said 'the world is governed by market forces' he meant the invisible hand of Adam Smith, not Roosevelt's 'invisible government' of big business pulling strings behind the scenes. But in *The Visible Hand: The managerial revolution in American business* (1977), Alfred Chandler described how hierarchical, managerial corporate structures of the United States came to dominate the world economy because they were more efficient than markets.

Legal and political factors were a significant influence on the growth of big business. Large corporations developed through the interaction of government policy, technological innovation, management science, individual entrepreneurs, available skills and market conditions in different countries (Chandler, Amatori and Hikino, 1997).

Markets are highly sensitive to rules made by governments. People will trade art, arms, drugs, influence, secrets, slaves, cuddly toys or whatever makes a profit. How markets are governed determines the balance between risk and reward that makes profit possible. Rulers throughout the ages have learnt to strike bargains with business. In return for permission to trade they levy taxes, borrow money and extract donations for pet projects or political funds. It is a relationship understood by rulers as diverse as Chinese communists, Indian nationalists and American conservatives. The balance between freedom to trade and protection of people, nature or other values is a central political challenge for every age, as new discoveries and desires change what is possible.

Most states seek to create rules that favour businesses they think will benefit their nation. This creates many varieties of capitalism and shades of socialism (see Hall and Soskice, 2001; Campbell *et al.*, 2006; Marshall *et al.*, 2008; Elsner and Hanappi, 2008; Mjøset, 2011). The apparent laissez-faire of the United Kingdom and United States is no less a political choice than the state-led planning of Japan, Korea, France or China.

The internal politics of big businesses are often as important for citizens as the politics of their elected chamber, so that corporate 'units of rule' deserve as much study as the politics of nations. Adam Smith, founder of free market economics, famously observed:

> *The proposal of any new law or regulation of commerce which comes from this order [wealthy merchants and master manufacturers], ought always to be listened to with great precaution, and ought never to be adopted till after having been long and carefully examined, not only with the most scrupulous, but most suspicious attention. It comes from an order of men,*

whose interest is never exactly the same with that of the public, who have generally an interest to deceive and even to oppress the public, and who accordingly have, upon many occasions, both deceived and oppressed it.

(Smith, [1776, 1904] 1976: 278)

'A merchant', Smith wrote, 'is not necessarily the citizen of any particular country. It is in a great measure indifferent to him from what place he carries on his trade; and a very trifling disgust will make him remove his capital, and together with it all the industry which it supports, from one country to another' (Smith, [1776, 1904] 1976: 444). Smith's words still resonate centuries later. Thousands of companies have moved production to low cost-locations and periodically threaten to move their headquarters over regulations or taxes.

Global businesses naturally seek the most hospitable and tax-efficient locations. They employ professional activists to deal with the complex politics of accountancy, law, management, taxation, trade, risk, environment, corporate social responsibility and other areas. They work closely with policymakers to promote favourable rules.

Businesses are more deeply engaged in developing rules of global governance than government officials or pressure groups, and certainly more than elected politicians. As a result, global rules for trade, industry and finance are more robust than for environment, employment, human rights or even security. Institutions such as the World Trade Organization (WTO), World Intellectual Property Organization (WIPO) and investor-state resolution mechanisms are more powerful than the International Labour Organization, UN Children's Fund (UNICEF) or humanitarian agencies, due to sustained political action by business.

The power broker business: Lobbying, consulting and professional persuasion

Ever since mass production made mass markets possible, businesses have used persuasion to promote their products, reputation and political interests. Advertising is the most widespread mass communication in the world. It uses creativity, research and now big data to influence target audiences. Advertising finances much of the internet, press, television and political parties. It creates a cognitive filter for how people understand the world.

In *Manipulating Public Opinion*, the founder of public relations, Edward Bernays, argued that the:

> *conscious and intelligent manipulation of the organized habits and opinions of the masses is an important element in democratic society. Those who manipulate this unseen mechanism of society constitute an invisible government which is the true ruling power of our country ... In almost every act of our daily lives, whether in the sphere of politics or business, in our social conduct or our ethical thinking, we are dominated by the relatively small number of persons ... It is they who pull the wires which control the public mind.*
>
> (1928, in Peters and Simonson, 2004: 37)

Politicians adopted commercial marketing methods long after businesses adopted politicians to further their causes. Political marketing is a well-developed discipline, used by both business and premier league politicians to influence public opinion and decisions. In *Consumer Democracy: The marketing of politics*, Margaret Scammell argued that political marketing can enhance democratic politics (2014), by improving political competition, political literacy and understanding of 'what works' to empower citizens as political consumers.

Business leaders employ a wide range of professions to 'pull the wires which control the public mind':

- **Public relations** (PR) professionals promote their point of view to the press, public, politicians, opinion formers or other target audiences.
- **Public affairs** staff build relationships with politicians and decision-makers.
- **Lobbyists** are public affairs specialists who influence decisions by government or other bodies.
- **Political consultants** and **strategists** like Crosby Texter primarily work political campaigns and parties, but also business, charities, unions and anyone else who wants to win political and public support.
- **Management consultants** are by far the biggest group, who mostly deal with internal office politics or battles between firms in mergers and acquisitions (see chapter 6).
- **Professionals** in accountancy, law, tax, corporate social responsibility and other disciplines devise schemes to protect corporate interests within the public realm, and occasionally to 'deceive and even to oppress the public', as Adam Smith put it.
- **Researchers** in think tanks and universities are funded to create 'thought leadership' and policy options on issues, influencing through

conferences, seminars and policy papers (Stone and Denham, 2004: 3, 42; see also Abelson, 2002).

Each of these disciplines aims to inform and educate politicians, policymakers, opinion formers and the public about the value of their clients, promoting their reputation and influence. These professional political operators are more numerous, and often better paid, than staff of political parties. Together they make up the influence industry and power broking business, mediating between the political system and their clients.

How big is the power broker business?

The lobbying and public relations business is many times bigger than the political parties in most countries. Reliable information is hard to find, partly because definitions of the industry vary widely. The Holmes Report 2016 suggested the global public relations industry was worth almost $14 billion and employed more than 80,000 people in 2015, while the US Bureau of Labor Statistics estimates there were more than 7,000 PR firms in 2012 in the United States alone, with a turnover of $10.5 billion, excluding internal or in-house communications.

The UK influence industry employed about 62,000 people in 2013, with an estimated turnover of £10 billion (PR Week, 18 December 2013), of which about 73 per cent was in-house. The charity sector employed about 5,000 campaigners, less than ten per cent of the total. In *A Quiet Word: Lobbying, crony capitalism and broken politics in Britain* (2014), Cave and Rowell gave a polemical account of the influence industry in British politics, providing numerous case studies of lobbyists, their campaigns, strategy and tactics. Although some of their evidence and analysis is weak, they highlight legitimate concerns about lobbying.

Spending on lobbying and PR in the United Kingdom is about a hundred times more than spending by political parties. The three main political parties from 2001–11 spent an average of £68 million a year according to one eminent source (Kelly, 2011) or £110 million a year from 2005–9 according to Democratic Audit (Wilks-Heeg and Crone, 2007: 7), when the combined turnover of the three main parties was £349 million. Large individual donations accounted for 25 to 60 per cent of the two larger parties' income over the last decade, showing the importance of corporate and personal wealth in party politics.

Like parties and the media, businesses are also in competition with each other, so they are not a unified block. Industry associations and umbrella bodies like the Confederation of British Industry, Institute of Directors, Federation of Small Business or British Bankers Association also advocate for business interests.

Inequality of influence

The growth of lobbying reflects the complexity and power of government. The central issue for citizens is not professional lobbying, since decision-makers need to know what impact their decisions may have on business as much as ordinary citizens. What matters is that unequal access to decision-makers distorts democracy.

A detailed study of 1,779 policy cases in the United States between 1981 and 2002 has shown how unequal this influence can be. Professors Martin Gilens and Benjamin Page studied how often people at different income levels and organized interest groups saw their policy preferences enacted. This showed that 'a proposed policy change with low support among economically elite Americans (one-out-of-five in favour) is adopted only about 18 per cent of the time, while a proposed change with high support (four-out-of-five in favour) is adopted about 45 per cent of the time' (Gilens and Page, 2014: 572). They concluded, 'When a majority of citizens disagrees with economic elites or with organized interests, they generally lose. Moreover, because of the strong status quo bias built into the US political system, even when fairly large majorities of Americans favour policy change, they generally do not get it' (576). 'Ordinary citizens' they say 'have little or no independent influence on policy at all. By contrast, economic elites are estimated to have a quite substantial, highly significant, independent impact' (572). For example, a majority of Americans have supported greater gun control for decades, but the influence of the gun industry and National Rifle Association has made it politically impossible. Katherine Rushton in *The Daily Telegraph* (Rushton, 2014) and other commentators reported that this research showed that America is an oligopoly, not a democracy.

An earlier study by Professor Frederick Solt showed that 'higher levels of income inequality powerfully depress political interest, the frequency of political discussion, and participation in elections among all but the most affluent citizens, providing compelling evidence that greater economic inequality yields greater political inequality' (Solt, 2008).

In their highly technical study of 'The Persistence of Power, Elites and Institutions', Daron Acemoglu and James Robinson (2008) showed how elites who lose power as a result of democratization 'increase their investments in *de facto* power, for example by controlling local law enforcement, mobilizing non-state armed actors, lobbying, or capturing the party system. This will enables them to continue their control of the political process.' This leads to a *captured democracy* that protects economic institutions that favour the elite, a finding supported by other studies (Baumgartner *et al.*, 2009; Benabou, 2000; Bonica *el al.*, 2013).

These studies have profound implications for practical politics. It means that to have an effective voice low-income citizens need to either win support from economic elites or change the rules governing money in politics, and create a sufficiently powerful organization to win political power and protect state institutions from capture by vested interests.

Responsible lobbying

For democracy to work, it needs measures to redress imbalance between powerful interests and ordinary citizens, such as:

- Make lobbying open, so that everyone can see who is lobbying whom about what.
- Give citizens the means to represent their interests as effectively as business and other powerful interests, through practical political education and support.
- Make the politics of business accountable, through consistent, fair rules to ensure accuracy, integrity and transparency.

Edward Bernays, founder of public relations quoted above, said later in life that those 'who heavily influence the channels of communication and action in a media dominated society should be held accountable and responsible for their influence' (1992). If businesses are not accountable for the way they take part in public politics, democracy is impossible. In closed, authoritarian societies business power brokers are more likely to rely on bribes, back door deals and pure power politics. We should expect better in democracies.

Money talks: Campaign finance

'Talking with politicians is a fine thing', as Justin Dart, Chairman of Dart Industries, said in 1978 'but with a little money they hear you better' (Andres, 1985). The more you give, the better they hear. Political parties, candidates, election campaigns and policy development all cost money. Generous donations ensure you are heard. Business and wealthy individuals are the main source of funding for parties in many countries. In the United States more than 60 per cent of the *Forbes 500* biggest businesses and most trade unions fund Political Action Committees (PACs) to promote their interests.

The relationship between money and influence is not linear. Politicians focus on their electorate and their political priorities, and then seek funding. Money can tip the balance, but political ability matters more. Businesses want a return on their investment, but crude attempts to buy influence can backfire. 'Cash for access' is a recurrent issue in democracies. Some analysts argue that campaign contributions should be seen as a legislative subsidy to 'assist natural allies in achieving their own, coincident objectives' (Hall and Deardorff, 2006). Others say 'campaign contributions are not a form of policy-buying, but are rather a form of political participation and consumption' (Ansolabehere *et al.*, 2003). Either way, sponsors strengthen parties that support their interests. Money buys better communications, research and facilities to improve party chances, just as in football wealthy teams buy the best players and poor teams stand little chance of breaking through.

To understand the relationship between business and politics you need to follow the money: who gives what to whom, and what happens as a result.

Trust in business and politics

Trust in business is fundamental to their influence with the public, politicians and governments. Commenting on the power of corporations, Stephen Wilks noted, 'Democratic legitimacy ... appears to be emerging from "brand legitimacy"' (Wilks, 2013: 258). 'Brand legitimacy' is more than a marketing tool for selling products, but promotes a vision of the good life created by corporations in slogans like 'I'm lovin' it' (McDonalds), 'Things go better with Coke' and 'Life tastes good' (Coca-Cola) or 'Just Do It' (Nike). In *No Logo* (1990) Naomi Klein presented a critical analysis of the power of corporate branding that became an international bestseller and reference book for the anti-globalization movement. But 25 years later corporate branding is more pervasive than ever. Brand images are modern icons that adorn almost every art form, sport, T-shirt, website, public place and political space.

In most countries business leaders are trusted more than government leaders, by 58 per cent to 44 per cent on average in 2014. Trust in business was above 75 per cent in the United Kingdom, Canada, Sweden (79 per cent) and Germany (80 per cent), but low in Brazil (42 per cent), India (35 per cent) and Mexico (34 per cent) (Edelman, 2014). This is not just due to propaganda. Businesses are extremely sensitive to attacks on their reputation. They often respond faster than thick-skinned politicians, because they are tested daily in the marketplace and risk losing market share or going under if they lose public support. Companies that fail to respond to customers' changing demands are likely to fold, like Atari, Blockbuster, Kodak, Leman Brothers, Ratners, Schlitz beer, Woolworth's and many others. Only 71 companies from the original *Fortune 500* in 1955 remained in 2014 (14 per cent), and most of these have changed utterly.

The relative good standing of business compared with governments reflects fundamental differences between business and politics, summarized in Table 5.1.

Table 5.1: Ten differences between business and governments

Governments	Business
Serve everyone, regardless of ability to pay	Serve only people who pay
Provide a wide range of diverse services to the whole population with many different needs and demands	Concentrate on fewer products or services, and withdraw from unprofitable areas or difficult customers
Provide services to unwilling customers, such as prisons, tax collection, inspection, etc.	Only serve customers who buy what they produce
Relentless public scrutiny and media attention	Most executives and decision-making are outside the media spotlight
Political leaders constantly pilloried in cartoons, comedy and commentary	Business leaders treated with respect by commentators
Politicians constantly attack each other. Publicity by governments is treated with suspicion by the public and criticized by opposition parties and commentators.	Companies only promote positive features of their own products and rarely criticize competitors. They invest heavily in brand promotion and reputation management.
Benefits or outcomes often difficult to measure	Bottom line and shareholder value easy to measure
Failing public services are often difficult to close or restructure and limp along for decades	Failing businesses closed quickly, sometimes leaving the public sector to pick up the pieces

Used to standing up to relentless opposition and complaints, less likely to admit mistakes and more likely to pick up the pieces from business failures	Often better and more experienced at dealing with risk, customer complaints and scandals, and offloading risks on to the state
Often slow to innovate, due to large number of stakeholders to be satisfied and the veto power of interest groups	Focus on customer service and innovation

These structural differences make business appear more reliable and trustworthy than politics, but they are fundamentally diverse. Politicians and governments can learn from business, about being enterprising and innovative and dealing with failure faster. But most of the time people do not see what goes on in business, where political battles can be more brutal than party politics. This is glimpsed briefly in hostile take-overs, boardroom shakeouts or the conquest of new markets, although the 'quiet politics' of business takeovers is mostly 'shielded from public view' (Culpepper, 2011: xv). Alistair McAlpine's *The New Machiavelli* provided a raucous guide to politics in business by an insider (2000).

Political education by the media

One industry has a particularly influential role in practical politics: the media. Television, press and increasingly the internet are the public's main source of political education. They are also the main channel for politicians to communicate with the public. And they give their owners, editors and commentators the means to influence the political agenda. These three roles are often in conflict.

Ownership, control and use of the media are critical battle grounds in politics. One-party states like China exercise direct control over the media; authoritarian states like Russia and Turkey use intimidation, but in democracies money largely decides who can publish what for whom.

Political parties devote much effort to seeking favourable coverage for themselves and damaging exposure of rivals. Major parties use focus groups, opinion polls and kite flying to test messages with voters. They plan a long campaign to set the media agenda in the run up to an election, and plot daily topics on their communications grid. This has been extensively described by its practitioners, including Philip Gould, one of New Labour's campaign advisers, in *The Unfinished Revolution* (1998); Damian McBride, political aide to Gordon Brown from 1999 to 2009, in *A Decade of Policy, Plots and Spin* (2013); Steven Foster (2010: 34); and most fully in Alastair Campbell's diaries (2007, 2010, 2011, 2012). Piers Morgan tells his side of the stories as editor of the *News of the World* and *Daily Mirror* in *The Insider: The private diaries of a scandalous decade* (2005). Richard Desmond said that when he bought the *Daily Express* in 2000, the Prime Minister, Tony Blair, rang to invite him for a celebratory drink and persuaded him to support Labour in the election a year later (Desmond, 2015).

Every newspaper, broadcaster and news website is also a political arena, fraught with argument about personalities, resources, lines to take and priorities between subjects, guided by the proprietor's preferences. Editorial meetings are important political forums. Decisions about what stories to investigate, what to put on the front page, the content of leader columns and who to commission as columnists are part of a nation's political process. Coverage of politics competes with advertising, business, celebrities, human interest, sport and other topics in the internal politics of media companies.

Trust in media and politicians

Viewers, readers and listeners tend to trust the media more than politicians (Edelman, 2013) and may be more loyal to their paper than a party, although this varies widely depending on which media and which politician. Papers have to keep readers' support every day, parties only every few years. Most readers interact with their paper or its website more than with any political party or elected representative, and may feel it represents their views better than any politician. In the United Kingdom 20 million adults (38 per cent) read a newspaper daily, and two-thirds (66 per cent) every week (June 2015), with growing numbers accessing news online. This means they have more readers than there are supporters for all the political parties put together. More affluent people (social grade ABC1) are 20 per cent more likely to read a paper than lower income groups (C2DE), and will read the more extensive broadsheet press.

Media owners are proud of their papers' robust role in politics. As *The Sun* boasted after John Major's 1992 election victory, 'IT'S THE SUN WOT WON IT', although its chairman Rupert Murdoch later said the headline was 'tasteless and wrong'. Readers also like their paper to take a stand on issues – like the *Daily Mail*'s campaigns over Stephen Lawrence's murderers or bad behaviour by the banks after 2008. In the 2016 EU referendum campaign the *Daily Express, Daily Mail, The Sun* and *The Daily Telegraph* actively campaigned for the UK to leave the EU.

As a public service, the BBC is obliged to be politically neutral with a duty to educate and inform. As a result the BBC is the most trusted of news outlets. But it also has internal politics and a public agenda that is occasionally challenged from left and right (Higgins, 2014).

The internet is disrupting traditional media, pushing some newspapers out of print, creating additional revenue streams and making it easier for the public and pressure groups to have a voice through Twitter, blogs and comment pages. Campaigning websites like Avaaz, Change.org, MoveOn and 38 Degrees have hundreds of millions of subscribers – more than parties – who have won numerous campaign victories (see www.change.org/impact; 38 Degrees, 2014). In Italy the *Movimento 5 Stelle* (Five Star Movement or M5S) largely built its base and developed its programme online since 2009, then won the second largest number of votes of any party in the 2013 general election and 2014 European election, and the mayoral elections in Rome and Turin in 2016. Essex MP Douglas Carswell predicted that digital media means *The End of Politics and the Birth of Democracy* (2012), by cutting out 'meddlesome middlemen' in the media and government to give people direct control over the goods and services they want. But traditional political parties and campaigners are also investing heavily in using new media to reach target audiences, so it is hard to predict how far power will really shift.

Citizens need to learn media literacy to understand how it works, how to use the media to have their say about issues of the day and how to win and use power accountably. The press and television, particularly the BBC, could also play a bigger role in giving citizens impartial information on how the system works, contentious issues and how to have an effective voice in politics.

Conclusion: Political education and the powerful
This chapter has provided evidence that:

- Leaders develop political abilities from an early age, through their families, schools, university, apprenticeships and mentors in politics and business.
- Powerful politicians and business leaders employ experienced coaches, consultants and advisers to help them win political battles.
- Governments create the rules that influence the way that markets work, so that businesses need to engage in politics under any political system.

- The 'power broking business' of political consultants, public relations and lobbyists provide high-level political education and support to those who can afford it.
- The power broking business is many times bigger (and probably more influential) than political parties in democratic countries.
- Big businesses are a major force in politics, acting as 'governing institutions' that may be more powerful than elected politicians, particularly at an international level.
- Branding and public relations have an important role in the influence of business.
- Businesses tend to be more trusted than politicians or governments due to differences in how they work and are scrutinized.
- The media are simultaneously the public's main source of political education, politicians' main means of communicating with the public and a platform for proprietors to promote their interests.
- Social media are starting to disrupt traditional forms of political organization.

In this context individual citizens are completely outgunned by professional players from business and politics. Charities, faith groups, pressure groups, trade unions and other civil society associations can strengthen citizens' voices on issues they care about. But even pressure groups with professional staff are like village football teams pitched against premier league clubs. This imbalance in political influence raises profound questions about the health of democracies.

There are many different ways in which this could be addressed, but the very least is that all citizens should be able to develop the skills, knowledge and confidence to have an equal voice with the most powerful. Education can help to create greater equality of influence necessary for democracy.

LEARN MORE ABOUT LOBBYING

Read

Lobbying: The art of political persuasion by Lionel Zetter (2014 [2008]), probably the most comprehensive, practical and up-to-date handbook, covering the United Kingdom, United States, Europe, Asia and the Gulf, including refreshingly frank tips and a lot of reference material.

Public Affairs in Practice: A practical guide to lobbying by Stuart Thomson and Steve John (2006) of the Institute of Public Relations, covers the essentials of lobbying in the United Kingdom and Europe plus chapters on developing a campaign to bring about policy change, the role of stakeholder relations and corporate social responsibility (CSR). It includes the codes of conduct and regulations of professional lobbyists.

Practice

Choose a cause you believe in and then volunteer or work for a campaign run by someone with a successful track record. In the United Kingdom these are often advertised at: www.w4mpjobs.org and www.work4anMP.org (and include work with MPs). Check the credentials of the organization and individual by asking a specialist in the field.

Pick a cause and choose a specific, practical short-term objective within it, such as getting a local councillor to take up an issue, a statement of support from a politician, a short amendment to a Bill in Parliament, evidence before a Select Committee, an answer to a question or action by someone in authority.

Use the web to identify your targets (officials, politicians) and an achievable objective, and then organize to achieve it.

Chapter 6

All politics is office politics

In this chapter you will learn:

- About the politics of two great debt crises
- Why all politics comes down to office politics
- How changing the story about an issue changes the politics
- How whistle-blowers take an issue from the office into public politics
- How blowing the trumpet promotes policy and practice
- How a 'Core Group' controls any organization (and how to find them)
- About the 'bargain of mutual commitment' between leaders and the rest
- Why accountants and management consultants are 'political educators' of office politics
- Why management thinking has more influence than political ideologies

Case studies: Jubilee 2000 and the Great Crash

This chapter tells the stories behind two debt crises: the ten-year Jubilee campaign to write off $100 billion owed by the world's poorest people, and the ten months it took governments to pledge 11 trillion dollars to rescue some of the world's richest people after the Great Crash of 2008.

The story began in July 1944, when British economist John Maynard Keynes lost a political argument with US Treasury officials at a conference in Bretton Woods about ground rules for two new institutions, the International Monetary Fund (IMF) and the World Bank. Keynes predicted that the US proposals would lead to unpayable debts between nations, but the Americans had the power to insist on their rules. Seventy years later the world is still struggling with unpayable debt as a result of this flawed decision. This is a powerful example of how rules for supra-political institutions shape reality long after they are made, and the difference that winning or losing a political battle can make.

Debt interest became a burden for many poor countries in the 1980s. Money flowed from the world's poorest nations into its richest. A growing number of academics, churches, development agencies and international solidarity groups took up the issue. There were many conferences, demonstrations and publications. People set up organizations such as the US Debt Crisis Network (1985–90); the European Network on Debt and Development; the UK Debt Crisis Network (DCN) formed in 1990; AFRODAD, in 1996; and more. But they had little impact on the $70bn of debt held by the IMF and World Bank.

The UK Debt Crisis Network recognized that the lack of a single overarching campaign was a weakness. After Ed Mayo of the New Economics Foundation became chair in 1992, the Network shifted emphasis from a policy-based network to campaigning and launched a petition to mobilize support for a joint call to action. It was funded by individuals who pooled money for progressive projects through the Network for Social Change.

Meanwhile, in February 1990, Martin Dent, a politics lecturer at Keele University, wrote a short paper called 'Why we are founding Jubilee 2000' and asked his students to sign a petition calling for cancellation of the unpayable debts of the poorest countries. Dent was 64, an old Etonian and former colonial civil servant in Nigeria, who had taught at Keele since 1963, and a devout Christian. He saw unpayable debt as a kind of slavery. 'Jubilee' was the ancient Jewish practice of cancelling debts and releasing slaves every 50 years (Leviticus 25: 10). The idea of a linking a 'Debt Jubilee' to the millennial year (a 'Kairos moment', or 'Special Time'), had been suggested by his friend Dr Michael Schluter, who founded the Jubilee Centre in 1983. Dent worked full time on the campaign after his retirement in 1990. He wrote to every MP, High Commissioner, Ambassador and many church leaders, as well as others campaigning on the issue. In 1993 he met Bill Peters, a former high commissioner in Malawi and chair of the Society for the Propagation of the Gospel. Together they involved more people to form the Jubilee 2000 Charitable Trust in 1996, which raised money and employed a few staff.

In 1997 the two campaigns merged. Although some of the new group suggested changing the name to a more secular 'Debt-Free 2000', Jubilee 2000 became the rallying cry for the wider campaign. 'Jubilee' reframed the argument over debt. Pope John Paul endorsed it; the Anglican Synod supported it; priests urged parishioners to support it; stars like Bob Geldof, Bono, Willie Colón, Youssou N'Dour and many others gave benefit concerts; even Republican Senator Jesse Helms backed it. Large NGOs like Christian Aid and Oxfam provided high-quality research and campaign materials, as well as links with Southern NGOs.

The campaign had a very specific focus: to cut debts of 52 countries and improve the World Bank's initiative for Heavily Indebted Poorer Countries (HIPC), not to abolish the Bretton Woods institutions. Ann Pettifor, campaign co-ordinator, said, 'Designing a campaign is like looking at a diamond. The specialists, they look at the diamonds for two years before they cut them and then they get the maximum reflection from the diamonds. So you would have to cut the problem in the way that would get the maximum reflection.' The message was positioned to 'be radical enough to mobilize people but not so radical that you were marginalized'. It presented the issue in human, accessible and emotional terms, using short, punchy sentences (Grenier, 2003: 93–4).

Inevitably there were internal arguments about aims, organization and conduct of the campaign. There were tensions between smaller organizations and the large NGOs who mainly funded it. Some big aid agencies were anxious it was competing for funds, media coverage and public support. Its informal, horizontal way of working tested their hierarchical management structures. It was also challenged by Jubilee South, a network of activists in Africa and Latin America, who called for repudiation of the debt as illegitimate, reparations for colonialism and rejection of the global financial institutions. There was another rift with Jubilee 2000/USA, who wanted to support Congressman Jim Leach's bill that included conditions for debt relief.

But the campaign stayed united. A meeting in Rome in 1998 created a loose international alliance to share information, intelligence and thinking on policy as well as the Jubilee 2000 name and logo. Co-ordination was mostly informal. In June 1998 a joyful human chain of 50,000 to 70,000 people encircled the G7 meeting in Birmingham and leaders of the Jubilee campaign met with Prime Minister Tony Blair. The following year 100,000 people surrounded the G8 summit in Cologne, Germany. The summit agreed to cancel $111 billion of debt, half the $260bn now owed. Christian Aid said it would take 1,370 Red Nose Days to raise the same amount of money. The campaign enabled the world's poorest countries to spend more money on education, medical care and poverty reduction.

By the end of 2000, ten years after Martin Dent started his petition, there were Jubilee campaigns in 69 countries, the UK Coalition had 110 member organizations and more than 24.2 million people from 166 countries had signed the petition. In 2001 Dent quoted from his ancestor Thomas Fowell Buxton (1786–1845), a social reformer, member of parliament and campaigner against the slave trade, that 'with ordinary talents and extraordinary perseverance, all things are attainable'.

After the Millennium the Jubilee 2000 coalition was wound down amid controversy. Several national and international groupings continued. Jubilee 2000's own self-assessment was that 'the unpayable debt will not be cancelled in full until we have changed the process whereby debt cancellation is agreed. Future campaigns, therefore, will have to tackle the deep structural injustices of international financial relationships' (Jubilee 2000 Coalition, 2000: 7). But the problem identified by Keynes in 1944 happened again and again, most recently in the financial crisis of 2007.

Reflections

Jubilee 2000 was the world's biggest civil society campaign since the abolition of slavery. There are disputes about how much debt was cancelled, but it was substantial. The campaign improved relationships between the world's richest and poorest countries, although many problems (and debts) remain. Five years later in 2005, the world leaders' G8 meeting in Gleneagles agreed to cancel debt for Highly Indebted Poor Countries (HIPCs) following another mobilization, Make Poverty History.

The campaign has many important lessons and is worth studying closely. A few key points are:

- The Jubilee concept reframed the issue to make the most of the millennium moment.
- Churches, aid agencies and trade unions created a broad coalition that reached millions of people across the political spectrum and the world.
- Support for the petition created a mandate to speak with world leaders and push the issue up their agenda.
- The organizers of the UK Debt Crisis Network, Martin Dent, Bill Peters, Ann Pettifor and others didn't give up, while leadership of the IMF, World Bank and G7 countries changed during the ten-year campaign.
- The campaign had a clear focus that the G7 Governments could act on (cancellation of unpayable debts of the 52 poorest countries), a target date (2000) and strong evidence.
- The coalition held together, despite or because of its loose governance structure; it maintained a clear, achievable focus that balanced many different interests across five continents; and it achieved a significant result.

The campaign was driven by passionate people who mobilized millions to influence the most powerful political leaders in the world. But the decisive battle grounds were not the public conferences, petitions, public meetings or even demonstrations, important as they were. The critical encounters were in the 'office politics' of the many agencies involved. If the Network for Social Change or big aid agencies had not backed the campaign, would it have taken off? If the proposal to rename the merged campaign had succeeded, would it have won such broad support? What if governments had decided to resist, as they did when a broad coalition campaigned for the Brandt Report in 1980? What if the IMF and World Bank had stuck to their rules and refused to budge?

Many equally worthy campaigns have not got off the ground, including several modelled on Jubilee 2000, because they were not able to get enough of the key ingredients together. Decisive factors for Jubilee 2000 were the commitments by many organizations to provide staff and resources for a broad-based coalition, its focus on a clear objective and its resonant names. Chris Stalker, a campaigner at Oxfam, says that 60 per cent or more of any campaign takes place within an organization, to persuade colleagues, managers and the board to commit the resources needed to 'cut the diamond', in Ann Pettifor's memorable phrase.

All politics is office politics (almost)

Tip O'Neill, long serving Democratic Speaker of the US House of Representatives (1977–87), famously said 'All politics is local', the title of his book about rules of politics (1994). But most of his stories are actually about office politics in Congress, the Democratic Party or other agencies. One of his tips is 'It's easier to run for office than to run the office'. Another is 'Don't give speeches that are pure bunk', in other words, just about local issues. This was about Senator Felix Walker from Buncombe County North Carolina, who in 1820 gave a long speech. When asked why, he replied, 'I am speaking to Buncombe', and the phrase *bunkum* became another word for claptrap. The reality is that politicians need to secure their base through local politics, but power politics takes place in the offices of leaders, factions, ministries, media, businesses, unions and agencies where decisions are made.

Office politics are the internal politics of any organization. They influence decisions about strategy, priorities, budgets, structure, staff, rewards, sanctions, ground rules and external relationships. Survival at the top of any organization depends on strategic alliances and control over sources of power in the organization. This includes the ability to bring in revenue and deal with its external environment successfully. Work in any organization involves both getting on with the job (producing goods or services) and influencing others about priorities, policies and resources. The higher you are, the more office politics you do. Those at the very top are usually engaged full time in office politics. Most office politics is routine negotiation through established structures, but organizations also have their back-channels, hidden hierarchies and baronies that don't appear on any organizational chart. When concerns about risks or wrongdoing at work are taken out of the office into the public domain through whistleblowing they may become public politics.

Public politics in the media, parliament and constituencies are only the visible tip of the democratic process. A good speech and well-staged campaign can be decisive in winning support and taking power. But behind the scenes are the directors, speech writers and managers who keep the machinery of politics running. Beneath the stage and behind the organizers are the power centres, in offices where leading politicians work with policy advisers and strategists like Lyndon Crosby or Frank Luntz to decide what to do. Beyond them are the offices of the permanent government, the civil service and agencies that actually run state institutions. The ultimate success or failure of any public victory in politics depends on effective office politics in the machinery of government, which translates policy into spending plans, institutions and job roles. Around them are the offices of other power centres – banks, businesses, media, local government, public services, trade unions and non-profits – that have their own internal politics. Big demonstrations like Jubilee 2000, Million Man March or Stop the War usually start with the office politics that decide to launch a campaign.

A great deal of public politics is about one office trying to influence the politics of another office. People within aid agencies had to influence staff of other agencies to join forces through Jubilee 2000, which in turn influenced government offices to lobby senior officials in the IMF and World Bank. Ambitious political parties are tightly controlled from the leaders' office, whose mission is to occupy the offices of state through a well-run election campaign. Most political battles are resolved eyeball to eyeball, when key players face each other and agree, compromise or decide to fight. The course of big public battles can turn on the decision of a few people at the centre to support or oppose a colleague, such as the decision by Michael Gove and Boris Johnson to lead the UK campaign to leave the European Union in 2016. But most political battles are scarcely seen outside the offices where they are waged.

Office politics goes on in every workplace. The manoeuvrings in any business, charity, church, newspaper or political party require similar skills. All organizations are different, of course. Some are tyrannies, ruled by fear; some are participative, with countless committees, consultations and hidden hierarchies; others are creative chaos; and a few are well run. But all are 'units of rule', with their own constitutions, laws, cultures and customs. Some of these private polities are more enduring and more powerful than the public politics of the state.

Understanding office politics is essential for three main reasons:

1. **Power is exercised through institutions** – banks, corporations, states, political parties, armies, security services, intergovernmental agencies, media empires, trades unions, alliances and change agencies. Even the most powerful people in the world rely on institutions to achieve their goals. The office politics of institutions can frustrate even the mighty and amplify the influence of the powerless.

2. **Most day-to-day politics takes place in offices,** and in corridors, cafés, bars, clubs, conferences, hotels, dinner parties, social networks or other extensions of the office. Public politics are a crucial test in the democratic process, but most of the heavy lifting takes place behind closed doors. It is often too late to save or sink a proposal by the time it goes public. Knowing how to do office politics is one of the secrets of success in most walks of life, including public politics.

3. **How offices work makes a big difference to society.** Because our world is run through institutions, both private and public, people need to be good at office politics to get things done. Effective politics is about creating and running institutions (offices) capable of providing the security, goods and services that people need to live well.

> *Effective politics is about creating and running institutions (offices) capable of providing the security, goods and services people need to live well.*

Office politics inside big bureaucracies like the UK Health Service, Chinese Communist Party, Google, Microsoft, BP and other *Fortune 500* companies can affect more people than most elections. Bureaucratic battles are rarely visible, but they can be as gruelling as any election campaign, and just as important.

The ability to navigate the office politics of your own organization and understand the office politics of those you want to influence are essential in any regime, time or place. Office politics is everywhere and affects everyone, from the shop floor to the Oval office, Kremlin or Zhongnanhai. Some politicians triumph in the politics of their party to gain the highest offices of state, but fail in the office politics of government to achieve much with their power.

Office politics are not a trivial side show to the real politics of state. They are the frontline of executive action. The 'supra-politics' of finance, law and national security are conducted in offices that set system conditions for everything else. They created the unpayable debts of developing countries in the first place, and responded to the public demands of Jubilee 2000. The financial crash of 2008 was sown in the office politics of institutions created to minimize risk. The intrigues of office politics are no less intense in non-democratic societies, only more concealed. But the consequences of winning or losing office battles can be a matter of life or death in any country.

The financial crash of 2008 provides many dramatic case studies of how office politics have shaped – and shaken – the world. Political battles within financial institutions and regulators nearly destroyed the capitalist system.

Case study: The campaign for derivatives

While Jubilee 2000 was challenging governments to cut a debt burden of about $100 billion on the world's poorest nations, another campaign was wrangling within banks and regulators that eventually got governments to pledge $11 trillion – 10,000 times more – to relieve debts of the world's richest banks.

Gillian Tett's *Fool's Gold* (2009) tells the inside story of how Peter Hancock and his multinational team of traders navigated the internal politics of J.P. Morgan to create credit derivatives in the early 1990s, then mobilized other banks to lobby against the threat of regulation. In 1990 Hancock was a 32-year-old British banker in J.P. Morgan's New York headquarters. He led the derivatives team, creating financial products to help companies manage risks associated with debt. The regulatory authorities were expressing concerns about derivatives, so a coalition of bankers, the International Swaps and Derivatives Association (ISDA), started to lobby. Their first opportunity was an invitation to lead a study of derivatives with an influential group of economists, academics and bankers called the Group of Thirty (G30), funded by the Rockefeller Foundation and led by Paul Volker, former chair of the Federal Reserve Bank (from 1979–87). Hancock and J.P. Morgan staff led the G30 study. It was published in 1993, an influential three-volume guide to derivatives. They argued for self-regulation by the industry. This was a victory in office politics.

During 1992 and 1993 the deal value of derivatives had grown from $5.3 trillion to $8.5 trillion a year, almost equal to a third of global GDP ($25tr). The chairman of the Bank of Canada warned that derivatives were 'a time bomb that could explode just like the Latin-American Debt Crisis'. America's General Accounting Office published its own 196-page study of derivatives warning of systemic risks. Officials at the New York Federal Reserve also wanted regulation. Politicians on both sides of Congress submitted four bills proposing regulations. Bill Clinton had taken a tough line on Wall Street in his campaign for the presidency in 1992. Peter Hancock and the derivatives trade were under threat. But the ISDA lobby was well connected. The head of Clinton's National Economic Council was Robert Rubin, a former arbitrageur at Goldman Sachs. Rubin reassured Clinton that regulation was unnecessary and went on to lead the deregulation of Wall Street. Thus the seeds for the 2008 financial crisis were sown by a political victory within the offices of the Clinton administration (Tett, 2009: 27–47; Roberts, 2014).

Hancock's derivatives team then solved a political problem created by an international rule (the Basel I accord of 1988) to hold capital reserves for corporate loans. They invented the 'credit default swap', an arrangement with another bank to offload risk through an insurance policy. Regulators loved it, because it seemed to spread risk. Other banks loved it, because it was easy money. The derivatives team loved it, because it created a new income stream. But the politics of persuading senior J.P. Morgan officials was difficult. Then a new CEO in 1995 changed the political landscape at J.P. Morgan, giving the derivatives team more power to exploit their invention. Political battles with 'dinosaurs' in the bank continued, although dinosaur caution eventually saved J.P. Morgan from the worst excesses of Wall Street.

Tett, a social anthropologist by training, concluded that 'while plenty of greedy bankers play crucial parts in the drama … the real tragedy of this story is that so many of those swept up in the lunacy were not acting out of deliberately bad motives' (xviii). She explained what happened in terms of Bourdieu's *Outline of a Theory of Practice* (1977 [1972]), which observed that elites tend to control a society by influencing the way it talks about itself, its discourse and cognitive map, as much as through power and wealth. How it talks also influences what is *not* mentioned in public, because it is taboo, boring or completely taken for granted. 'Areas of social silence, in other words, are crucial to support a story that a society is telling itself, such as that about the credit boom' (xiii). Breaking this silence is an essential step in changing the balance of power.

Changing the story

The art of politics involves controlling the story, the narrative that frames an issue for policymakers and the public. The authors of the financial crash first created new stories within banking, out-manoeuvring 'dinosaur' risk managers within their own banks, captivating regulators and then enchanting politicians like Bill Clinton, Tony Blair and Gordon Brown. Jubilee 2000 changed the story about the debt burden on the poor, but it was a $100 billion sideshow compared with the multi-trillion derivatives market. After 2010 the political stories have changed again, to towering debt mountains, austerity and fiscal discipline. The narrative among central bankers is much more interesting, about global co-operation, crisis management, printing money (quantitative easing) and keeping the system going, but that is another storybook.

The 2007 crash wiped about 13 per cent from global production, reduced world trade by a fifth and led to the collapse of countless companies, including more than 500 US banks, Lehman Brothers, Bears Stearns and AIG (compared with just ten bank failures over the previous five years) (FDIC, 2015). The crash cost millions of people their jobs, a decade of financial austerity across Europe and a multi-trillion dollar rescue of private banks by taxpayers: in 2009 the IMF estimated that Western governments had pledged $11 trillion to support banks, although most was not used (Tett, 2009: 307). The origins and scale of the crisis were due to political decisions by governments to deregulate financial markets, which enabled financial institutions to create unsustainable credit. The scale of austerity was also a consequence of political decisions by governments. But the office politics of the banking crisis is more important than the public politics of state regulation, because finance knows no borders and can always find a loophole, tax haven, financial instrument or shadow system to get round it. Mortgage bonds, credit derivatives and default swaps were all ways of getting round well-intentioned regulatory constraints.

More than 300 books have been written about the financial crisis. Many show how ambition, greed and power-lust drove the office politics that took banks over the edge. They describe political battles fought and lost within and between institutions that let it happen. After the crash governments jumped to rescue failing banks, pledging vast sums to shore up plunging balance sheets. Most of the intense bargaining between bankers, politicians and civil servants was inter-office politics, behind closed doors. Public politics played a relatively small part, and then mainly in America, where legislators scrutinize the executive more actively. US Treasury Secretary Hank Paulson, another former senior partner at Goldman Sachs, had to persuade Congress to approve a $700 billion bailout package, the Troubled Asset Relief Programme (TARP). In the United Kingdom the Chancellor Alistair Darling and the Governor of the central bank Mervyn King made statements to parliament and the press, like dispatches from the battle front. Most elected politicians were spectators, not participants in the politics of the crisis (Edmonds *et al.*, 2010). Parliamentarians investigated what happened and recommended reforms after the big decisions had already been taken.

Political decisions over the banking crash in Greece, Iceland, Ireland, China, the European Union, United Kingdom and United States showed very different responses to the crisis. In Greece politicians and people were intensely involved, but powerless against the officials of the IMF, European Union and other member states. China, the United States and United Kingdom had the power to print money to stimulate their economies. In Iceland politicians let the banks collapse, 29 senior bankers were sentenced to prison and the economy regenerated, like a forest after a fire. In Ireland and the United Kingdom governments decided to bail out the banks behind closed doors, then got Parliament to approve spending cuts to pay for it.

Alan Greenspan, chairman of the US Federal Reserve until 2006, was the most powerful person in the politics of finance while the crisis was brewing. He admitted that his 'ideology was not right':

> *I made a mistake in presuming that the self-interests of organizations, specifically banks and others, were such that they were best capable of protecting their own shareholders and their equity in the firms. ... I discovered a flaw in the model that I perceived is the critical functioning structure that defines how the world works.*
>
> (HOGRC, 23 October 2008)

This flawed model was central to the institutional dynamics that created the crisis, but there is little evidence that the model has fundamentally changed since. Political movements such as Occupy, Syriza in Greece and Podemos in Spain have challenged it on the streets and at the ballot box, to little effect so far. Economists like Nouriel Roubini (2010), Joseph Stiglitz (2010), Mark Blyth (2013), Paul Krugman (2013), Raghuram Rajan (2010), Martin Wolf (2015) and many others have analysed its flaws and proposed solutions, warning that another crisis is likely unless they are addressed. Rajan, a former chief economist at the IMF who warned of the impending crisis in 2005, even proposed that 'multilateral institutions like the IMF and World Bank should take a cue from the movements promoting actions against climate change and supporting aid to poor countries' to campaign against the global trade imbalances that cause recurrent crises. In other words, mount a Jubilee 2000-style campaign to correct the flaw in the system created when Keynes lost his battle with the US Treasury in 1944, and change the story about global finance.

Taking office politics into the open

The line between office politics and public politics is crossed every time someone takes an issue from the office into the public domain. Jubilee 2000 took the debt crisis from the offices of the IMF and World Bank on to the street, so that the world leaders couldn't miss it when they went into meetings of the G7. The battle over derivatives was mostly conducted in the offices of banks, regulators and the US National Economic Council. There were many warnings of risks to the financial system, but they were barely heard in public politics (Hansell and Muehring, 1992; Lewis, 2010; Harrison, 2005; Rajan, 2010; Roubini and Mihm, 2010; Cable, 2010). None disturbed the dominant story about the City's success, the 'end of boom and bust', home ownership and rising wealth as told by those in power. Critics were ignored, silenced or dismissed. A few mavericks, like Burry and Eisman, bet against the system and made a lot of money, as dramatized in the film of *The Big Short*. The collective silence of the City, regulators and governments screened out the alarm signals until it was too late.

What happens in Wall Street, Whitehall and Washington is mostly office politics. Intrigues within banks, corporations, hospitals, universities and non-profits occasionally erupt in public, but are often ignored. But to overlook politicking within offices is to miss the most powerful politics in practice, with sometimes fatal consequences.

Blowing the whistle

Often we only hear about wrongdoing because an insider passes information to someone outside, crossing from office politics into public politics, often via the office politics of another organization such as a newspaper, pressure group or politician. Investigative journalists have a crucial role in shedding light on private politics that powerful people don't want the public to see. Whistleblowing can change the course of national politics, such as the Watergate scandal that ended President Nixon's career (1972–4), Enron (2001) or Edward Snowden's exposure of secret surveillance (2013). The practical politics of whistleblowing are different if you are in a position of governing, the organization in which wrongdoing is taking place, in an intermediary organization or government, or if you are a challenger, or indeed a whistleblower.

It takes courage to reveal wrongdoing by colleagues. People who raise concerns internally, like Sherron Watkins at Enron, are easily sidelined and can suffer reprisals. Raising concerns externally can be even more risky, and may not make much difference. Public criticism can damage or destroy an organization, without necessarily solving the problem.

Many organizations now recognize the benefits of encouraging internal whistleblowing to protect staff who identify concerns and address problems early. After a series of scandals in the health service, the UK government created a 'duty of candour' on health professionals to reveal mistakes and wrongdoing. The airline industry developed an approach to flight safety called 'Just Culture', which encourages staff to be open about mistakes (GAIN WG, 2004), now part of EU law (Regulation 691/2010).

Whistleblowing is increasingly recognized as a public good, protected by law. In the US whistleblowers can be rewarded with about 16 per cent of the fines levied. In 2012 the former banker Bradley Ray was paid a $104 million reward by the US Inland Revenue for blowing the whistle on a tax fraud case in the Swiss bank UBS. Cheryl Eckard, a former employee of drug maker GlaxoSmithKline, was paid $96 million for revealing manufacturing faults.

Raising concerns at work is a significant act of office politics. Sometimes it is possible to change things through official channels, so always try them first if safe to do so. But often wrongdoing can only be dealt with by people inside and outside the organization working together.

Blowing the trumpet

For every example of harmful office politics, there are many people using office politics to make a positive difference. Many business books use stories of corporate success or failure to demonstrate general principles, such as *Built to Last* (1994) and *Good to Great* (2001) by Jim Collins, *Toyota Production System* by Taiichi Ohno and *Reengineering the Corporation* (2006) by Michael Hammer and James Champy. These are text books in office politics for executives.

One of the most famous of this type was Tom Peters and Bob Waterman's study of 43 outstanding clients of McKinsey Consulting, *In Search of Excellence* (1982). They identified eight themes such as A Bias for Action, Close to the Customer, Managing by Walking About, and Productivity through People. The book sold three million copies in its first four years. It became an inspiration for corporation renewal and flat, flexible organizations that valued staff and customers.

In Search of Excellence is also a case study in the office politics of McKinsey, where Peters and Waterman worked, as described in Peters' 'confessions' (2001). It took off because they were in the margins, a long way from 'headquarters politics' that 'invariably and inevitably "bland up" and then kill any worthwhile project'. It had 'lower expectations, far less political baggage, and much less management scrutiny'. Second, it did not set out to prove a theory: 'I went out and talked to genuinely smart, remarkably interesting, first-rate people.' Third, the choice of companies was based on insight, not metrics: the McKinsey mantra. Finally, Peters had an agenda, which was to challenge the 'hierarchy and command-and-control, top-down business operation' preached by business guru Peter Drucker, the statistics and systems of Robert McNamara and the bureaucracy of Xerox, 'Chase Manhattan Bank, Western Electric, and most of McKinsey's typical clients'. It was against all the 'conventional thinking that was running American business back in 1981, the bean-counter mentality', Taylorism and scientific management. It was for passion, values, 'management by wandering around. It was anthropology, not statistical analysis!'

'We got away with it because Bob Waterman and I wore dark McKinsey suits with skinny McKinsey ties and spoke proper McKinsey consulting business-speak. *Search* is a McKinsey-looking book. It has a black cover with a conservative white typeface. Our message was revolutionary, but our credentials and our look were traditional.' A radical message in conservative packaging is often more effective than the self-proclaimed revolutionary who attracts attention (and opposition).

Above all, the book was about new ways of doing business, which they observed at Hewlett Packard, 3M, Dana Corp and 40 other companies: 'we were in search of excellence. Not competitive advantage. Not economic growth. Not market dominance or strategic differentiation. Not maximized shareholder value. Excellence. It's just as true today. Business isn't some disembodied bloodless enterprise. Profit is fine – a sign that the customer honours the value of what we do. But "enterprise" (a lovely word) is about heart. About beauty. It's about art. About people throwing themselves on the line. It's about passion and the selfless pursuit of an ideal.' This vision of business has inspired many corporate leaders to create more humane, progressive organizations. In other words, it was an exercise in practical politics aimed at changing corporate culture, which it did.

Another influential collection of 'hero stories' in office politics is David Osborne and Ted Gaebler's *Reinventing Government: How the entrepreneurial spirit is transforming the public sector* (1993), which tells numerous stories from across the United States to identify 36 options for providing better public services.

Good case studies of organizational change from within provide insights and inspiration for different ways of doing things in your own institution, although simply transferring lessons from one place to another is a recipe for failure. Nothing can beat the value of a sound method, informed observation and action tailored to the specific circumstances of a particular organization.

The Core Group

The key to office politics is knowing *who* has power and what they want. In *Who Really Matters: The Core Group theory of power, privilege and success*, Art Kleiner (2003) looked at the actual behaviour and accomplishments of organizations, including companies, unions, government agencies and schools. Kleiner showed that 'every organization is continually acting to fulfil the perceived needs and priorities of its Core Group' (4), which are more important than its stated mission. This explains why, for example, some hospitals and care homes can tolerate abuse of patients, why churches founded on the principle that God is love could kill and torture in God's name, why banks almost wrecked the financial system and why political parties in government usually fail to achieve their stated aims. Only when the Core Group's priorities are fully in line with the organization's mission does it stand a chance of achieving them. This is a profound insight for anyone seeking to influence organizations, from the inside or outside.

Kleiner identifies the 'bargain of mutual commitment' as a key driver of organizations: 'The people of the organization agree to make decisions on behalf of the Core Group, while the Core Group members agree to dedicate themselves as leaders to the organization's best interests. When it works, the result of this arrangement is greatness' (8, 49). Things go wrong when the Core Group pursue other interests.

The Core Group sets the organization's direction and '*the organization becomes whatever its people perceive that the Core Group needs and wants it to become*' (8, italics in original). In *Power at Work: The art of making things happen*, leadership consultant Jo Owen described how:

> something odd happens when you finally become partner or CEO. Suddenly all your jokes become funnier. Your taste in art, food and wine becomes excellent. Your judgement and ideas become better. ... When you have an idea, you may be alarmed to find that people have gone away and acted on it, even though it was no more than a passing thought.

(2007: 146)

The Core Group is a handbook for high-level office politics, for people at or near the top and in the middle. It is full of stories, strategies and exercises to understand how to achieve change in an organization. The heart of this process is the 'bargain of mutual commitment' in which the staff or members of the organization give legitimacy and power to a Core Group in exchange for results. Kleiner observed that most people legitimize their boss and the status quo because they tend not to think they have a choice, their jobs depend on it and 'cognitive complexity' – to do otherwise is just too demanding (49). This psychology corresponds with research that shows that relatively powerless people often explain their position in society and accept the status quo in what is known as 'system justification theory' (Jost *et al.*, 2004), or what Marx called false consciousness.

The person at the top is not necessarily leader of the Core Group or even a member. Some chiefs are merely figureheads, as entertainingly portrayed in the television series *Yes Minister*. People who work in an organization, even at a junior level, sense who is in the Core Group and know when power shifts. Membership of the Core Group can change suddenly as a result of internal political battles invisible from the outside. Sometimes members of the Core Group themselves don't know who is in or who is on their way out, as British Prime Minister Margaret Thatcher discovered on 21 November 1990 when senior ministers told her one by one that she was unlikely to win another leadership contest. The 'bargain of mutual commitment' with her MPs had broken and she was thrown out of the Core Group.

Kleiner wrote, 'People seriously trying to influence an organization can only be effective if they understand how the Core Group's priorities are perceived, and how those perceptions differ from the Core Group's actual intentions.' He then provided advice on how to influence it: become a deliberate *intervener* (or change agent), solve problems and build legitimacy with others in the organization without threatening the Core Group (Kleiner, 2003: 189–97).

Kleiner's analysis is based on his work on learning organizations with Peter Senge, his study of attempts to change corporations from within, described in *The Art of Heretics* (1996) and his experience as a consultant to many Core Groups. Consultants can be seen as the leading educators and coaches in office politics.

Political ability and culture in organizations

Political ability matters at every level in any organization. Some chiefs fight their way to the top only to be trapped by their position, unable to use their power effectively. Others dominate their organizations internally only to lead them to failure, as at Enron, RBS, Lehman Brothers, GEC and countless once powerful companies. The founder of Apple computers, Steve Jobs, was deposed as chairman in 1985, returning as CEO in 1997. His successor Tim Cook ousted his vice president and retail chief 'as internal politics and dissent reached a key pitch' (Arthur, 2012). Party leaders watch their back as rivals manoeuvre to force their hand or take their place. In almost every organization political skill is more important for success or failure than position, even at the very top.

All organizations are different, and the political abilities needed vary greatly between organizations, in different parts of the same organization and at different times in the life of an organization. Politics is also very different in the middle, bottom or outside an organization, requiring different skills. Someone who is skilful at rising through the ranks may lack abilities to lead from the top, while the driving ambition that built up an organization may fail when it reaches a steady state or hits a crisis.

The nature and use of power also varies according to position: the higher you are, the more politics you do. The main job of people at or near the top of any institution – whether it is a charity, church, pressure group, political party, government department or business – is almost entirely political. Many organizations share responsibility for internal and external politics between two posts, such as Chair and Chief Executive, President and Vice-President. In government, ministers lead the public, outward-facing politics, while civil servants manage the internal politics of getting things done. People lower down the organization have to do what they're told but ignore office politics at their peril, since their job may be changed or abolished as a result of battles at the top.

To be effective, you need to understand both the political culture of your own organization and the organizations you wish to influence, and not just at the top.

Who are the educators for office politics?

Most people learn the politics of their organization by being part of it, picking up its customs, norms and values though everyday interaction. If they don't learn how things are done, they either don't last or adopt a maverick role, like fools in a medieval court.

The most intense office politics is within business, particularly large multinational corporations. The constant pressures of competition, innovation, regulation and changing consumer demand means that corporations are almost continuously reorganizing, merging or breaking up. The average company listed in the Standard and Poor's 500 index of leading US companies has a lifespan of less than 18 years, down from 67 in the 1920s and 61 years in 1958 (Foster and Kaplan, 2001). Managing organizational change is all about office politics, so it is not surprising that most education for office politics takes place inside corporations, for people with leadership roles.

Like politicians, business leaders make decisions about priorities and strategy; they reconcile competing interests of customers, staff, shareholders, their supply chain, local communities and other stakeholders; and they pursue the common good of the firm, their polity, as well as their own interests. Unlike politicians, who are constantly challenged by opposition parties, business leaders expect their decisions to be carried out. Nevertheless, it is tough at the top, and business leaders have access to the most extensive (and expensive) education in practical politics to help them.

Public relations and lobbying, described in the previous chapter, provide political support in the external environment. Most of this deals with the office politics of government, regulators, media and other agencies, in the hidden dimensions of public politics.

But help with internal politics is equally important. In addition to coaching, mentoring and management trainig, business leaders draw on three sources of education and intelligence for internal politics:

1. **Accountancy** provides statistical analyses for both internal management and external accountability to shareholders, regulators and the public. Although largely technical, the design of accounting systems is one of the most powerful areas and political of 'supra-politics' in organizations and society.

2. **Management consultancy** and business schools provide strategic advice, instruction and detailed support for office politics.

3. **Industry analysts** provide in-depth data and scrutiny of the economic and political environment in which they work, as well as innovations in technology, production processes, materials and marketing, to inform office politics.

The following sections look at each of these in turn.

The politics of accounting

'Follow the money' is a basic rule for detectives, journalists, politics and business. The phrase was popularized by the book and film of the Watergate scandal, *All the President's Men* (1974), echoing the Latin *cui bono*, meaning 'who benefits?' The flow of money tells you the source of power, who controls resources and how they gain from any activity. To achieve something in an organization, you need a line in the budget to pay for it. To hold someone to account, you need to control the purse strings that permit them to act. The art of the accountant is to show how money flows and suggest how it can be used to achieve your aims. Accountancy provides intelligence for the use of resources, which is the beating heart of office politics.

Accounting rules played a devastating role in the international debt crises of the 1980s and 2008. Derivatives, collateral debt obligations and subprime mortgages were made possible by accounting practices. Companies use accountants to minimize tax, allocate costs and income between different jurisdictions through transfer pricing; maximize bonuses and pursue pet projects. Senior executives at Enron, WorldCom, Tesco and other companies abused accounting rules to misrepresent their performance. Governments use accounting tricks to hide spending, bury mistakes or display their commitment to doing something about an issue.

Rulers since ancient times have recorded income from taxes, so that states are among the first organizations to collect data and develop accounting. The word 'statistics' actually comes from the German *Staat*. In the Soviet Union numerical data was the chief instrument for planning the economy for almost 70 years. Over the past 20 years Western politicians have increasingly used targets and statistical data in their efforts to control public services.

Traders and bankers developed accounting to manage risk and the flow of goods and money through their business. The growth of shareholding, professional management and delegation of responsibility in big organizations increased the role of accountants and auditors to provide a 'true and fair' view of a company's business.

Thus the affairs of state and commerce developed the foundations of accounting. Numbers are the navigation instruments of big organizations. Accountancy provides a 'governance dashboard' of measures to analyse what is happening and decide what to do. In practical politics the choice of measures, how they are presented and used, are more important than any ideology, because numbers have an aura of objectivity that influences behaviour more directly than ideas. Accountancy and statistical analysis are therefore two of the most powerful instruments of politics.

The accountant's role is to give organizations the information needed to achieve their aims. Most of this information is financial, because money is the easiest and most widely used measure. But money is only a proxy for many different things. Over the past 50 years greater recognition of the complexity of the world and power of accounting has developed to take account of the environment, social well-being and even happiness. Handbooks such as *Accounting for the Environment* (Gray, 2007 [1993]) provide a practical guide to help managers include environmental impact in their decision-making.

In business, accountancy has also developed to take account of intangible assets. When a company is valued on the stock exchange or sold, a figure has to be found to account for the difference between the value of its physical assets (buildings, machinery, etc) and what it is worth to someone willing to buy it. Accountants have developed rules for measuring 'goodwill' and other intangible assets such as:

- economic competencies such as brand equity, firm-specific human capital, networks, organizational know-how that increases efficiency, and aspects of advertising and marketing
- computerized information such as software and databases
- intellectual property including research, patents, copyrights, designs and trademarks.

The value of global companies like Apple, Google and Microsoft is now almost entirely accounted for by intangible assets. The World Bank estimates that intangible capital is now the most important form of wealth worldwide and a significant factor in productivity growth.

Accounting enables people to 'follow what matters' for their organization and society. It provides detailed feedback on whatever aspects of an organization's performance are considered important. The numerical picture and story that it tells, as interpreted by accountants and executives, is a foundation of credibility in a company, or even the whole economy. When the numbers are challenged and found wanting, as the journalist Bethany McLean did in *Fortune* magazine about Enron, or some financial analysts did about subprime mortgages, then credibility collapses.

Accounting is an underestimated instrument of practical politics. It can reveal the costs of existing policies and the benefits of an alternative, like the case for investing in early childhood under the Head Start programme, which showed that spending $1 saved $6 later; it can uncover tax avoidance, like Tax Justice campaigner Richard Murphy; it can show the impact of tax and spending policies; or be used to track down corruption in any organization. The ability to analyse and understand figures is a key skill in any area of practical politics.

Management consultancy: Education for office politics

Consultancies like Accenture, Bain, Deloitte, McKinsey and PWC offer in-depth analysis, executive coaching and support for office politics at the pinnacle of corporate governance. Corporate strategy and change management in the relentless process of improving products, productivity and profitability are all part of the practical politics of running large complex organizations in a competitive environment. The politics is largely top-down, more Machiavelli than Mill, but it is often more sophisticated than the politics of political parties and pressure groups.

There are about 30 large multinational consultancies like McKinsey, but most firms are relatively small. IBIS*World* (motto: 'Where knowledge is power') reported that the United Kingdom had 124,725 consultancy businesses employing 343,749 people, in a local market worth £47 billion revenue in May 2015, suggesting that the global market could be worth more than $500 billion. Consultancy.uk estimated the global consulting market as $230 billion in 2015, with Europe worth $82 billion and the United Kingdom $19.4 billion in 2014 and the US market $89 billion in 2013.

Management consultancy covers a broad range of work, including strategic and organizational planning, marketing, information technology, human resources and business processes. Some of these are technical, but all change involves internal politics. The largest segment is Operations Management, followed by Financial Advisory and IT. The most prestigious area of Strategy Consulting represents less than 15 per cent of the market, but is most influential.

Consultants, ideology and organization

Management consultants are much more than corporate coaches and problem solvers. They provide philosophies, strategies and 'thought leadership' with profound influence on the world. As the 'visible hand' of corporate management spanned the global economy over the past century or more, its systems and ways of thinking spread to many other institutions, including churches, governments and non-profits (Chandler, 1977). In practice, their influence may be greater than any overtly political doctrines:

- Frederick Winslow Taylor was one of the first management consultants. His book *Principles of Scientific Management* (1911) advocated time and motion studies, standardization of production, training and piecework payment. It influenced Henry Ford, Harvard Business School and a generation of business leaders. The first leader of Communist Russia, Lenin, advocated Taylorism to 'cut by three-fourths the working time of the organized workers and make them four times better off than they are today' (Lenin, 1914).

- When the US wanted to secure Japan as an ally after World War II, General McArthur sent engineers and management consultants to help Japanese managers rebuild their industries. Consultants like W.E. Deming, J.J. Juran and Charles Protzman helped to create an 'economic miracle' by applying the best American management practices of the 'visible hand' (Hopper and Hopper, 2009: 109–24; Cohen, 1987; Reischauer, 1974).

- The consulting firm McKinsey grew globally alongside American corporations, helping companies to merge, restructure, cut costs, shed staff and increase profits, as well as spreading corporation practices to governments, non-profits and businesses worldwide, vividly described in Duff McDonald's *The Firm: The inside story of McKinsey* (2014), a case study of the Core Groups within one influential firm. For example, when executives at General Motors wanted to raise their pay in 1951, they hired McKinsey to produce a study on executive compensation, which then justified a pay explosion at the top of American business.

- Peter Drucker (1909–2005) is often described as 'the founder of modern management', credited with influential concepts such as:
  ○ management by objectives and self-control (1954)
  ○ decentralization and simplification of organizations
  ○ outsourcing 'back room' activities to companies for whom they are 'front room' business
  ○ the concept of knowledge workers (1959: 122)
  ○ New Public Management (1969), an approach to public administration that dominated the discipline from the 1980s, including New Labour in the United Kingdom
  ○ the role of non-profits, which he called the third sector (1989).

Drucker was a professor of politics and philosophy from 1942 to 1949; professor of management from 1950 to 1971 in New York; and then developed one of the first executive MBA programmes at Claremont Graduate School, California, in 1971. His breakthrough was a two-year social-scientific 'political audit' of General Motors, published as *Concept of the Corporation* (1946). This popularized GM's multidivisional structure and other management techniques. Although his prescriptions were unpopular within GM, Drucker's consultancy for leaders of General Motors,

Sears, General Electric, IBM, the American Red Cross, Salvation Army and many others was both the basis of his knowledge and his influence, extended through his teaching, 39 books and several institutions, including the Drucker Institute, Peter F. Drucker and Masatoshi Ito Graduate School of Management, and the Peter F. Drucker Academy (Drucker, 1954, 1959, 1969, 1973, 1989a, 1989b, 2001, 2010).

- Peters and Waterman's *In Search of Excellence* (1982), Peter Senge's *Fifth Discipline: The Art and practice of the learning organization* (1990) and W. Edward Deming's systems thinking and 'profound knowledge' of *The New Economics* (1993) were part of a counter-revolution in organizational thinking, challenging the orthodoxy of Taylor, McKinsey and Drucker.

These are just a few examples of powerful influence of doctrines and practices promoted by consultants serving Core Groups in large organizations. McDonald described McKinsey as a 'CEO Factory' for the number of alumni running companies with more than $1 billion in annual sales (more than 150 in 2011) (McDonald, 2013). Many powerful people also move between business consulting, management and politics, such as former Republican US Governor of Massachusetts (2003–7) and presidential candidate Mitt Romney (Bain Consulting); UK Conservative party leader and Foreign Secretary William Hague (McKinsey); Arthur Mutambara, former head of the Movement for Democratic Change in Zimbabwe (McKinsey); and many others.

Drucker wrote that 'in modern society there is no other leadership group but managers. If the managers of our major institutions, and especially of business, do not take responsibility for the common good, no one else can or will' (1973: 325). This statement confirms the centrality of office politics as well as Aristotle's proposition that the purpose of politics should include a concept of the public good.

The office politics of many businesses, government agencies and non-profits are still dominated by traditional models of command and control, New Public Management, Strategic Planning and other concepts developed and promoted by management consultants. Dealing with them takes a great deal of skill and experience, because the practices are often more powerful than the people who use them. Understanding and then changing the model of organizational thinking that governs an institution can have a powerful part in practical politics.

Summary

Office politics is the most widespread form of politics, present inside every organization. The higher you are in an organization, the more your work is concerned with office politics. Every organization has a 'core group' who decide its priorities and purpose (which may be different from its stated purpose) and a 'bargain of mutual commitment' between the core and the rest. Challenging the core group from within is risky and often fails, but it is possible to influence the core group by becoming an effective intervener, by solving problems and by changing the story without threatening the core group.

A great deal of public politics is about people in one office (or set of offices) trying to influence other offices to do something. Office politics sometimes enters public politics when someone blows the whistle to expose wrongdoing or blows the trumpet to promote a concept of practice.

Education for office politics is provided by accountants, management consultants and industry analysts, who mainly work for business leaders. These professions probably have more influence on practical politics than any overt political ideology.

Three powerful tools of practical politics are:
* changing the story about an issue
* analysing the money flows
* understanding the core group and its management model.

Learn more about doing office politics

There are countless books on organizational change, including sector-specific guides for schools, non-profits, health services, environment, etc. The following are recommended to stimulate thought and deep learning about the nature and purpose of organizations:

Art Kleiner's *Who Really Matters: The Core Group theory of power, privilege and success* (2003) is a basic text for understanding office politics.

Geoff Mulgan's *The Art of Public Strategy: Mobilising power and knowledge for the common good* (2009) is about strategies, systems and thinking for public service organizations by the former head of policy and director of the UK Government's Strategy Unit under Prime Minister Tony Blair, which concludes with ten principles for any public leader (258). His *Good and Bad Power: The ideals and betrayals of government* (2006) is also worth reading.

David Boyle (2012) *The Human Element: Ten new rules to kick start our failing organizations,* is about the critical role of people in making systems work, full of stories from organizations as diverse as General Electric, the 'Upside Down Management' of Timpson's shops and Edgar Cahn's peer tutors and youth courts that empower disaffected young people to help others.

Inside the office

Michael D. Watkins (2013) [2003] *The First 90 Days.* Harvard Business Review Press. A practical guide for anyone promoted into a leadership role or joining a new organization.

Jo Owen (2007) *Power at Work: The art of making things happen.* Pearson Education. Full of insights and tips for thriving in any organization.

Patrick Forsyth (2006) *Manage Your Boss.* Marshall Cavendish Business. 'Eight steps to creating the ideal working relationship'.

Tom Lambert (1996) *The Power of Influence: Intensive influencing skills at work.* Nicholas Brealey. A practical course book on the psychology of influencing.

Oliver James (2013) *Office Politics: How to thrive in a world of lying, backstabbing and dirty tricks.* Vermilion; Penguin. A psychologist explores the dark sides of office politics to help understand power games and dynamics at work and how to navigate it.

Chapter 7

Power and its uses

This chapter aims to show how to unlock power and use it to increase the well-being of all.

In this chapter you will learn:

- Why the powerful don't always get their way
- The difference between hard, sticky, soft and free power
- Why violence is almost always a failure of politics
- That power is the ability to get the outcome one wants
- Three parts of power: agency, organization and context
- Six main instruments of power
- Why the use of force is a failure of democratic politics
- Fourteen sources of power and how to use them
- How to use 'power petals' to find sideways routes to influence
- The many dimensions of power
- The importance of increasing power and freedom for all.

The main case studies are the Project for the New American Century and Save the Children.

Case study: Project for a New American Century (PNAC)

In spring 1997 William Kristol, Robert Kagan and a few other men set up a non-profit educational organization to promote US global leadership called Project for the New American Century. Kagan and Kristol were influential conservative commentators who had had senior posts under Presidents Reagan and George H.W. Bush, and wanted to influence the foreign policy of President Clinton.

Their published aims were 'dedicated to a few fundamental propositions: that American leadership is good both for America and for the world; and that such leadership requires military strength, diplomatic energy and commitment to moral principle'. The Project:

intends, through issue briefs, research papers, advocacy journalism, conferences and seminars, to explain what American world leadership entails. It will also strive to rally support for a vigorous and principled policy of American international involvement and to stimulate useful public debate on foreign and defence policy and America's role in the world.

(PNAC, 1970)

Their Statement of Principles, signed by 25 prominent conservatives, argued that the United States 'needs to shape circumstances before crises emerge, and to meet threats before they become dire'. It set out a four-point call to action:

1. Increase defence spending.

2. Strengthen ties to democratic allies and challenge regimes hostile to American interests and values.

3. Promote political and economic freedom abroad.

4. Preserve and extend 'an international order friendly to our security, our prosperity, and our principles'.

Their campaign was influential. One of their specific goals was the overthrow of Saddam Hussain's dictatorship in Iraq. Congress passed the Iraq Liberation Act (H.R. 4655) by an overwhelming majority in 1998, making regime change US policy and providing up to $97 million for Iraqi opposition groups to 'establish a program to support a transition to democracy'. President Clinton authorized Operation Desert Fox, a four-day bombing campaign to destroy Iraq's nuclear, chemical and biological weapons programmes.

In September 2000 the PNAC published a 'grand strategy' to 'secure and expand the "zones of democratic peace"; to deter the rise of a new great power competitor; to defend key regions of Europe, East Asia and the Middle East; and to preserve American pre-eminence through the coming transformation of war made possible by new technologies'. But the process of transformation would be long without 'some catastrophic catalyzing event – like a new Pearl Harbor' (PNAC, 2000).

The PNAC campaign was boosted by George W. Bush's election to the Presidency in 1999. Ten of the 25 signatories joined his administration (2001–9), including Vice President Dick Cheney, Defence Secretary Donald Rumsfeld and his deputy Paul Wolfowitz.

After al-Qaeda murdered 2,977 people by attacking the Twin Towers and Pentagon on 11 September 2001 (9/11), the PNAC urged President Bush to remove Saddam Hussein from power, 'even if evidence does not link Iraq directly to the attack' (20 September 2001).

There was a lot of office politics about Iraq in both the Clinton and Bush administrations. Iraq competed with other issues, and after 9/11 Afghanistan was top priority. But Dick Cheney and other PNAC signatories were in the ruling Core Group and kept Iraq on the agenda. Kristol regularly met Karl Rove, Bush's chief political adviser, urging Bush to act. Advocates of war with Iraq kept up pressure through the press.

Many in the administration had doubts, including Secretary of State Colin Powell and CIA Director George Tenet. But once the decision to go to war was taken by President Bush, the US government mounted an intense campaign to keep US public opinion on side and build an international 'alliance of the willing' in the face of growing opposition across the world. In March 2003 the US-led invasion toppled Saddam Hussein's government, without UN backing. In January 2005 the PNAC called on Congress to substantially increase US forces in Iraq by 'at least 25,000 troops each year over the next several years'. After 9/11 American defence spending rose from 3.5 per cent of GDP to 4.6 per cent by 2005 for the invasion of Iraq, then 5.0 per cent in 2008, and peaked at 5.7 per cent in 2011 with the renewed focus on Afghanistan.

In 2006 the PNAC Director, Gary Schmitt, said it had 'done its job' and it closed. In 2009 Kagan and Kristol created a new think tank, the Foreign Policy Initiative, to 'promote an active US foreign policy committed to robust support for democratic allies, human rights, a strong American military equipped to meet the challenges of the twenty-first century'. In July 2015 it published a warning on 'Iran and its Terror Proxies: A clear and present danger', arguing for military intervention.

Reflections

Two objectives of the Project for the New American Century were achieved: a significant increase in defence spending and the overthrow of Saddam Hussain's regime. But it failed to secure American global leadership, deter the rise of a new great power competitor or expand the 'zones of democratic peace'. On the contrary, China, Russia, Iran and North Korea were emboldened by US intervention in Iraq, which sapped America's political and economic capital. Freedom House has reported a decline in freedom and democracy every year since the war.

It is debatable whether the 2003 Iraq war happened as a result of the PNAC campaign or other factors. But the Project's insistent message about regime change, targeted at opinion formers and political leaders, contributed to the dominant narrative across political parties and the media even before

9/11. Its supporters inside the Core Group of the Bush Presidency certainly influenced the decision to go to war.

The Project's failure was eloquently described by one of its original signatories, Francis Fukuyama. He wrote in the *Wall Street Journal*:

> *The war was a mistake. By invading Iraq in the manner it did, the United States exacerbated all of the threats it faced prior to 2003. Recruitment into terrorist cells shot up all over the world. North Korea and Iran accelerated their development of nuclear weapons. Indeed, Iran has emerged as the dominant regional power in the Persian Gulf once the United States removed its major rival from the scene and put its Shi'ite clients into power in Baghdad.*
>
> (2008)

The US decision to ignore the UN created a precedent for Russia to invade Georgia in 2008 and annex Crimea in 2014, and for China to project its power across the South China Seas by building islands and an airbase in disputed waters. Since the conflict, American defence spending was also cut to below 3.5 per cent of GDP by 2014. Fukuyama made his case more fully in *After the Neocons: America at the crossroads* (2006).

The Project may even have helped end the American Century. Far from strengthening the United States as the dominant power in a unipolar world, the Iraq war encouraged others to assert their power. It destabilized the region and enflamed conflict between Muslims and the West, between Shia and Sunni, as well as Muslims and Christians across Africa. Historians may look back at this as the world's biggest political mistake since Chairman Mao's Great Leap Forward in 1958.

Lessons

People will take many different lessons from these events. The 2003 Iraq war has become a defining narrative, and myth, for political movements in the Middle East, Russia, China, Europe and the United States, where it will infuse politics for generations. I draw three main lessons for practical political education:

- Immense power is not enough to achieve your objectives.
- Sometimes winning a campaign leads to failure.
- The price of political mistakes can be high.

It is possible that the war prevented greater suffering from Saddam's regime, but unlikely. The total cost includes the deaths of more than 134,000 civilians in direct war violence; the lives of 4,488 US service members, at least 3,400 US contractors and hundreds of thousands suffering injury or trauma for the rest of their lives (the United States has more than 675,000 disability claims from veterans of the two wars), as well as indirect deaths due to increased vulnerability to disease or injury; about 1.5 million Iraqis uprooted from their homes, many of whom left the country, including half the country's doctors; and the 150 per cent rise in the infant mortality rate from 1990 to 2005. The financial cost to the US taxpayer was over $2.2 trillion, plus $1.7 trillion cumulative interest on the war debt for the next 40 years, and the opportunity cost of diverting resources from more productive purposes (www.costsofwar.org; Lutz, 2013). The biggest cost is long-term: destabilization of the region, the Syrian civil war, the rise of Daesh/Islamic State and justification for endless war by alienated Muslims across the world. The main victor was probably Osama Bin Laden and *jihadist* militants who wanted to bankrupt America by provoking conflagration with the West (Gartenstein-Ross, 2011, 2014a, 2014b; see also Jihadology. net and the Global Terrorism Index). For opponents of war there are also lessons, such as:

- There were many steps on the way to war, over a long period, and it would have been easier to stop or slow them before the PNAC narrative about Iraq became dominant.
- The dominant narrative set the frame for the decision long before it was made.
- Internal disagreements (office politics) continued until the decision was taken, so that advocacy for alternatives to war within the decision-making elite might have stopped it.
- Once the commitment was made, the allies united behind the decision (very few resigned, like UK Foreign Secretary Robin Cook).

Finally, there is a general point about democratic politics: in retrospect, successful opposition to the war would have benefited everyone: it might have given UN weapons inspectors time to neutralize the Iraqi regime; a better way to hold Saddam Hussain accountable for his crimes could have been found; President Bush and Prime Minister Blair might have left office with their reputations intact; and the West would not have inspired the resurgence of militant Islam.

Understanding power

Many people are daunted by the power of their boss, let alone governments or corporations. Many campaigners feel they are crying in the wilderness or beating their head against brick walls. They may have marched, signed petitions and lobbied without getting anywhere. They see politicians or companies doing things they consider harmful but feel powerless to stop them.

The citadels of power frequented by Kristol, Kagan and Cheney are utterly remote for most people. But the PNAC was a political campaign no less than Brake, Citizens UK, Jubilee 2000 or the Bristol school students. They had more access to people in power than most campaigners, and vast resources were mobilized behind their goals. Yet they utterly failed to achieve their objectives.

Practical politics is above all about the ability to make things happen. This means using power well. Bernard Crick defined power as 'the ability to achieve a premeditated intention' and 'influence over others' (2000: 82, 187), similar to Bertrand Russell's 'power is the ability to produce intended effects' (Russell, 1938). The sociologist Max Weber saw power as 'the probability that one actor within a social relationship will be in a position to carry out his own will even despite resistance' (1922: 53). Joseph Nye, former chairman of the US National Intelligence Council and Assistant Secretary of Defence in the Clinton administration, defined power as 'the ability to get the outcome one wants' (Nye, 2004: 1).

> *Power is the ability to get the outcome one wants.*

The Iraq war showed that overwhelming force is not enough to get the 'outcome one wants'. Supporters of the Project for a New American Century had access to President Bush, Congress and the media to campaign for war on Iraq. They overcame resistance within the administration and carried out their will despite resistance from millions of protesters and most governments of the world. And yet the world's most powerful state, with the most sophisticated weapons and biggest military budget in history, failed to achieve its goals.

Most people have more modest ambitions – to make their neighbourhoods and hospitals safe, protect the environment, promote animal welfare, end FGM and a thousand other causes. They also have less access to people in power, money or technology. But in representative democracies, with freedom to organize, publish and campaign, it is possible for anyone to use power better than Kagan, Kristal and the PNAC. You just have to be smarter. In authoritarian societies it is harder to organize, and challenging those in power can be fatal, so the practice of politics has to be smarter still. Understanding the nature of power and how to use it to get a worthwhile outcome is central to practical politics.

The parable of the elements illustrates the subtlety of power: the four elements of sun, wind, rain and thunder argue about which is most powerful and suggest a test: a man is walking across a field and whoever can remove his coat is strongest. Rain, wind and thunder drench, lash and buffet him in turn, but he just holds the coat tighter. Then the sun shines and he takes it off: gentle warmth – soft power – is strongest.

Creating power to bring about the outcome you want needs different elements depending on the context, people and institutions you want to change – sun and rain to make things grow, wind to blow sails and fire to melt or destroy. The following sections explore ten elements of power in more depth.

What is the nature of power?

The cry of a newborn baby has power to move people. A baby is totally dependent on others for everything. Babies have similar needs, but how well adults respond depends on circumstances. A baby born in Singapore can expect to live 34 years longer than one born in the shanty towns of Sierra Leone. But the cry of a suffering child can be amplified by charities, the media and politicians to mobilize support from across the world. Eglantyne Jebb, founder of Save the Children, said the cry of a child is the only international language the world understands.

A baby's cry offers a profound insight into the nature of power. The child's power to get its needs met depends entirely on circumstances, not its ability to cry. Countries like Singapore, Sweden and Japan are better organized to help children flourish than Somalia, Sierra Leone or the Washington Highlands in America's capital. The infant mortality rate in Somalia is more than 50 times higher than in Singapore. This is not because people care less, but because social conditions mean people have less power to give children what they need.

The cry of a child taps into the power of society to respond. Social organization makes it easy for parents in Singapore to get clean water, healthy food, medical help, toys and everything a child needs. This is it not just about poverty, because some poor countries, like Cuba, have lower infant mortality and longer life expectancy than Somalia or even poor areas of the United States. The child's power to have its needs met depends on society's ability to direct resources where and when they are needed, through families, markets, businesses, community associations, state agencies and non-profits. If there are unmet needs, people can set up a charity, start a business or go into politics to improve children's prospects. But in some countries bureaucracy, corruption or violence makes this choice difficult, while conditions elsewhere make it easy. These could be called conditions for freedom.

Everyone has some power to act – the baby to cry, parents to respond, agencies to intervene – but the extent of their power depends on organizations available and choices open to them. Better organizations and more choices mean more power to act. These factors depend how society is organized, as a result of political decisions over decades.

Power, therefore, consists of several elements: an individual's ability to act, organizations that amplify actions and the choices open to people. No one is completely powerless, but effective power comes from organizations – families, firms, cities, states, health services, non-profits, gangs, the financial system, law, internet and myriad agencies that create or block choice and opportunity. When organizations work well, in conditions of good governance, power to do well is increased; when they work badly, society is poorer. Thus social power has three parts:

1. **Agency**: people's ability to act.
2. **Organization**: social entities that amplify (or dampen) their actions.
3. **Context**: circumstances that make it possible for individuals and organizations to act.

These are like the key, lock and engines of power: the key is your ability to act, the lock is the context and organization makes things happen. To use another metaphor, you may have the ability to drive and a car (organization), but without roads (context) you can't go far.

Eglantyne Jebb responded to the cries of refugee children after World War I in 1919 and founded the International Save the Children Union in 1920. She drafted the Declaration of the Rights of the Child, adopted by the League of Nations in 1924 (the first human rights document approved by an inter-governmental institution). She used her contacts and abilities to unlock the power of people to hear and respond to a baby's cry in the moment, and then created an organization to amplify people's power to respond. Her legacy of international law and organization continues her work, so that the power of her action almost a century ago still has influence today. The world around us is run by agencies created by people who responded to a need.

What is the purpose of power?

To influence people in power, you need to understand why they want it: what do they want to achieve, for themselves and others? This is often different from their stated purpose, as discussed in the section on the Core Group in chapter 6.

People seek power for many reasons – status, wealth, achievement, duty, insecurity, revenge, cruelty or to do good – and often a mixture. The philosopher Bertrand Russell thought that 'of the infinite desires of man, the chief are the desires for power and glory' (1938: 11). Advocates for a New American Century were clearly motivated by power. But many people prefer a quiet life and are content to blame others for anything that goes wrong, while Eglantyne Jebb was motivated to prevent suffering. All, in different ways, were trying to meet needs, in themselves and the world.

Understanding what needs an individual or organization wants to meet can therefore help to see why they want power. These needs may be psychological or material, or a mixture of both. But recognizing and addressing the reason why people want something can help resolve a political conflict.

> *The easiest way of finding out the purpose of power is to ask:*
> **Who benefits? (Cui Bono?)**
>
> *Look at who gains what from particular arrangements to see the interests and purposes of those who wield power and you will understand what they are likely to do.*

Political systems can end when their leaders lose faith in its purpose, as in East Germany, the Soviet Union or apartheid South Africa, while institutions with a strong sense of purpose continue for centuries, like many faiths. Although their actual purpose may change over time, they keep going so long that people imbue them with meaning that meets their needs. Skilled political operators know how to change the purpose of an organization to meet changing needs, aspirations or circumstances, or how to harness the ambitions of a Core Group to meet their particular purpose.

I take Aristotle's view that politics should aim at 'the highest of all goods achievable' (Nicomanchean Ethics, 1094–5). The purpose of power is therefore to do good, for your family, society and all humanity. A 'good society' is one where these are in line, and doing the best for yourself benefits everyone. But since people have different views of the 'highest of all goods', democratic politics and practical political education should enable people to decide what they are and how to achieve them.

Questions about what is 'good' are about values, the 'know why' of any action or organization.

What are the instruments of power?

Instruments of power are the means that individuals and organizations use to get their way and bring about the result they want. John Kenneth Galbraith (1908–2006) was a Washington insider like Kagan and Kristal, but in the Democratic administrations of Presidents Roosevelt, Truman, Kennedy and Johnson. He had worked for the conservative Republican publisher of *Time* and *Fortune* magazines, Henry Luce, for five years from 1943. He served as US ambassador to India under Kennedy from 1961 to 1963. He was a leading economist of his time, publishing influential books. His insights into *The Anatomy of Power* are grounded in 40 years' experience of power at the centre or watching from the ringside. Joseph Nye (b. 1937), another influential Harvard professor and Washington Democratic Party insider, has also written widely on power, coining the term 'soft power' for the ability to attract and persuade through culture, values and ideals. Their thinking on the practical politics of power is as good as any.

Galbraith described three instruments of power (1983: 4–6) as:

1. **Coercion,** which he called 'condign power' and Nye called hard or command power: the 'ability to change what others do' by force, sanctions or threats (Nye, 2004: 7).

2. **Compensatory power,** 'which wins submission by the offer of affirmative reward' including praise, payment or privilege; Galbraith and Nye saw this as a form of hard power, incentives for people to do something they would prefer not to do. However, it may be more accurate to call it 'sticky power', between soft and hard.

3. **Conditioned power,** which is exercised by changing belief, through 'persuasion, education, or the social commitment to what seems natural, proper or right', what Noam Chomsky called 'manufactured consent' (Herman and Chomsky, 2002) and Nye called soft power.

Carrot and stick are the common terms for compensation and coercion. They are currencies of office power everywhere, widely used in both authoritarian and democratic societies. The power of organizations –

corporations, government agencies and the military – is largely based on compensatory power: loyalty bought with a pay check, but cemented by conditioned power through belief. Galbraith observed that capitalist societies use 'massive deployment of compensatory power' to mobilize millions of workers and purchase 'legislators and other public officials [to win] ... the power of the state' (1983: 115), bolstered by conditioned power through 'the public relations and advertising effort of large firms' (141). In his view the 'social conditioning of corporate propaganda' was often counter-productive and cultivated disbelief (142), but this was over-optimistic. The everyday experience of most people in most societies is the 'sticky power' of earning a living and fitting in with people. 'Sticky power' includes the compensatory power of pay and the soft power of loyalty or conformity to groups to which you belong, as well as the social conditioning of commerce.

Soft power is by far the most widespread instrument of power today. Soft power was analysed almost a century ago by Edward Bernays in 'Manipulating public opinion' (1928) and is the basis of the public relations industry and electoral politics (see chapter 5). Galbraith identified the media, along with families, education, religion and advertising, as instruments of conditioned or soft power. 'Much of what is called political power' he reflected, 'is, in practice, the illusions if power. So also is the power of the press' (70). Most effective power, he argued, is concealed in powerful organizations.

Galbraith argued that 'power creates its own resistance and acts to limit its own effectiveness' (72). People on the weaker side of a power relationship can change the balance of power through politics. Galbraith described the diffusion of power in modern society as a result of the rise of organization as a source of power and affluence: 'As personality gives way to organization, there is, inevitably, a wider participation in the exercise of power' (1983: 183). Corporations and public agencies concentrate power and distribute it through managers and frontline staff. Affluence has also 'weakened the role of property and therewith of compensatory power. With affluence, consumers and workers have alternatives' (186). The diffusion of power gives rise to more democratic instruments of power, which can redress the balance between those who wield power and those who submit to it. Challenge and co-operation create countervailing power to make society better at dealing with problems and, potentially, increase freedom for all.

In *American Capitalism: The concept of countervailing power* (1952), Galbraith argued that big business was necessary for technological progress, but 'countervailing power' was essential to prevent companies from abusing power. Countervailing power includes government regulation, collective bargaining by unions and, above all, competition from other companies.

Democracy depends on countervailing power, to challenge, question and hold those in power to account. As societies rely less on force and more on conditioned or soft power, countervailing power needs to become more sophisticated. Near universal access to information through the internet makes the domination of communication from a few sources increasingly difficult, so that exercising power needs to engage people. As two RAND analysts argue, 'In the information age, "co-operative" advantages will become increasingly important' and 'societies that improve their abilities to co-operate with friends and allies may also gain competitive advantages against rivals' (Arquilla and Ronfeldt, 1999: 42, quoted in Nye, 2004: 20). Any group that can build co-operative relationships across society is therefore likely to have more power than those who merely command force.

In terms of practical politics today, I would therefore identify three other instruments of power:

1. **Challenge power** is the act of speaking up, defying or taking on those who wield power, like Jesus confronting money changers in the temple, English barons forcing King John to accept the Magna Carta in 1215, the Jubilee 2000 petition or even Deng Xiaoping's challenges to Maoist orthodoxy in China in the 1960s and again from 1977. Challenge may rely on force (like the barons), persuasion (like Jubilee 2000) or political cunning (like Deng), but it is distinct from them. It is an act of disruption that puts an issue on the agenda and defies those in power, which is why it is often suppressed. It is a countervailing power that curbs abuse.

2. **System power** is the invisible power of institutions and social conditions that influence what people do without thinking. It is the power of a tap that brings fresh, clean water into your home, the power of roads, electric pylons, Wi-Fi and postal services. People in the West take it for granted, but notice when it is missing. It is also the power of electoral systems and constitutions, which determine the outcome of a ballot. It is Herbert Simon's social capital, which generates the wealth of societies.

3. **Co-operative or consensual power** is exercised by people acting freely together to achieve common objectives, who take initiatives out of their own sense of power, neither submitting nor commanding. This is not 'power over' but 'power with', and may be the most effective power of all.

In today's complex, interconnected world, even absolute rulers experience some greater power that they must submit to or at least take into account. No one has unrestrained power everywhere. Rulers are increasingly constrained by both international law and internal politics. Many people abuse power, from domestic violence and local officials to executives in ENRON, FIFA or the Kremlin. Democracy is about creating political systems that expose wrongdoing, hold power to account, end abuse and enable people to use power for productive purposes within rules accepted by the majority. The ideal of a democratic society is one based on freedom and equality, in which power is exercised by consent and people make things happen out of their own free will, using power to create a world that works for everyone.

To summarize, instruments of power can be drawn on a spectrum, from force to freedom:

```
Force          Pay    Reward              Loyalty           Commitment
|--------------------|------------|------------------------|-------------------------|---->
Hard           Sticky       Soft                    Free
```

This is not a political left–right spectrum, but there may be a progression from societies ruled by force to ones in which all citizens are free. Freedom is made possible by pluralism and effective institutions. People gain greater power over their own lives through shared institutions that respond to the cry of every child, protect the weak and meet needs. Greater freedom for all depends on institutions governed by the rule of law, public accountability and good conduct.

FORCE AND VIOLENCE IN POLITICS

Force is often seen as the ultimate power, as in the much quoted 'War is merely the continuation of politics by other means' (von Clausewitz, 1832) or Chairman Mao's slogan 'Political power grows out of the barrel of a gun' (1938: II). But force can often backfire and end up weakening those who use it, as the United States learnt in Vietnam (1968–74) and Iraq (2003–14). Chenoweth and Stephan's analysis of 232 resistance campaigns showed that non-violent campaigns were nearly twice as likely to succeed as violent ones, and that 'violent insurgent success prohibits or reverses democracy while increasing the likelihood for recurrent civil war' (2011: 6–7, 218–19).

Force is always a failure of politics. Although coercion, conflict, war and violence must be understood in political terms, they are like bribery and corruption in business. Yes, corruption oils the wheels of commerce, and in some countries it may be the only way to do business, but it is bad practice. Likewise force may be *realpolitik*, but it should not be accepted in democratic politics. Force is still one of the most widespread instruments of political power in the world, from the balance of power between nations and nuclear missile arsenals to the prison guards of North Korea and Jihadi beheadings in Syria. Many political traditions see violence as the only way to overthrow repressive regimes. But winning power through violence tends to perpetuate violence. Political regimes 'differ in the level and types of violence they generate' (Tilly, 2003: 9) and collective violence may be a natural response to injustice. This does not make it the best response.

Democratic politics is about peaceful resolution of differences and reducing coercion at all levels, from neighbourhood gangs and office bullying to threats, terror and war in world politics. This is, of course, a debatable view and many would argue that it is not possible to protect society or change anything without force. To which my response is that if societies invest more in developing opportunities and skills for peaceful politics, then people would feel less need to resort to violence and states would need less force to protect themselves or their citizens. The peace process in Northern Ireland is an example of the benefits of reducing violence by creating political structures in which differences can be addressed (White, 2013). The end of dictatorships in Latin America, apartheid in South Africa and Indonesian rule over East Timor (Timor-Leste) are other examples.

Good politics is ultimately about making things happen without coercion. At best, democratic politics creates win–win bargains in which different interests compromise for a common good. The following section looks in more detail at where power comes from and how to use it.

What are the sources of power?

Galbraith described sources of power as 'the attributes or institutions that differentiate those who wield power from those who submit to it'. He identified three primary sources – personality, property (including income) and organization. Of these, he regarded organization as 'the most important source of power in modern societies' (1983: 6). I suggest that since his time a fourth category of power has become clearer – the power of expertise, information, reputation and ideas – that I'll call intelligence.

I have used Galbraith's three headings plus intelligence to identify 14 sources of power below. Each of these is a political asset that can be cultivated by any individual or organization to increase their power and influence. They are more elaborate versions of sun, wind and rain. Any course in practical politics needs to develop the ability to use these well.

Personality

❤ **Confidence** and self-belief are enormous assets for gaining and holding power, which is why the education of elites puts so much emphasis on character and leadership. These traits are evident among powerful leaders such as Churchill, Roosevelt, Deng Xiaoping or Putin, as well as people who challenge power, such as Mahatma Ghandi, Nelson Mandela, Steve Biko, Martin Luther King, Lech Walesa or Malala Yousafzai. Confidence is a product of circumstances, of family, school and wider social circle that builds people up or pulls them down. Almost anyone can develop their confidence and inspire confidence in others, through drama, singing, sport, personal development and political action. Do not underestimate the benefits of building confidence as a foundation for any kind of politics. If you are low in confidence, you can develop strength through expertise, organizing ability or other sources of power, which build confidence in turn.

✓ **Initiative** is the power of asking a question, making a suggestion and taking action, like the Rochdale Pioneers who founded the co-op movement; Rosa Park's defiance of racial segregation or Mary William's decision to set up Brake; or the child's cry and Eglantyne Jebb's response. Taking action, however small, creates movement. Dave Elliott, an Open University lecturer and a founder of the sustainable energy movement and *Undercurrents* magazine (1972) in the United Kingdom, described it as a 'ripple revolution'. Fifty years later these pioneering initiatives are like giant waves sweeping through civil society, industry and government. The art of taking initiative needs to be studied closely and practised repeatedly: what small steps can you take to further your cause today?

✌ **Leadership** is sustained initiative, taking responsibility for the direction and action of a group or movement. Leadership is distinct from position. Many people in positions of power are poor leaders, while some people lead through words, deeds or personality without any formal power, such as leaders of the women's movement in the 1970s, the Iranian Ayatollah Khomeini before 1979 or Professor Milton Freidman, who led a monetarist revolution in economic thinking. Practical politics can benefit from studying different kinds of leadership at all levels of society.

★ **Celebrity** is a projection of personality associated with stars of sport and screen, with deep roots in the stories of prophets, saints, martyrs, heroes and villains of the pre-television age. Charismatic politicians tell stories about what kind of society we are and what matters. Some campaigners become celebrities, like Kids Company founder Camila Batmanghelidjh. Others use their celebrity status to campaign, like Angelina Jolie (sexual violence), Joanna Lumley (Gurkhas), Princess Diana (landmines), Bono, Russell Brand, Donald Trump and many others. People project celebrity onto others to empower qualities they value, while celebrities can use it to bring about or resist change. Do you or your contacts know any celebrities who are likely to support your cause? How would you approach them? What would the association with you do for them? Could you or a member of your team develop stand-out features to promote your cause?

Property

ð **Resources** – money, tools and other assets are material foundations of power, providing incentive for people to do things. Wealthy individuals, companies, organizations and countries clearly exercise a great deal of power. But possession of wealth is not sufficient to achieve the outcomes they want if they lack the ability, or others outsmart them. To use resources well takes personality, expertise and organization. Control of natural resources gives countries like Saudi Arabia a great deal of power, but can also be a curse (Humphreys *et al.*, 2007). Smart states like Hong Kong and Singapore do more with few natural resources. Nevertheless, increased concentration of wealth is a major factor for any form of politics. What resources do you really need? Where and how could you get access to them? How can you use them effectively?

$€£ **Revenue** – a regular, reliable income stream gives any political project security: owning premises, producing goods or providing a service creates financial independence. For example, the Electoral Reform Society administers elections for organizations, the Adam Smith Institute provides consultancy in privatization and Living Wage Mark earns income from accreditation. What service can you provide that furthers

127

your cause? Alternatively, are there potential donors or sponsors? Could a fundraiser help your campaign take off?

Organization

✣ **Collective action** is the power of people acting together with a shared goal. Throughout history people with big ambitions to change society have formed a group, alliance or movement to make things happen. Political parties, the co-operative movement, trade unions and Jubilee 2000 are examples of collective action. But states, cities, corporations and armies are also units of collective action. The question for anyone seeking change is, which organization could do most to bring about the change you want?

🏛 **Position** gives control over decisions, money, staff and other resources, but also responsibilities and pressures to serve the institution or system. People need skill and expertise as well as contacts and confidence to use any position successfully. In other words, you need to be good at office politics. A career in an organization dedicated to your cause is one way to advance it.

🏳 **Discipline** and focus are a significant source of organizational power: Galbraith wrote 'the fewer purposes the organization pursues … the greater its internal discipline will be'. He observed that conservative organizations are likely to be more effective due to 'the greater conservative instinct for discipline. The conservative mood accepts the established beliefs, … the liberal instinct is to question, challenge, and debate' (150–1).

🏵 A **network** of contacts enables people to exert influence beyond their formal power or expertise: *who* you know can be the fastest route to making things happen. Building relationships, a database of contacts and networking effectively can be a fast track to impact, particularly if you have expertise and reputation.

Intelligence

🔦 **Expertise** creates its own power. Bacon's dictum that 'Knowledge is power' has proved itself in the scientific and technological innovations that continue to revolutionize society and challenge politics to catch up. Organizations like Amnesty International, Heritage Foundation, Migration Watch, Transparency International, Worldwatch Institute and more than 6,618 think tanks worldwide seek to influence others through the credibility of their research (McGann, 2015). People also exercise power within organizations, professions and the media by controlling information, becoming the 'go to' expert or opinion former on an issue. What skill, knowledge or information can you provide to be an authority in your field?

● **Reputation,** name recognition and brand are valuable assets for individuals and organizations. Like celebrity, they project soft power, but can be easily damaged. They have can have great commercial as well as political value, and are therefore an important focus for practical politics.

💻 **Information** is in a class of its own as a source of power: Galbraith remarked that agencies of government that have no capacity to manage information have no power comparable with those that do (152–3); the ability of private companies and states to aggregate vast quantities of information gives them great power, which can be used for good in solving economic, medical and social problems, but also capacity for coercion and manipulation. In politics information gives parties the ability to target voters, and gives citizens the potential for greater transparency and engagement. The press, social media and whistle blowers like WikiLeaks and Edward Snowden have a huge impact by putting information into the public domain.

⇔ **Ideas** remain potent forces in politics, particularly when promoted by a charismatic personality and effective organization. Ideas have power to both motivate and organize people. Big ideas such as Buddhism, Christianity, Islam, the nation, freedom, communism, co-operation and free markets have rallied people for a cause and transformed continents.

The source of all power is in relationships between people that enable a call for action to get a response that achieves the desired outcomes. Organizations are communication structures through which calls for action are carried out, but they do not always produce the desired outcomes. Large hierarchical structures command people from the centre, but messages get mangled and subordinates learn how to give their superiors the illusion of control while doing their own thing. The most effective organizations do not need command and control to bring about results, because they have a clear purpose and are organized to empower people to respond effectively. Markets work because they enable people to mobilize resources to respond to other people's needs as expressed through purchasing power. Markets are often more powerful than state-run economies because they handle information and diversity of demand better than bureaucracies. Large corporations (bureaucracies) deliver at scale by creating systems to rapidly convey calls for action from customers through supply chains, as described by Chandler in *The Visible Hand* (1977). But markets don't respond to people with little or no money, so the political system creates relationships that give people power based on equal citizenship rather than money.

Political systems design is the art of creating organizations and systems to use power for a purpose. Management consultancy seeks to do this for corporate power, as discussed in the last chapter. Political consultants, scientists and activists do it for the public sphere, but this gets less attention. Practical political education could do this for all citizens.

The source of all power is in relationships between people that enable a call for action to get a response that achieves the desired outcomes.

Power gradients

Most organizations have steep power gradients from top to bottom. People at the top exercise much greater power than those immediately below, while those at the bottom usually have very little power, even over their own work. Although every organization is different, the power gap between tiers tends to fall exponentially, so that even the third tier down has relatively little power compared with the top (see Figure 7.1). Real hierarchies are often different from official ones. The Core Group may constrain the person at the top, as discussed in chapter six and illustrated in the television series *Yes Minister*. Knowing who is in the Core Group, how they work and what they want is therefore crucial in practical politics.

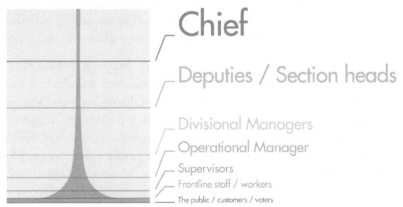

Figure 7.1: Power within many organizations is concentrated at the centre

Daunting as they are, all hierarchies are vulnerable. Core Groups may be toppled from within if they lose support of key groups or fail to deal with threats from outside. Powerful regimes have been toppled by citizens' action, including dictatorships in Greece (1974), Portugal (1974), Spain (1975–82), Philippines (1986), Latin America, Eastern Europe (1979), apartheid South Africa (1994), Tunisia (2011) and many others. Effective campaigning has persuaded mighty corporations to adopt fair trade, sustainable development, the living wage and other policies. Powerful institutions like the World Bank, G8 and even NATO have been influenced by citizens' action.

But most power structures are resilient and can survive determined challenges. Timing, skill, persistence and courage can succeed against incredible odds, which is where learning practical politics can make a difference. By understanding the power dynamics of organizations you want to influence, anyone can bring about change. Many of the skills of influencing hierarchical organizations are outlined in the previous chapter. The following section suggests sideways routes to reach people in powerful positions.

Spheres of power (power petals)

People at the top of any large institution are often closer to people at the top of other institutions than to people at the bottom of their own. Charles Arnold-Baker (1967: 34) showed this as 'power petals' representing different social spheres and institutions with overlapping peaks at the centre (see Figure 7.2).

The 'petals' today are different, and the number of people at the centre may even be smaller than in 1967, but as a rough guide it offers insights for practical politics. At a global level each state, transnational corporation and organization has overlapping 'power petals' run by a relatively small global elite. In *Superclass* David Rothkopf (2008) identified 6,000 people who qualify. At this level, most prime ministers are mere petitioners at the edges of power, straining to influence the mightiest on the planet. British Prime Minister John Major and the Bank of England were no match for hedge fund manager George Soros, who made more than a billion pounds profit by short selling sterling in September 1992 (Mallaby, 2010). When Tony Blair, Gordon Brown and David Cameron aspired to become Prime Minister, they wooed Rupert Murdoch, owner of News International, as assiduously as the electorate (Blair, 2010; Watson and Hickman, 2012; Tiffen, 2014).

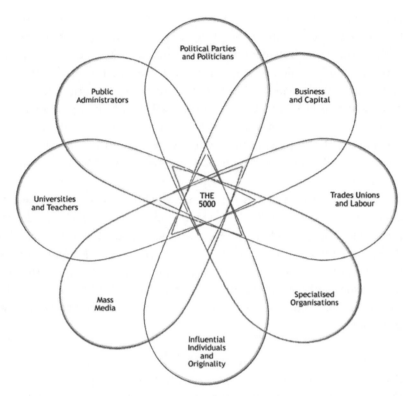

Figure 7.2: 'Power Petals' from Charles Arnold-Baker, *The 5000 and the Power Tangle* (1967)

Analysing 'power petals' at any level helps to identify the institutions and individuals that influence decisions about your cause and how to reach them. Sometimes it can be easier to reach key decision makers in your own organization through another area altogether. For example, it is easier to talk with leaders in many faith communities than it is for shop floor workers in a multinational corporation to communicate with their chief executive. In open societies people move at different power levels in different spheres, so that a powerful CEO or politician may be an ordinary member of a faith community or club, while a frontline worker can become a celebrity sports champion or leading lay member of their faith. These differences in accessibility offer fast tracks to influence, which are widely used by elites and are open to skilful citizens. Thus the end of apartheid in South Africa owed as much to influences among the Afrikaner church and business leaders as to direct pressure from the worldwide resistance movement. Jubilee 2000 reached millions through their faith more than political structures.

Levels of power: Local, institutional, national, continental or global

Our globalized world means that power is exercised at many levels through international treaties and institutions, multinational polities like the European Union and NATO, and transnational corporations (TNCs), non-governmental organizations (NGOs) and faith communities. International decisions have as much influence on our daily lives as national and local politics, through the price of fuel and food or control of disease, conflict and climate. Many people understand the intricacies of international football or other sports, but do not know how politics works at a global level or how it affects their lives.

Every level, from neighbourhood to global, has its own complexities and personalities, so it is important to understand the intricacies of the level you want to influence. But every level is also influenced from above and below. So whatever issue you are engaged in, you need to look at the connections between agencies and institutions that govern that issue, to find examples, policies, networks or allies to support your cause. If your government has signed up to an international agreement, use it as a lever. If someone elsewhere in the world is doing what you want to do, use it as an example. Action at a local level in one place can spread very fast if communicated well and it resonates with people elsewhere, like the student protests of 1968, the Occupy Movement, participatory budgeting and campaigns against FGM. Global agreements can also give local campaigners a focus, like Charter 77, Agenda 21 and the Sustainable Development Goals.

Global governance is conducted through thousands of institutions that regulate many aspects of our lives. It is largely run by officials from governments and business (Hurd, 2010; Rittberger *et al.*, 2012), but civil society and academics are a growing influence. Communications technology means that global decision-making is increasingly accessible to citizens. International organizations like Amnesty International, Friends of the Earth and the World Wild Fund for Nature act as multipliers, replicating messages and models of action across national boundaries, as do companies, global media and governments.

Political spaces: What access to power do people have?

John Gaventa *et al.* (2011) use the image of a cube to describe different dimensions of power (see Figure 7.3), distinguishing between **closed, invited and claimed** spaces. Closed space refers to decisions taken behind doors, with little or no public involvement. Invited spaces are institutionalized forms of participation, organized by those with greater power on their terms. 'Claimed spaces' are 'those which relatively powerless or excluded groups create for themselves' (16). The authors see these in terms of social movements through which marginalized groups create political space for themselves. The history of democratic politics is also a process of people prising open decision-making space to a wider public. Moving the boundary of formerly 'closed' spaces creates more visible, transparent and accountable decision-making.

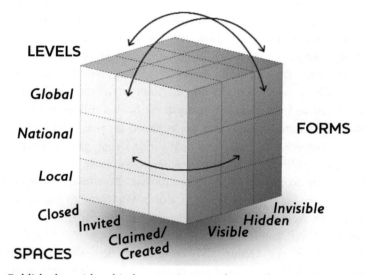

Published with kind permission from the Institute of Development Studies

Figure 7.3: The 'Power Cube' framework

✍ The Power Cube can be used to explore power dynamics through a variety of activities described at www.powercube.net.

Perhaps the most important observation from the Power Cube is that relatively powerless groups can create political space to build a base from which to challenge established powers. Thus the women's movement punctured the glass ceiling of all-male elites; the Solidarity trade union swept out Poland's Communist rulers and elected its leader, Lech Walesa, as president of Poland; the ANC built a base to take power in South Africa; the Workers' Party of Brazil propelled its leader, Luiz Lula, to become president of Brazil (2003–11). The fluid realities of power do not correspond to neat squares, as the authors recognize, and their case studies identify more categories on each side of the cube, but it offers a rough guide to different dimensions of power, described in the following three sub-sections.

Who takes part? What are visible, hidden and invisible forms of power?

Another face of the Power Cube draws on the work of Steven Lukes in *Power: A radical view* (2005 [1974]), who argued that power must be understood not only in terms of who participates, but also who does not. In Lukes's view power has three faces – the public face that we all see as the theatre of politics; a hidden face, that keeps issues off of the agenda of decision-making arenas; and a deceptive third face, through which the relatively powerless accept their own condition and do not recognize or act on their own interests. This 'false consciousness' is described as a form of self-preservation, through which people with little power protect themselves from forces much greater than themselves, also analysed by system justification theory (Jost *et al.,* 2004). The most important question, however, is how people with relatively little power can learn how to use it to protect themselves and create a better world.

> ✋ For educators, the question is how people excluded from power can understand their situation and strengthen their voice as politically equal citizens in unequal societies. Under the Brazilian dictatorship in the 1960s, Paulo Freire did this through 'conscientization' in adult literacy (1970, 1993) while Augusto Boal used participatory theatre (1979, 1998). In the United States Saul Alinsky trained the 'have-nots' to take power through community organizing (1971). In apartheid South Africa Steve Biko used Black Consciousness for psychological liberation (1986). Training for Transformation is an approach to community organizing that enables people to 'read their reality and write their own history' inspired by Freire and developed in Africa since 1975 by Anne Hope and Sally Timmel (1984, 1999, 2014), still used in Ireland, Africa and elsewhere.

Degrees of freedom How much scope do people have to exercise power?

Different circumstances allow people varying degrees of freedom. Open societies and institutions allow more freedom than closed ones. People who own property and have a reliable income have more freedom than those who are poor. People at the top of a hierarchy have more freedom than those at the bottom, although people outside hierarchies may have most of all. People's ability to exercise freedom depends on the resources available to them, their position in society, external environment and the rules or constitution that governs them.

People's freedom within institutions also varies widely, and changes over time. Some armed forces permit homosexuality, while many ban it; some companies encourage whistleblowing, others punish it; some organizations allow people to manage their own time and speak freely, while many impose tight controls. The relationship between freedom and effectiveness of organizations is even more complex than for countries, and varies widely between types of organization, so that the freedom of an academic institute is inappropriate for a secret service or police force. But how much freedom and power people have in any institution can be changed.

Most people have more freedom than they realize, but feel constrained by circumstances, lack of ability or fear of the consequences of taking action. Understanding the constraints, power gradients and degrees of freedom at different levels within their organization, community and nation of expanding freedom, learning how an organization or political system really works increases people's ability to influence it, however little formal power they may have.

Conclusion

People need power to solve problems and do things. The more power people have, the more they can do. Over the past century humanity has dramatically increased its power to grow food, make things, travel, treat illness, prolong life and communicate. These achievements have been due to political arrangements that increased freedom for science, technology, enterprise, politics and public services. Humanity has also increased its power to kill people, pollute nature and warm the planet. These forces are also governed by our political arrangements. The future of our species depends on how well we organize and use power at all levels of society, from families and firms to global governance.

Power in society is constantly changing, as individuals, groups, organizations and nations rise and fall, technologies come and go or people take action to address problems. To take part in politics you need a good map of the agencies and actors who influence what matters to you. Any political project needs to map the powers that influence the desired outcome. Political strategists, lobbyists, the military, investors, development agencies and community organizers use a variety of activities and tools to map power and influence. Power mapping is also used in some therapeutic traditions 'where the impact of social adversity and inequalities can outweigh benefits of individualized psychotherapy' (Brown, 2010; Smail, 2005).

For practical politics a fresh map needs to be drawn for each situation, as in engineering or business. Relying on maps drawn by others or from times past, whether the CIA, *Economist* or Marx, is to risk getting lost. This chapter has offered some of the questions about the nature of power, where to find it and how to use it. The final part of this book looks in more detail how to learn and teach practical politics in different settings.

LEARN MORE ABOUT POWER

List occasions when you experienced a) a sense of power, and b) powerlessness. Look at each experience and identify factors that gave you or others power, including force, language, position, self-worth, situation and surprise. Go through each experience of powerlessness and imagine what you could have done differently to achieve more equal power, if anything, or what else could have changed the balance of power, such as different norms of behaviour, laws or actions.

This exercise can be done alone, in pairs or in groups, and can be used to analyse power dynamics in different situations, including historical events, contemporary politics, fiction, film and organizations.

Power mapping

Study case studies of different power mapping tools (and if possible practise using them), such as:

1. Stakeholder Analysis: see, for example, MMU Stakeholder Analysis Toolkit: www2.mmu.ac.uk/media/mmuacuk/content/documents/bit/Stakeholder-analysis-toolkit-v3.pdf, relevant for planning any kind of change project or campaign.

2. DfID's Political Economic Analysis: www.odi.org/sites/odi.org.uk/files/odi-assets/events-documents/3501.pdf

3. Bode, B. (2007) *Power Analysis in the Context of Rights-Based Programming*. CARE Bangladesh.

4. Hyden, G. (2005) 'Why do things happen the way they do? A power analysis of Tanzania'. http://xa.yimg.com/kq/groups/20674633/1114493356/name/Goran+Hyden_Power+Analysis_Tanzania.pdf

5. Participatory rural appraisal (Chambers, 1983, 1997), power analysis (Gaventa, 2006; Powercube, 2011) and net-maps (Schiffer and Waale, 2008) for work with local communities.

6. Power structure research (Mills, 1956; Domhoff, 2012, 2013, 2016; Rothkopf, 2008; Sampson, 2004) on the wider political and social context at a local, national or global level.

Create a stakeholder analysis and power map of an issue that concerns you.

Part Three
Learning for democracy

3

This section shows how to make education for practical politics available to all.

Three chapters show how to support learning for democracy through:

1. Universities (Chapter 8)
2. Schools (Chapter 9)
3. Charities, local authorities, political parties and the media (Chapter 10)

The final chapters address three sets of questions:

4. How do you create demand for practical political education?
5. How do you create a curriculum for it?
6. How do you get institutional and political support?

The Civic University
Practical political education by universities and colleges

In this chapter you will learn:

- How Innocence Projects teach law by addressing miscarriages of justice
- Why high-level practical knowledge will become central for universities
- About parallels between practical politics and business education
- About key policy commitments to education for democracy

About examples of existing provision, including:

- Service learning and civic engagement
- Policy and research centres as 'intelligence services for democracy'
- Institutes of Politics, Schools of Government and specialist programmes
- How Massive Open Online Courses (MOOCs) could bring practical politics to a wider audience

The chapter concludes by showing how robust ethics can underpin education for practical politics.

Case study: Innocence Projects – Learning about justice

Bob Dylan's famous ballad *Hurricane* tells the story of Rubin 'Hurricane' Carter, imprisoned in 1966 and released 19 years later by a federal judge in 1985 because the conviction was 'tainted by racial bias and the withholding of information' (NYT, 1988). In 2016 the numbers of innocent people in US jails was between 46,000 and 100,000 (2.3–5 per cent), according to estimates by Michigan Law School. Many law students are learning about justice by gathering evidence to release them.

Students at the Cardozo Law School in New York get academic credits and real-world experience by working for a judge, government agency or non-profit. The school's Center for Rights and Justice (CRJ) co-ordinates more than 25 initiatives for justice through research, public policy reform and client advocacy. Its best known programme aims to free innocent people from prison and 'reform the system responsible for their unjust imprisonment'.

The Project was founded in 1992 by two professors, Barry Scheck and Peter Neufeld. It became an independent non-profit in 2004, affiliated with the law school. It has seven full-time attorneys working on nearly 300 active cases, with about 20 law students on a year-long programme.

Since 1989 more than 1,745 people have been exonerated of serious crime, according to the National Registry of Exonerations, founded by two professors at Michigan University Law School in 2012. Hundreds were released as a result of innocence initiatives. Many had spent more than ten years in prison. Twenty had been sentenced to death.

A Network of 21 innocence organizations was formed in 2005. It now has 70 member organizations worldwide. Many work with educational institutions to give students real-world experience. The Network fosters mutual support among innocence efforts, a 'brief bank' of legal arguments to educate courts and a guide to Starting an Innocence Organization.

Legal clinical education was pioneered in 1910 at Northwestern University by Dean John Henry Wigmore. This is now the Bluhm Legal Clinic, where most of its 200 students gain experience by representing clients. Students also take part in simulations of legal cases with experienced practitioners and work with faculty to challenge the fairness of legal institutions and propose reform (see video at https://youtu.be/bT2mswsT5co). Students can also do specialist legal work with children and families, the environment, international human rights or mediation. Its Center on Wrongful Conviction of Youth (CWCY) does outreach, advocacy, education and litigation for young people. One of its cases featured in a ten-part Netflix documentary, *Making a Murderer*.

At Northwestern's School of Journalism, Professor David Protess ran a famous investigative journalism course with the Legal Clinic. Students worked in groups of four on cases of suspected wrongful convictions, and this had a remarkable impact. In the Ford Heights case, four men who had spent almost two decades on death row for a double murder were exonerated as a result of evidence gathered by students, as documented by Protess and Rob Warden in *A Promise of Justice* (1998). 'The biggest eye-opener for students is the extent to which people can get railroaded,' Protess said. 'One man out of seven [sent to death row] is proven innocent. I believe there are more.' The case led Illinois Governor George Ryan to declare a moratorium on executions in 2003, commuting 150 death sentences to life in prison. Governor Pat Quinn abolished the death penalty in 2011 as a direct result of this initiative.

Portess's students uncovered evidence that saved five men from death row and at least another six from prison. But in a controversial twist the project was accused of distorting evidence and framing another suspect. Portess lost his job at the university and now leads the Chicago Innocence Centre, founded in 2011 and not a member of the Network, while the controversy continues.

Lessons

Innocence initiatives enable students to learn high level skills through real projects, helping to solve problems in the criminal justice system as well as gaining a deeper understanding of law and equipping them for employment. I draw several lessons from these projects:

- Combining education with service enriches both, but needs experienced practitioners and effective support for students and the public to benefit.
- Adequate funding is essential: legal investigation, representation and campaigning need time, expertise and commitment. These projects rely on a variety of funding sources and invest in building relationships with donors. The NY project, for example, has an annual budget of $12 million, of which about 80 per cent is from individuals and less than five per cent from the law school.
- Institutional support is critical. Projects seem to work best as stand-alone non-profits in partnership with practitioners and university departments. This provides autonomy to focus on their core mission, accountable to an independent board. However, projects take time to build expertise, systems and donor relationships, so they may need to incubate within a university or other organization before becoming independent.
- The Network enables projects to support each other, share expertise and promote their cause worldwide.

There are many examples from other subjects where students combine learning with practice for a social purpose, but they are still the exception. Practical projects develop basic political skills of teamwork, negotiation, leadership and communication, as well as some understanding of the political context of the subject. Extending opportunities of this kind is one way to develop education for practical politics.

Finally, the unresolved controversy over Professor Protess's investigative journalism programme raises ethical and safeguarding issues, which are discussed at the end of this chapter.

Teaching practical wisdom

Practical knowledge is sometimes seen as marginal to the purpose of universities, but people who combine learning with doing are creating the future now. High-level practical knowledge is changing the world through innovation and influence. In many disciplines subject knowledge soon goes out of date, but abilities to apply core principles, research a topic, analyse, question, present a case, work in teams, carry out projects, negotiate and influence others are increasingly sought after.

Higher education has traditionally taught advanced vocational professions like the priesthood, law and medicine, then engineering, teaching and other subjects. Academic learning and scholarship are themselves advanced vocational skills, which dominated universities as a result of their role in civil service recruitment (Ellis, 2013) and peer-reviewed research for employment, funding and ranking among universities. But demand for vocational subjects such as accounting, advertising, business studies, computing, journalism, law and marketing is growing. Degree-level apprenticeships are likely to become attractive as a cost-effective route to high-level practical knowledge.

The closest parallel to learning practical politics is business education. The motto of Cranfield University School of Management is 'Transforming Knowledge into Action'. Its mission is to 'transform the practice of management around the world by creating and disseminating applied knowledge'. Harvard Business School's mission is 'to educate leaders who make a difference in the world'. The best business schools use real-life problems, projects, placements and case studies to develop practical knowledge and bring about change.

Universities establish enterprise units to help academics develop the commercial potential of research. Business links flourish through joint ventures and economic clusters (Porter, 1998; Paytas *et al.,* 2004). In *The Global University* (2012) Adam Nelson argued that 'the idea that universities operate as firms in a global marketplace has become axiomatic for most scholars of higher education, even if some continue to challenge the normalization of this paradigm' (11). Nelson cites numerous scholars in support (Bok, 2004; Breton and Lambert, 2003; Geiger, 2004; Priest and St John, 2006; Slaughter and Leslie, 1999). Some have argued that the autonomous university is in ruins (Delanty, 2001; Readings, 1996). The risk is that if universities become too closely aligned with business they will lose academic freedom under the constraints of commercial confidentiality and short-term priorities of the market.

Developing the civic role of universities and education for democracy would balance their commercial role. Practical politics could develop a triple role as business expertise has done, as a subject of study, as a way of increasing the impact of research and as an active contribution to society. Providing practical politics on a similar scale as business education would transform university regions and help solve many problems facing humanity. Innovation in democracy and politics would help people make the best use of the innovations in finance, science and technology that are driving social change.

Higher education for democracy

As independent institutions dedicated to non-partisan pursuit of knowledge, pushing the boundaries of democracy should be as important as pushing the boundaries of science, medicine or business. Universities in the US and Europe have already started this journey.

In the United States the Truman *Commission on Higher Education for American Democracy* (1948) established a network of public community colleges. Campus Compact was founded in 1985 to promote the civic purposes of higher education and 'renew our role as agents of our democracy'. It has a membership of 1,200 college presidents and 34 Campus Compact affiliates that link academic courses to community service learning. The American Democracy Project (ADP) was started in 2002 by the American Association of State Colleges and Universities (AASCU) in collaboration with *The New York Times*. It includes some 250 public colleges and universities, reaching more than one and a half million students. Its Political Engagement Project aims to develop political efficacy and 'prepare students to become informed, engaged, and active citizens'. The US Department of Education (2012) published a *Road Map and Call to Action* for 'civic learning and democratic engagement from grade school to graduate school, with special attention to the federal role and civic learning in higher education' available at www.ed.gov/civic-learning. It urges 'action civics' (O'Connor and Duncan, 2011), with numerous examples of practical political education, and sets out nine steps for action. The report quotes Tony Wagner, co-director of the Change Leadership Group at the Harvard Graduate School of Education, who said, '[There is a] happy convergence between the skills most needed in the global knowledge economy and those most needed to keep our democracy safe and vibrant.'

In 2010 Ministers of the Council of Europe launched a *Charter on Education for Democratic Citizenship and Human Rights Education* that declared that 'Member states should promote, with due respect for the principle of academic freedom, the inclusion of education for democratic citizenship and human rights education in higher education institutions, in particular for future education professionals' (Article 7) and 'democratic governance in all educational institutions both as a desirable and beneficial method of governance in its own right and as a practical means of learning and experiencing democracy and respect for human rights' (Article 8). The Council sees universities as a 'site of citizenship' and 'preparation for life as active citizens in democratic societies' as one of four major purposes of higher education (the others are preparation for the labour market, personal development and the development of a broad, advanced knowledge base). The Bologna process of the EU and European University Association also recognize the civic role of universities. Sir Christopher Snowden, President of Universities UK, has said, 'Higher education impacts on wider policy objectives including those related to health, citizenship, community cohesion, national security, social mobility, and wider society'.

Governments say that education for democracy matters, but have done little to promote it. Universities can fulfil these aspirations by expanding existing provision, as outlined below. The following sections briefly highlight provision aimed at each of my four categories of political activity – submitting, following or supporting, challenging and governing or leading.

Learning through social action

Innocence initiatives are excellent examples of how higher education can serve people who are utterly powerless. Wrongfully convicted prisoners are forced to submit, like the targets of child abuse, domestic violence, FGM, forced labour, torture and other victims of injustice. Focusing on problems in the university's neighbourhood and more widely would identify opportunities for learning practical politics and developing high-level knowledge in a wide range of disciplines.

American universities and community colleges have a strong tradition of civic engagement, with 40–75 per cent of students involved in social action, compared with 15–30 per cent in the United Kingdom. Campus Compact promotes public and community service to develop students' citizenship skills, create community partnerships and provide resources and training for faculty to integrate civic and community-based learning into the curriculum. Community engagement is defined as 'collaboration between institutions of higher education and their larger communities (local, regional/ state, national, global) for the mutually beneficial exchange of knowledge and resources in a context of partnership and reciprocity' (Driscoll, 2006).

In *Civic Engagement in Higher Education* (2009), Barbara Jacoby and colleagues describe numerous examples of civic engagement, showing how democratic practices can be integrated into courses across disciplines. US research also shows significant gains in academic achievement as well as civic engagement after leaving college (Eyler *et al.*, 1999, 2001; Kuh, 2007).

Service learning is a form of community-based experiential learning that has grown rapidly over the past two decades. When done well it blends structured learning with community action and reflection to develop character, problem-solving skills and civic responsibility (Eyler *et al.*, 1999; Butin, 2010). However, a study of more than 600 service learning programmes showed that only one per cent focused on specifically political concerns (Colby *et al.*, 2007: 5). To address this Cipolle (2010) offers 'a road map to social change through service-learning" (p.9) to create a programme that 'fosters students' critical consciousness and their commitment to engage in social change' (p.xi). She outlines a three-stage process that enables students to develop a more complex 'systemic view of the causes of injustice and inequity' (p.11).

Educating for Democracy (Colby *et al.*, 2007) makes a compelling case for education in practical politics, drawing on research and the Political Engagement Project (PEP). These 21 projects in learning for responsible democratic participation were funded by the Carnegie Foundation. The study showed that education for political development increases political understanding, skill, motivation and involvement while contributing to general academic learning. The authors argue that 'liberal education must liberate, not indoctrinate' (xi). Significantly, the project 'did not change party identification or political ideology' (5), which will disappoint some and reassure others. *Educating for Democracy* describes how to teach practical politics without imposing particular ideologies and offers guidelines for faculty to help students engage in politics. It describes how to create an environment for open inquiry; how to teach political knowledge, understanding and participation skills; and how to increase the likelihood that political learning lasts beyond graduation. It provides details of five pedagogical strategies, including:

- political discussion and deliberation
- political research and action projects
- invited speakers and mentors
- external placements, internships and service learning
- structured reflection.

The Political Engagement Project developed skills relevant to both electoral politics and direct forms of democracy, such as working with a school board or community group, including:

- political influence and action
- political analysis and judgement
- communication and leadership
- teamwork and collaboration.

The authors report 'We were not surprised that the category of skills for which students reported the lowest facility at the pretest were those of political influence and action, followed by skills of political analysis and judgement' but by the end of the programme 'Students made statistically significant gains in all four skills categories, showing the largest gains in political influence and action' (15) for which they had begun with the lowest scores.

Intelligence services for democracy

Politics needs research and policy analysis to inform action. Governments and industry can afford to do it, but citizens who want to question or challenge policies have difficulty finding reliable and accessible analysis. However, universities are creating centres for practitioners and researchers to work together in a growing range of policy areas, such as cities, diplomacy, government, health, housing, human rights, responsible tourism, science and sustainable development. For example, the University of Bath Institute for Policy Research (IPR), fosters inter-disciplinary research to address major policy challenges and support global policy research networks. The Centre for Social Justice and Community Action at Durham University brings together researchers from several disciplines and community partners to develop research, teaching, public engagement and staff development for social justice, with a focus on participatory action research. Institutes such as the Cardoso Center for Rights and Justice, the independent Centre for Cities, Columbia's Earth Institute, Harvard's Poverty Action Lab, International Inequalities Institute at LSE or TERI University in New Delhi are actively engaged in practical solutions to problems with a political dimension.

Specialist research centres gather knowledge to inform public debate and action, such as the National Registry of Exonerations, Costs of War at Brown University or the Partner Abuse State of Knowledge Project on family violence run by a network of academics. The independent Institute for Fiscal Studies is the leading authority on tax and spending in the UK.

During the referendum on independence in Scotland, university centres had a vital role in providing impartial information to the public through public debates, the media and online, more than research papers.

These activities could be called 'intelligence services for democracy', enabling citizens to have a more informed voice in decisions. However, opportunities to learn political skills to use this information effectively are still scarce.

The Bipartisan Policy Center (BPC) is a non-profit set up by senior Democratic and Republican politicians in America to 'find actionable solutions to the nation's key challenges'. It aims to drive 'principled solutions through rigorous analysis, reasoned negotiation and respectful dialogue'. It 'combines politically balanced policymaking with strong, proactive advocacy and outreach' to confront challenges 'from the national debt to national security'. It acts as a convenor, research focus and support network for elected politicians working across party divisions to find long-term solutions. In 2010 it launched a Democracy Project to promote civic education and service.

Student-organized activities are traditionally more important for developing politics skills of the elite. Many political leaders learnt to campaign, debate and organize through student-run societies and youth wings of political parties. Many pressure groups also provide campaign training, such as People & Planet, Campaign Bootcamp, Oxfam, Friends of the Earth, or the Tea Party Patriots.

Learning to lead and govern

A growing number of universities offer high-level practical political education, such as Chicago University's new non-partisan Institute of Politics, founded by Barack Obama's chief strategist David Axelrod to 'ignite in young people a passion for politics and public service'; LSE's Department of Government; and Harvard's Kennedy School of Government, which convenes a Global Public Innovation Network from ten countries. Skills for governing are also taught in public affairs, political communication and Masters in Public Policy as well as business-orientated programmes for corporate social responsibility, leadership and management. Philosophy, Politics and Economics (PPE) provides an intellectual grounding for aspiring political leaders, but its focus is less practical.

It is also important to recognize the wide-ranging contribution of academics to government, such as Madeleine Albright, Milton Freedman, J.K. Galbraith, Henry Kissinger and Condoleezza Rice, who have provided strategic advice or served in the highest offices of state, then returned to teaching and research.

Building capacity for democratic citizenship

The demands of our age mean that provision for practical political education will grow, through think tanks, pressure groups, the media and business if not in higher education. The biggest challenge is to create opportunities for ordinary citizens, so that increasing provision doesn't widen the participation gap between the majority and the elite. Universities that recognize this are developing community engagement, making learning available online and supporting networks to tackle social problems with adult educators, civil society, cities and other agencies.

Massive Open Online Courses (MOOCs) make higher education courses available worldwide at low cost. Courses in practical politics include Making Government Work in Hard Places from Princeton (NovoEd), the Moral Foundations of Politics from Yale on Coursera or Causes of War from Kings College London (FutureLearn). Although MOOCs tend to attract people who already have higher education, they offer anyone high-quality material for self-organized study. To make the most of these resources, universities, broadcasters, adult education providers or civil society could train 'barefoot educators' to facilitate study circles for low income groups on issues that concern them, using methods of Paulo Freire, the Folk High School movement or action learning (see chapter 10).

Universities are also creating global learning networks, such as the University-Community Partnership for Social Action Research, which connects students, university faculty, community activists and governmental officials working on the UN Millennium Development Goals (MDGs) in 75 countries. It aims to educate community leaders by providing an online library of resources and facilitating cross-sector collaboration, networking and multicultural dialogues, co-ordinated by the Arizona State University. The International Community Action Network (ICAN), founded in 1997 by McGill University, promotes social justice, equality and civil society through 'Rights-Based Community Practice' (RBCP) in the Middle East in order to develop peace, security and healthy societies (see www.mcgill.ca/ ican/ican-international-community-action-network). The United Nations Academic Impact (UNAI) initiative aims to align scholarship and research with the UN and each other according to ten principles including human rights, global citizenship, poverty reduction, sustainable development, peace and conflict resolution. It currently involves more than 900 institutions in more than 100 countries and some 40 academic networks.

Celebrating practical political education

This outline shows the wide range of provision for practical politics, from service learning to policy development, leadership and government, although not always identified with politics or democracy. America's Campus Compact has the clearest commitment to addressing critical issues and advancing the civic purpose of higher education, but it is small scale compared with enterprise education. While it is possible to learn business skills at every level, there are still relatively few opportunities to develop political skills. Most politics courses focus on theory and knowledge rather than practice, while education rarely practices the pedagogy of power. But innocence initiatives, service learning, policy centres and institutes of government show that it is possible to combine high-level learning with action. We need to recognize and develop this range of provision as part of an unfolding new discipline that enriches democratic citizenship and governance.

Ethics for learning through action

To learn practical politics, you have to do it for real. Like team sports, you can't just talk strategy. People train to win. Similarly, the best enterprise education enables people to develop business ideas in the market. This raises ethical issues that must be addressed to support learners, teachers and the institution as well as the public.

The strongest defence of practical political education is to make it an ethical, empirical and non-partisan discipline that enables people to take action based on evidence and judgement, along the following lines.

First, the Nolan principles of public life, drawn up after Britain's cash for questions scandal in 1994, provide clear guidelines for anyone in politics. They are accountability, honesty, integrity, leadership, objectivity, openness and selflessness. The Universal Declaration of Human Rights offers a broader framework and reference point.

Second, projects in practical political education should follow an ethics process, to address questions such as:

1. Is the evidence robust? Is the case strong?

2. Is the project consistent with the Nolan principles of accountability, honesty, integrity, leadership, objectivity, openness and selflessness?

3. How long is the project likely to last? How will you know it has succeeded? Is it feasible within the time available? What will you do if

it takes longer? If there is a chance it could take longer than planned, is there a smaller project within it that you could start with?

4. What's the worst that could happen? Who could counter-attack, and how will you respond?

The ethics process could have two stages, first with a peer group of participants on the programme. If there is any possibility of controversy, it should involve someone in authority at the institution, such as a head of department, ethics committee or other independent person.

Third, it has to be clear that the participants (learners) are acting as citizens, not for the education institution. The educator is an adviser or mentor, not part of their project. This may involve a written undertaking setting out roles and responsibilities as well as any safeguarding issues.

For controversial projects senior people in the institution need to know about the programme and be able to respond quickly if the project comes under political attack. If necessary, board members should be aware of it and be prepared to back it, like the head of the Bristol school where students ran a campaign against female genital mutilation. Occasionally this may be uncomfortable for institutions, but they are more likely to gain credit for their commitment to democratic politics.

LEARN MORE ABOUT INFLUENCING HIGHER EDUCATIONS AND FACILITATORS

Influence your course programme

Students: decide what you ideally want to do after you have completed your studies and find out what influencing and political skills, knowledge and theory are most useful in that role by asking people who are doing it or by looking online (use the first thing that comes into your head if you can't decide what work you want to do).

How much of your current course programme equips you to do practical politics? Go through every module and make a rough estimate of what proportion of time is spent on a) theory, ideas and general principles; b) knowledge of political institutions and problems; c) knowledge of practical skills and strategies; and d) practice and experience.

Note how much of it is concerned with the politics of 1) governing and leadership; 2) challenging and questioning; 3) following and supporting; and 4) submission.

Consider whether your course programme equips you to do what you want to do later and negotiate the content with others on the programme and the people responsible for it, bearing in mind that you can never know what will be useful later and some knowledge is worthwhile for its own sake.

Tutors: look at the destinations of your graduates and assess the political skills required, then do a similar assessment of your programme and increase opportunities for learning practical politics accordingly.

Influence your institution

Read the Council of Europe *Charter on Education for Democratic Citizenship,* the US *Road Map* for civic learning and democratic engagement or other relevant policy documents.

Identify all learning for democratic engagement and practical politics of your department or institution, and gather evidence of outcomes for students, the community or social problems in at least one area of practice.

Identify at least one opportunity to enhance civic learning or democratic engagement and draw up a strategy to influence people with the authority to develop it, with reference to relevant policy documents.

Chapter 9

Foundations for learning democracy

This chapter is about political education in schools, and:

- The political battle between 'traditional' and democratic or 'progressive' education
- How democratic schools raise attainment
- Why politics and democracy need to be on the school timetable
- Political education and indoctrination
- The experience of citizenship and political education in England
- Three reasons why education for practical politics and democracy are likely to flourish in the future

Democratic education: A battle of ideas

Over a century ago the American educator John Dewey argued that schools should 'be a miniature community, an embryonic society' in which pupils develop 'social power and insight' (1900: 15–16). Dewey practised his ideas in a 'Laboratory School' at Chicago University as well as private and public schools. In *Democracy and Education,* he wrote about the school community 'freeing individual capacity in a progressive growth directed to social aims' (1916: 95).

'Democracy cannot flourish where the chief influences in selecting subject matter of instruction are utilitarian ends narrowly conceived for the masses, and, for the higher education of the few, the traditions of a specialized cultivated class' (185).

'But an education which acknowledges the full intellectual and social meaning of a vocation would include instruction in the historic background of present conditions; ... and study of economics, civics, and politics, to bring the future worker into touch with the problems of the day and the various methods proposed for its improvement. Above all, it would train power of re-adaptation to changing conditions so that future workers would not become blindly subject to a fate imposed upon them' (Dewey, 1916: 306).

Dewey inspired generations of teachers. He was a pioneer in the 'progressive', child-centred education movement and frequently attacked by supporters of traditional subject-based education. In *Experience and Education*, Dewey observed 'the history of educational theory is marked by opposition between the idea that education is development from within and that it is formation from without' (1938: 1).

Dewey had a profound influence on educators worldwide. But in America his democratic approach clashed with the management style of civic leaders elected to school boards. They hired professional superintendents to run large school districts, using methods of consultants like Frederick Taylor. They rationalized schools into hierarchical systems, sorted pupils into ability streams and managed teachers like production workers. The introduction of national standardized testing from 1965 reinforced traditional teaching.

In England progressive education started in the private schools such as Bedales (1893) and Quaker schools. It spread across the state sector during the 1960s through teacher training colleges, local education authorities and the Schools Council (founded in 1962). It was boosted by the end of streaming in primary schools, political commitment to comprehensive secondary schools and the Plowden Report (1967), which recommended child-centred classroom methods (Galton, Simon and Croll 1980: 39).

The political backlash against Plowden was swift. Supporters of traditional schooling published *The Fight for Education* in 1969, which sold 89,000 copies. It was followed by four more 'Black Papers' on the 'crisis in education'. Their case was echoed by the press and influential figures in both main political parties. It was confirmed by negative press coverage of teaching practices at William Tyndale School in London in the mid-1970s and well-publicized research criticizing progressive methods in primary school teaching by Neville Bennett (Bennett, 1976). In October 1976 Labour Prime Minister James Callaghan called for a 'great debate' about the nature and purposes of education in a famous speech at Ruskin College (Callaghan, 1976). This was a tentative start of intervention by central government into the curriculum and organization of schools, which until then had been a matter for teachers, schools and elected Local Education Authorities. The Education Department wrote that 'the challenge now is to restore the rigour without damaging the real benefits of the child-centred developments' (DES, 1977: 8). In 1988 the Conservative government introduced a National Curriculum for state schools. Prime Minister John Major told his Party Conference in 1992, 'We will take no lectures from those who led the long march of mediocrity through our schools ... My belief is a return to basics in education. The progressive theorists have had their say, and ... they've had their day' (quoted in Alexander, 2009). Child-centred education was officially discouraged by the 1992 DES report *Curriculum Organization and Classroom Practice in Primary Schools*.

Twenty-five years later traditional approaches seemed utterly entrenched in England through the National Curriculum, external testing, league tables, frequent inspection and central control by ministers through regional school commissioners. However, wider social changes mean that democratic political education could be the best way to raise attainment and equip young people to thrive.

Schools in a global society

We live in a new global era. The internet, news and trade connect people more than ever, but we experience the world through different cultures. Diversity is a great strength, because different perspectives create new possibilities. But differences are also sources of conflict. As the world becomes more connected, many people demand barriers to keep others out. Groups want their own enclaves, based on nationality, faith or other identity. Hostility to others is often virulent, sometimes violent. Rising barriers reflect minds closing from fear and ignorance.

In this context schools can create microcosms of humanity, where people learn to live with difference and how to resolve conflicts by peaceful means. Schools in multicultural societies have the privilege of many faiths, languages and nationalities within their community, but all schools can reach across continents through school linking, service learning, an inclusive ethos and curriculum.

Every classroom is a 'unit of rule', nested within the school, neighbourhood, region, nation and wider world. Management theorist Charles Handy compared schools with city-states, displaying every form of governance from dictatorship to the direct democracy (Handy, 1987). The challenge is to create forms of governance that empower pupils, teachers and communities to thrive in our rapidly changing world.

Citizenship and educational achievement

A good education is the foundation of citizenship in any society. This means fluency with reading, writing, numbers, information technologies, the scientific method and creativity as well as knowledge of the world and practical politics. Schools are not necessary to learn. Online tools for learning, sharing, exploring, understanding and influencing are growing rapidly. People can learn online for free through Alison.com, Khan Academy,

MOOCs, TED talks or YouTube. A smartphone can access more knowledge than was available in universities a generation ago.

But schools are more than institutions for instruction. A creative school environment, diverse peer groups and good teaching open doors to learning in ways most people would find difficult on their own. Every school can be a centre for citizenship, culture, sports and community.

The quality of schooling for the majority of children is a critical issue for most societies and a major political battle ground, as shown by the conflict between 'progressive' and 'traditional' schooling outlined above. School improvement requires political skills to bring about change from within as well as outside-in. A review of research into North America's school systems concluded:

> *of all the factors that contribute to what students learn at school ... leadership is second in strength only to classroom instruction. Furthermore, effective leadership has the greatest impact in those circumstances (e.g., schools 'in trouble') in which it is most needed. ... Educational leadership, our review also makes clear, comes from many sources, not just the 'usual suspects' – superintendents and principals' but is distributed and shared.*
>
> (Leithwood *et al.*, 2004: 70)

The study emphasized 'the influence of student and family backgrounds on student success in school' and the need for school leaders 'to understand how schools and homes interconnect with each other and with the world' (46–50). These findings were confirmed by a unique 15-year study of improving schools in Chicago that showed the 'complex interplay of how schools are organized and interact with the local community to alter dramatically the odds for improving student achievement'. Five key factors identified were leadership, student-centred learning, professional capacity, effective teaching and strong parent–community ties.

Study after study also shows that family background explains as much as half the difference in student achievement (Alexander, 1997; Desforges, 2003; Feinstein, 2007). Although socio-economic status is strongly related to student learning and behaviour, evidence from the 1970 UK Birth Cohort Survey (BCS) and elsewhere shows that parental interest in their child's education has four times more influence on attainment at 16 than socio-economic background (Feinstein and Symons, 1999). Work with families complements efforts in the classroom, particular in areas where parents have had a bad experience or low expectations of education (Henderson and Mapp, 2002). Building relationships with parents is often the start for transforming a school and creating school cultures that support all students (Comer and Haynes, 1992; Epstein, 1995; Henderson and Mapp, 2002; Sebring *et al.*, 2006).

Teachers, pupils, parents and their communities can be agents of change, influencing achievement in ways that are beyond the reach of education officials and politicians. Community-led Initiatives such as Parent Mentors, Literacy Ambassadors and adult education, as well as political battles over the siting of a new school or leadership of a low-performing school, can drive school improvement from the bottom up (Warren and Mapp, 2011). In the US more than 200 community alliances are working with schools to raise educational outcomes (see Shirley, 1997; Orr, 2007). Citizens UK is using these experiences to work with schools in the United Kingdom (Jameson and Chapleau, 2011).

Leaders of democratic school improvement can also learn from Finland (Niikko, 2006; Sahlberg, 2015; Tuovinen, 2008), Michael Fullan's approach to school change (1992, 2001, 2006, 2012 [1993]), John Taylor Gatto (2000, 2002), John Holt (1990; 1995), William Glasser (1990) and Neil Postman and Charles Weingartner's inspiring *Teaching As a Subversive Activity* (1971).

What are citizenship schools?

A 'citizenship school' offers a sophisticated model of democracy, involving activities such as circle time, peer mediation, pupil responsibilities, project work, service learning, schools councils and parent forums. The starting point is a commitment to transform the way school is run by giving young people direct experience of decision-making and the issues they face in growing up. These must be real decisions, with real consequences, in which young people have to seek compromise and consensus among themselves as well as with adults. All schools teach people how to behave and take part in society through the 'hidden curriculum' of ethos, behaviour and rules (Jackson, 1991; Snyder, 1970; Gatto, 1992). Citizenship schools use this to empower pupils, parents, staff and local people (Alexander, 2001; Audsley *et al.*, 2013).

A ten-year study has shown that the most successful approach to citizenship education in the United Kingdom 'is embedded in the curriculum, has links to student participation across the school/college, and encourages links with the wider community' (Keating *et al.*, 2010). There is also evidence that schools where pupils are able to take responsibility and participate have higher attainment (Hannam, 2001a, 2001b; Houser, 2014).

Politics in the curriculum

Citizenship, civics and politics are often low status subjects, taught by teachers with little specialist training, unlike high status STEM subjects of Science, Technology, English and Maths. This is like saying the only skills that matter in football are on the pitch, not the manager, coach and referee who provide strategy, tactics and rules of the game. All are necessary for success.

Political education also has to be on the timetable for three main reasons. First, citizenship and politics are challenging subjects, which require specialist skills and knowledge. They need capable teachers who can handle controversial issues. Second, subjects on the timetable show what students will learn and why. Third, the timetable gives subjects status.

Politics on the timetable gives young people opportunities to discuss issues that matter to them and learn how they can have a say about them. Many young people are inspired by a cause, like the Bristol schoolgirls. It may be animal rights, the environment, homelessness, immigration, local issues or something at school. Whatever the issue, it can show the complexities and possibilities of political problem solving.

Ignoring young people's desire to act on issues can have damaging consequences. First, they are likely to act independently and join internet sites or groups that address things they care about. This can be positive, but white supremacists, Daesh/Islamic State or other groups can be attractive and dangerous. So it is best if young people's desire to take action is welcome at school. Second, if issues are discussed in the abstract and young people can't do anything about them, they become bored and switch off. They learn that other people do politics and they are mere spectators. Third, young people are often aware of problems that need to be addressed that adults may not be aware of, such as bullying, child abuse or substance misuse. Creating time in the school timetable where issues are addressed in a spirit of openness and respect enables young people to deal with them. Fourth, young people need to see that taking action can bring about change. If nothing happens after signing a petition, lobbying politicians or voting, people conclude that politics is pointless and they are powerless. The reality is that politics is more complicated than shopping. Clicking a petition won't deliver the result like Amazon. That's why young people need to learn about different kinds of action and experiment with them in a supportive, learning environment such as a school, youth club or community centre.

Political education and indoctrination

Many politicians are wary of political education. As the Crick Report on education for citizenship in England put it, 'Parents and the public generally may be worried about the possibility of bias and indoctrination' (Crick, 1998: 8, §1.9).

The reality is that the content of instruction is less influential than how pupils are treated and wider social values. In the former Soviet Union political education aimed to 'train genuine Communists capable of stamping out falsehood and prejudices and helping the working masses to vanquish the old system and build up a state without capitalists, without exploiters, and without landowners' (Lenin, 1920). But 'the Soviet regime had extremely limited success in its seventy-year effort to inculcate regime values among Soviet citizens' (Reisinger *et al.*, 1994: 184).

In China compulsory political education still teaches principles of Marxism-Leninism, Essentials of Mao Zedong's Thought and Deng Xiaoping's Theory. Since 2006 all pupils have been taught a value system known as the 'Eight Honours and Disgraces' to foster patriotic, diligent, disciplined and law-abiding citizens (Kennedy *et al.*, 2014: 68–70). Yet despite sustained moral instruction at school and college corruption is widespread (Transparency International, 2014). Teaching Marxism has not inhibited a largely capitalist market economy within a one-party state.

Education for democracy, on the other hand, aims to teach people to think critically, question authority (including teachers and rulers) and take part in politics. Democracy is the best inoculation against indoctrination.

Political education and democracy

Many young people may never engage with formal politics at all. In Africa about 65 per cent of the population are under 35 years, but the political participation of young people is consistent with other regions of the world (AfroBarometer). In the US Congressional elections of 2010 turnout by 18 to 24 year olds was just a fifth (21 per cent). In Britain less than 44 per cent of 18 to 24 year olds voted in the general elections of 2010 and 2015, compared with 65 per cent of people of all ages and almost 80 per cent of over-65s. A Hansard Society report showed that only a quarter of this age group were interested in politics, and lacked understanding about politics. Those who do not take part are mostly in lower socio-economic groups. This means that political priorities are set by older, wealthier sections of the population.

An international study of 140,000 Grade 8 students in 5,300 schools from 38 countries in Asia, Europe and Latin America showed that civic knowledge and civic engagement at school were positively associated with intentions to vote and less accepting of authoritarian government, corruption or law breaking. This evidence supports the view that civic and political education promotes democratic politics (Ainley *et al.*, 2013).

Political education in England

Most European societies include some political education from primary school, including active citizenship (NFER, 2002; Eurydice, 2012). England was unusual in Europe in not having a national commitment to teach citizenship until 2001, and nearly dropped the subject in 2014.

When Bernard Crick's former student David Blunkett became Secretary of State for Education in 1997 he invited Crick to chair an advisory group on education for citizenship in schools. The new subject was 'to include the nature and practices of participation in democracy; the duties, responsibilities and rights of individuals as citizens; and the value to individuals and society of community activity'.

The Crick Report provided a thoughtful, diplomatic discussion of this three-fold definition of citizenship. It was a sophisticated exercise in practical politics, securing support from across the political spectrum and the teaching profession. Its proposals were bold:

> We aim at no less than a change in the political culture of this country both nationally and locally: for people to think of themselves as active citizens, willing, able and equipped to have an influence in public life and with the critical capacities to weigh evidence before speaking and acting; to build on and to extend radically to young people the best in existing traditions of community involvement and public service, and to make them individually confident in finding new forms of involvement and action among themselves.
>
> (Crick, 1998: 7, §1.5)

Ten years later, a longitudinal study (CELS) showed that students see citizenship as about rights and responsibilities, and issues of identity and equality, rather than political literacy or participation (Keating *et al.*, 2010). My conversations with young people suggest that many find citizenship boring and they learn so little about politics that there are several campaigns for political education in schools. As CELS tactfully put it:

there are still some aspects of citizenship education which require further development, including improving the availability of teacher training; teacher confidence in teaching political literary topics, increasing the use of active teaching and learning methods and improving assessment policies and practices.

(3)

The study reported that 'the most successful approach is the "citizenship-rich" school, where citizenship is embedded in the curriculum, has links to student participation across the school/college, and encourages links with the wider community'. It also reported 'preliminary indications' that 'where young people receive "a lot" of citizenship education, [it] can have an impact on their citizenship outcomes, over and above the impact of other factors' (iii). Crick's ambition to change the political culture of his country is far from being achieved.

Opportunities for renewal

Despite the current dominance of 'traditional' schooling and difficulties of including citizenship, civics and politics in school timetables, there are at least three reasons to be hopeful about education for practical politics and democracy:

First, the worldwide trend to give schools greater autonomy enables them to become more democratic and develop practical political education. Schools recognize that pupil confidence, participation and voice increase attainment. In the United States charter schools such as Democracy Prep in Harlem, New York, and Trillium in Portland, Oregon, emphasize civic participation as well as academic achievement. In the UK there are now more than 444 co-operative trust schools based on democratic governance, equal participation and accountability (by mid-2013, more than double the number in 2011) (Woodin, 2012), out of 3,444 academy and free schools. The more democratic schools in Finland are among the highest achieving in the world.

Second, the pressures of standardized testing has increased emphasis on personalized learning, student empowerment, civic engagement, mindfulness and other methods previously dismissed as 'progressive'.

Third, demand for creativity, independent thinking and teamwork in a knowledge economy creates a new institutional logic that is less hierarchical, more open, flexible and collaborative. Smart policymakers and school leaders can see that everyone needs political skills of influencing, organizing, public speaking and negotiating.

Dewey's insights about democratic education and learning about 'problems of the day' are more relevant now than a century ago. Authoritarian capitalism, as pursued by China, Russia and other countries, presents a credible alternative to democratic freedoms and self-government. Western democracies have many flaws and often do not live up to their own ideals, but the values of pluralism, tolerance and human rights enables people of all faiths and none to thrive together.

LEARN MORE ABOUT CITIZENSHIP AND POLITICAL EDUCATION IN SCHOOLS

To understand citizenship and political education in schools:

- Volunteer to run a weekly discussion group about current affairs at a school, college or youth club: start by drawing up ground rules; invite students to choose a topic/issue to explore over a week in order to identify the actors and interests involved, analyse the power dynamics and tell the story of what happened; then discuss the issue; and ask what they think is likely to happen next.
- Work with a school on a one-off citizenship project such as a visit from a politician or to a council/parliament, training for peer-mediation, organizing a debate, exploring a topical issue, or voter registration, etc.
- Read national or state policies/guidelines for civic and political education, and then look at what is actually taught in local schools by talking with pupils and teachers and reading any studies or reports on current practice, in order to identify opportunities and constraints.
- Join or subscribe to a relevant organization (e.g. Citizenship Foundation, Association for Citizenship Teaching, School.Co-op, Youth Parliament, Young Mayor Network, Youth Council Network, Youth Voice in the UK, or the Alternative Education Resource Centre (AERO), Everyday Democracy or the Institute for Democratic Education in America in the USA) and take part in activities to strengthen democratic education through school.

In each case keep a diary and/or write a blog to record what happens and lessons learnt (get permission from other people involved), draw out any recommendations for action and share your findings with at least one person who can act on them.

Chapter 10

Whole life learning

In this chapter you will learn:

- Why and how 'whole life learning' will replace lifelong learning
- Why charities, civil society and non-profits need political skills
- How local government and public services can empower citizens
- How civic leaders and politicians can encourage learning for democracy
- How the media can improve public understanding of politics
- How adult education supports education for democratic politics

Case study: Medellín – city of innovation

The Columbian city of Medellín is a dramatic example of a city transformed through civic leadership, learning and grassroots empowerment. Before 2000 Medellín was the drugs and murder capital of the world, with 6,349 killings in 1991, 380 per 100,000 residents. It had a long history of corruption and appalling public services. Its sprawling slums, rising up steep hillsides, were gang warzones, no-go areas for police or military. Yet in 2012 it was recognized as 'Innovative City of the Year' by the *Wall St Journal* and a model of public administration by the Inter-American Development Bank.

Change started when power shifted from the national government to elected city mayors in 1988. Sergio Fajardo was a mathematician and journalist who challenged the city government to provide poor and rich with the same quality of education, transport and architecture. The city built a modern metro and cable-car system to connect poor neighbourhoods with the wealthier lower plains. In 2003 Fajardo was elected mayor on an anti-corruption platform. He had prepared a targeted programme of action: 'Once you get into power, you have to know exactly what you want to do.' He created 'civic-pacts' between city administrators and neighbourhoods to meet local needs and address problems such as school improvement. Community leaders and officials identified initiatives together and agreed who would do what. Local communities decided how to spend some of the city's budget in a participatory budgeting process. The civic pacts were designed as 'pedagogical exercises' to show what people had a right to expect from government and the importance of public participation.

> *'Once you get into power, you have to know exactly what you want to do.'*
>
> *Sergio Fajardo*

Medellín also has around 130,000 students in 35 institutions of higher education, both public and private, which contributed to regeneration. Columbia's Co-operative University is a private institution founded in 1958. It aims to 'improve the quality of life of communities through the solidarity economy' by 'training politically oriented professionals, that is, citizens who think and act autonomously about societal issues that promote the greater good'. Its values are solidarity, equality, respect for diversity and freedom.

The university runs community projects with people who do not have higher education. Professional development includes political awareness 'because we believe that politics is the key to encourage participation and focus collective energy, and to provide space for the expression of people's necessities and aspirations. It is a mechanism for making collective decisions and, in short, it is the way to rethink and restructure society for the good of all.' The university practises social responsibility 'to create a better, more inclusive world'. Its mission is 'the education of competent citizens in order to cope with the world dynamics; we contribute to the construction and spread of knowledge; we support the competitive development of the country through its organizations and we seek the improvement on life quality on communities through solidarity economy which founded us' (UCC website).

Enterprise, innovation, knowledge and social solidarity are recurrent themes in the city's regeneration. In 2010 Fajardo's successor and ally Alonso Salazar created an innovation park, Innovation Week and other projects to encourage new businesses in culture, fashion and new technology. The city's development is supported by public agencies and enterprises, including a state bank, local micro-finance agencies and a utility company that provides electricity, gas, water, sanitation and telecommunications.

Medellín still has problems, but it has the institutions and political capacity to address them (Devlin and Chaskel, 2007; Merin *et al.,* 2013; Dávila, 2013).

Whole life learning

To thrive in the modern world people need to learn all their lives. New means of communication, organizations and technologies spread faster than ever, constantly changing the balance of power between people, cities, countries and companies. Driverless cars, wearable computers, direct democracy and other inventions will transform our lives. Climate change, pollution, population, migration and other challenges are likely to create more crises, more often and more severe, than the 2008 financial crash or 2015 Syrian exodus. Political pressures on citizens and governments could be greater than ever.

In this context, conventional lifelong learning – people attending courses, retraining and continuing professional development – is not enough. People need to learn, adapt and develop every day in every walk of life.

The boundaries between institutions of learning are blurring. People keep up to date through the press, broadcasters, social media and web portals that curate and organize knowledge. High-quality specialist learning will always be at a premium, available online and through centres of excellence. Skilled coaches, facilitators and experienced teacher-practitioners are needed to distil, understand and use knowledge well, but this can be done online anywhere in the world. Face-to-face learning in groups will always matter, for social reasons and mutual support as well as questioning, thinking aloud and going more deeply into topics. 'Learning brands' like the BBC, City and Guilds, Coursera, Harvard, LSE, Open University, TED Talks or the WEA will evolve through partnerships and the internet to create more diverse opportunities for learning.

'Whole life' or 'lifewide' learning are more accurate descriptions of this emerging world, where technological and social change enable people to learn without knowing they are doing it (Jackson, 2011, 2016). Organizations and societies that enable people to become immersed in 'practical wisdom' and emerging worlds of learning have the best chance of overcoming problems and creating better futures for people.

Practical politics is already a premium subject in whole life learning, but not under that name and not available to most people. It is called influencing, leadership, lobbying, public affairs, advocacy and campaigning. It is mainly provided by management consultants and political strategists to corporate and political leaders, as described in chapter 5. But, like the 'civic pacts' of Medellín, community organizing, service learning or co-operative schools, it can also engage citizens at the grassroots.

The following six sections briefly describe how practical political education can increase the impact of non-profits, local government, political parties, civic leaders, the media and adult education.

Charities, non-profits and civil society

Non-profits are among the most effective and versatile vehicles for practical politics. However, many charities are like ambulances at the bottom of a cliff. They rescue people or animals, but let the harm continue. Some support long-term recovery and a few campaign to stop people falling over the cliff in the first place. The suffering addressed by charities is often a symptom of problems that are best solved by political action.

Many charities are wary of campaigning. Most spend very little time, money or training on it. A study of non-profits in the United States showed that over 70 per cent engaged in advocacy, but most (85 per cent) devoted less than two per cent of their budget to it and involved only a 'narrow band of organizational players', chiefly the executive director, so that clients or patrons were rarely or never involved (Salamon and Lessans Geller with Lorentz, 2008). This suggests that many non-profits are missing opportunities to make a difference.

Charities can be powerful voices for their cause, as the following examples show. But charity engagement in politics needs to be more strategic and sophisticated than party politics, or they risk losing their prime political asset: trust.

THREE SUCCESSFUL CHARITY CAMPAIGNS

Landmines: many charities have helped victims of the 110 million landmines in more than 75 countries since 1960, which killed 15,000 to 20,000 people a year (Walsh, 2003). But in 1992 the International Campaign to Ban Landmines (ICBL) was launched and just five years later the Mine Ban Treaty was signed by 122 states. By 2015 over 80 per cent of states had signed the treaty and destroyed stockpiles of more than 48 million mines. Hundreds of square kilometres of contaminated land have been cleared. The number of new casualties dropped to fewer than 5,000 in 2014, which means 12 people a day were still killed or maimed by remnants of war.

Debt: Christian Aid calculated that the Jubilee 2000 coalition to cut the debt burden on the world's poorest countries was worth more than a thousand years of regular fundraising. More than 24 million people from 166 countries signed the petition. As a result of the campaign lenders pledged to cancel $110 billion of debt and more than $88 billion of debt has been written off, more than $3,600 per signature.

Smoking: Cancer Campaigns calculates that its campaign to make UK workplaces smoke-free will save more lives than a new cancer treatment, at a fraction of the cost.

(Sources: Lofgren *et al.* (2008) and campaign websites)

Politicians often regard campaigning by charities with suspicion. As the Brazilian cardinal Dom Helder Camara said, 'When I give food to the poor, they call me a saint. When I ask why the poor have no food, they call me a communist' (Rocha, 2000: 53; Regan, 2002).

In the United Kingdom campaigning by charities is governed by sensible guidelines from the Charity Commission, but spending during elections is controlled by the bureaucratic Lobbying Act, 2014. Restrictions on the use of public funds for campaigning were introduced in 2016. There are justifiable concerns that charity campaigning could be used to bypass limits on election spending by political parties, but these restrictions are a blunt instrument that inhibits the benefits of charity campaigning.

In the United States charity campaigning is permitted by tax regulations, but lobbying to influence legislation is restricted (Smucker, 1999). (See www.independentsector.org/advocacy)

Advocacy makes charities great

Charities pioneered public services in education, health and social welfare, laying foundations for modern welfare societies. In many policy areas non-profits are still major players, providing services as well as lobbying. Their ability to combine service delivery with campaigning gives them greater authority than many politicians.

US research into 'What makes great non-profits great?' identified advocacy as the first of six key practices of high-impact non-profits (Crutchfield and McLeod Grant, 2008):

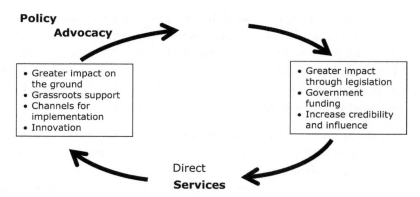

Figure 10.1: Experience, advocacy and impact in non-profits, based on *Forces for Good* (Crutchfield and McLeod Grant, 2008)

Andrews and Edwards (2004) describe advocacy in terms of five areas of policymaking:

1. agenda setting (establishing the issues considered for policy development or change)

2. gaining access to decision-making arenas

3. achieving favourable policies (the most commonly recognized advocacy goal)

4. monitoring and shaping implementation of policies; and

5. shifting long-term priorities of political institutions to support the long-term goals of advocacy organizations.

Kimberlin (2010: 176) quotes Donaldson's eight practices for progressive advocacy by non-profits (Donaldson, 2008):

1. Reflect on the social and policy context of services when developing advocacy.

2. Use the knowledge of constituents [beneficiaries] who are experts in the real-world problems and consequences of public policies that need to be created or changed.

3. Use frontline staff who are knowledgeable about the issues and can articulate the experience of constituents collectively and over time.

4. Work in coalitions to gain political cover for positions that are unpopular with agency funders and supporters.

5. Focus on your area of expertise for the greatest impact.

6. Dedicate full-time staff to ensure that advocacy activities have high priority and are not set aside by competing responsibilities.

7. Diversify funding in case controversial advocacy activities result in reduced funding from any single source.

8. Ensure full support from both staff and board leadership to commit financial and personnel resources needed.

This is sound advice for practical politics in many areas, not just for non-profits.

The advantages of non-profits as campaigning organizations are that they have a focused remit; they are not driven by short-term political timetables, and can take a longer view, if they have support from donors; they do not have to appeal to a majority of the population; and they do not have to try to reconcile their priority focus with competing interests, as in political parties.

People support non-profits to make the world a better place. Non-profits have more public support and trust than political parties, they involve more people as volunteers and raise more money. America's one million-plus non-profits received $300 billion in 2013 (Forbes, 2014), while the UK's 160,000 general charities had a combined income of about £37 billion in 2012 (Civil Society Almanac). For some, advocacy is 'the quintessential function of the voluntary sector' and 'a unique organizational competence' (Kramer, 1981, quoted in Salamon, 2002, p.1). They are also vital intermediary institutions that represent minorities and disempowered groups and help governments to respond by influencing public policies (Kimberlin, 2010; Boris and Krehely, 2002).

Weaknesses in charity campaigning

However, the practice is often less than the promise (Halpin, 2010). Charity campaigning can be motivated by fundraising rather than lasting change, more concerned with profile and income than impact. Charity income depends on making a splash and telling donors a good story, so that long campaigns about difficult problems get less support than high-profile causes with emotional appeal.

The public accountability of charities is often loose, with little independent scrutiny compared with the public or private sectors. Organizations that provide scrutiny, such as Charity Watch, Charity Navigator, Guidestar or Give.org run by BBB Wise Giving Alliance, could play a valuable role in assessing the impact of campaigns, but their evidence base is not yet reliable. The Centre for Effective Altruism at Oxford University, Animal Charity Evaluators, GiveWell, and the Life You Can Save are doing a great deal to focus on charity effectiveness.

The triple challenge for charities is to 1) develop capacity for advocacy and political skills among service users and supporters as well as staff; to 2) become 'problem realistic' and tackle root causes, which may take decades; and to 3) improve their public accountability (and often governance as well).

Who should promote practical political education in the charity sector?

The charity/non-profit sector is small compared with corporations and states, so they need to be smarter and more strategic. Six groups can play a significant role in developing practical politics by non-profits:

1. **Funders,** including trusts, governments and individuals, need to understand the benefits of advocacy and campaigning by charities and the kind of assessment, evaluation and capacity building needed (see *Critical Masses* by Lofgren *et al.* (2008), and *Closing in on change* (Hestbaek, 2014a)).

2. **Trustees** and board members need to ensure that campaigns are part of their overall strategy, are well thought-through, manage risk, have built-in evaluation and maintain public trust (Hestbaek, 2014b).

3. **Umbrella bodies** such as the Association of Chief Executives of Voluntary Organisations (ACEVO), Bond (the international development network), National Council for Voluntary Organisations (NCVO) and National Association for Voluntary and Community Action (NAVCA) in the United Kingdom, Alliance for Justice and Innocence Network in the United States, and the co-operative movement and others worldwide can share good practice, build capacity and develop long-term strategic campaigns.

4. **Capacity builders** such as Drasa in India (www.dasra.org/). New Philanthropy Capital in the United Kingdom and Give Well in the US (www.givewell.org/DIY/policy-and-advocacy).

5. **Non-profits** can provide education and support for their donors and beneficiaries to understand how politics works and to take part, and large organizations like Friends of the Earth, Greenpeace, I-India, Oxfam, Red Cross, United Way, UNICEF and WaterAid share their expertise with small groups and civil society.

6. **Politicians and civil servants** create the regulatory framework for the sector and need to distinguish between party political campaigning and the necessary advocacy role of charities for their beneficiaries and wider public purpose.

Local government and public services

What matters to most people is local – homes, roads, services and job opportunities, made possible by local politics. People often experience local authorities as remote, unresponsive and exclusive, creating the first and final barrier to active citizenship. But local government can be the first rung on the political ladder, a training ground and base for civic ambition. Local authorities and public services can overcome the democratic deficits described by Pippa Norris (Norris, 2011) by creating opportunities for people to take part and learn. As Bernard Crick wrote, 'Participation provides people with the skills and relationships so that they are better able to govern themselves.'

Studies from the United States have shown that participation reduces cynicism (Wang and Van Wart, 2007), increases trust in citizens by officials (Yang, 2005; Yang and Callahan, 2007) and improves citizens' skills and knowledge (Kathi and Cooper, 2005). It also improves local efficiency and effectiveness (Neshkova and Guo, 2012), as well as decisions and government responsiveness (Wang, 2002).

However, without outreach and support for marginalized citizens, better access to local decision-making only helps those who know their way around the system. Research by Demos confirms my own experience that 'those already well connected tend to get better connected' (Skidmore *et al.*, 2006: ix). Demos identified six 'network dynamics' that create barriers for those not involved and increase participation by those already involved. To address these they proposed a 'One per cent solution' – target the one per cent of the community who get things done, and design 'the formal structures of governance in a way that taps into the informal spaces of community life that they routinely inhabit ... [such as] the school gate, their place of worship, or their local newsagent or post office' to create 'an everyday bridge between ordinary people and more formal governance activities'. A 'local Community Governance Service', run by local community organizations, could recruit, train and support participants to 'diversify the pool of people involved in governance' (xv). As Education Secretary, David Blunkett set up a highly successful small grants programme for Community Champions that achieved some of these aims.

The Power Inquiry recommended setting up local Democracy Hubs 'where people can access information and advice to navigate their way through the democratic system' (Kennedy, 2006: 24, 151). Public services could also nominate 'democracy champions' to increase access to influence by local people. In 2010 the Labour government introduced a 'duty to promote democracy', promptly repealed by the incoming Conservative-Liberal Democrat coalition.

Political education by parties

Politicians are widely mistrusted, yet they are the main source of political education for the public. Parties try to set the political agenda, discredit their opponents, put their own spin on events and deflect attention from difficult issues. This is the opposite of education, concealing more than revealing. Yet, as Professor Goldman put it in 1959, 'political education is inevitable when competing propagandas go about unmasking each other' (Goldman, 2002: 261). Although pressure groups influence public debate more than in 1959 and the status of parties has fallen, parties still have a major role in public political education. This takes place in three areas, which are not always well-connected:

First is **internal policy debate**, conducted by the leadership, policy groups, research departments, think tanks, commentators and party activists. This battle of ideas informs the party's direction, priorities and programme. In the United Kingdom it is most visible at fringe meetings and bars of party conferences, then on social media and meetings throughout the year. It is mainly among party supporters, driven by personal ambition and commitment, often assisted by interest groups. This education is rarely formal, but involves high-level research, talks, seminars and debates aimed at influencing the party's programme. Traditionally this was done among the party elite, but social media is forcing parties to open policy development.

Second is **training to win elections**. At the top this involves campaign strategists who help the leadership hone and target their messages. Training for party members is usually instrumental, transmitting the party line from headquarters to activists on the ground. It involves relatively little discussion of policy and focuses on campaign strategy, message development and delivery, use of voter data, fundraising and getting out the vote. The US Republican Party has a national Campaign Management College to train party workers in 'the skills to succeed' (see www.gop.com/get-involved/political-education/).

Third is **public propaganda** – the soundbites, speeches, debates and photo-opportunities to create a convincing narrative about the party's view of the world. These have become highly orchestrated marketing campaigns targeted at swing voters and core supporters. Parties, to a large extent, have become marketing machines, selecting policies and messages most likely to win power (Lees-Marchment, 2001).

This may not be edifying, nor education as we know it, but party political combat and the media's running commentary is the only political education that most people get. Many people just switch off. But elections also force politicians to listen and engage with the public, to address people's hopes and fears and craft policies in response. Contests between parties test candidates' character, stamina and communication skills as well as their policies. These personal abilities matter as much as policies, since without political ability policies cannot be implemented. On election day the public will mark their performance with a cross. Pass or fail, in or out. It is a brutal exam.

Parties are important intermediaries between citizens and the state. They are the main means through which democracies reconcile conflicting priorities and develop programmes for government. Although interest groups have become much more important in influencing the state, and party manifestos are often carefully crafted shopping lists to appeal to different interests rather than a coherent programme, they are still needed.

In a fascinating study of civil society and politics in Germany before 1933, Sheri Berman argues that the combination of a flourishing civil society and weak political institutions enabled Hitler's National Socialist German Workers' Party (NSDAP or Nazis) to seize power and create a dictatorship (Berman, 1997).

Douglas Carswell, sole UKIP Member of Parliament in Britain, argued that traditional politics is dead and political parties have ceded power to unaccountable bureaucracies. 'It doesn't matter who you vote for, the same remote officials remain in charge' he wrote. 'Our system of democratic politics has been hollowed out from within. It has become a husk' (Carswell, 2012: 82–83). He argued that political parties have become centrally controlled mass brands that are losing market share to smaller parties (183–6). He advocated iPolitics and iState in which citizen-consumers tell their representatives and officials what they want, not once every few years in elections, but all the time, online. Carswell may be right. Challenger parties across Europe are taking votes, and sometimes control, from established parties. The state is also changing, becoming 'digital by default' and engaging people through social media.

But citizens will always need some form of collective organization to stand up for their values, develop policies, prepare a programme for government and do the politics needed to carry it out. Having more parties increases the need for political ability to navigate the rapids of public life. Small parties are more vulnerable to being blown apart by gaffes or wayward members. The permanent government of civil servants could increase their power among shifting sands of smaller parties. Without a collective voice individual citizens could have even less power to stand up to the big players of state and corporations.

Western governments fund political education in countries emerging from dictatorship to develop effective parties and political systems. Some of this is generic information, research and support for democratic systems, such as International IDEA, the International Institute for Democracy and Electoral Assistance, and the ACE Electoral Knowledge Network, an information portal and service to support and develop elections worldwide, both of which are intergovernmental organizations. Non-partisan support for political parties and systems is available from organizations like the Westminster Foundation for Democracy (UK), the National Endowment for Democracy and National Democratic Institute for International Affairs (US) and George Soros's Open Society Foundations. More partisan education and support is available from the International Republican Institute, which supports centre-right political parties, or the German *Stiftungen*. This kind of support is needed more widely in all democracies.

Civic leaders as representatives of democracy

Every elected politician also represents the practice politics. How they act, speak and treat each other matters as much as what they say. When politicians denigrate each other, they also diminish the political process. Politics is by its nature adversarial. People compete for power, position and policies to advance the interests of particular groups or their vision of society. Mockery, humour and sharp words are all part of democratic politics. Citizens have a responsibility to expose weakness, flawed policies, malpractice and incompetence in public life. A thick skin is necessary to survive public politics. Citizens also need to be sceptical, to question and challenge politicians, public officials and authorities. But the public also needs to understand what is going on and be able to take part as equal citizens.

Democratic politicians therefore have a responsibility to respect both their adversaries and the political system, particularly when they are passionately opposed to everything their opponent stands for or they want to change the system itself. This is not easy. Most political systems have developed rules of etiquette, so that members of the British House of

Commons call each other 'Honourable Member' and US Representatives refer to each other as 'friends' regardless of party, identifying them by constituency, not their name.

Given the lack of trust in politics, politicians need to do more to show people how the system works and make it more accessible, inclusive and effective in giving people power over their lives. Elected representatives at all levels should make it part of their job to talk about the role of politics at schools, community associations and in the media.

Many elected assemblies are developing education to increase understanding and participation in politics. For example, the Australian Parliamentary Education Office (PEO):

- teaches how parliament works through experiential learning
- produces resources and publications for classroom use or independent study
- assists members to inform constituents about the work of the federal Parliament.

In South Africa Parliamentary Democracy Offices (PDO) are based in the provinces to:

- conduct public education and provide information about Parliament and its work
- provide a platform for people to access and participate in the processes of Parliament
- facilitate public input and feedback
- provide ground and logistical support for parliamentary programmes and activities
- co-ordinate and co-operate with other spheres of government.

But parliamentarians themselves need to do more to make politics accessible and comprehensible to the public.

How politicians can promote practical political education

During elections the educational role of politicians is partisan, and barely qualifies as education, so that academic and media commentators have a vital role. But after an election campaign, winning candidates can promote the practice of politics by talking about:

- why and how they themselves got involved, to encourage others to take part
- how the political system works, the role of parties, legislatures, scrutiny committees and the executive branches of government

- the value of democratic politics as a public good
- their respect for people who campaign about things they care about, even when they themselves disagree with them
- how citizens can have an effective voice and can be heard by politicians.

Elected politicians can host public debates about political issues, inviting speakers with conflicting views to explore topical issues and deepen public understanding and participation. Politicians need to create bridges between people and government at every level, reducing barriers and opening doors to the formal political process. Educational institutions and community organizations can also create opportunities for students and the public to engage with politicians, question them on the political process and challenge their policies.

Political education through the media

All media have a role in political education, but it is partisan, so public service media like the BBC have a special responsibility. The complex and contested role of the media in politics is discussed in chapter 5. The BBC website, Radio 4 podcasts and some newspapers are a vast source of information and analysis of political affairs. What is missing are straightforward guides to help people navigate issues and find the best way to have their say.

For democracy to flourish, citizens need more than commentaries and analysis of the issues. They also need to know how they can influence decisions. To do this, politics needs to be presented as something anyone can do all year round, not just in elections every few years. Promoting public participation does not mean taking sides on the issues, but siding with the public. Citizens are ultimately responsible for how the country is governed and need to be better informed.

A free press and independent media are critical for democracy, providing a plurality of opinion and scrutinizing those in power. Information on how to campaign about issues makes politics more accessible and effective.

Adult political education

Adult and community education have long pioneered political education. In Scandinavia Folk High Schools are closely linked with the development of social democracy and national identity (infed.org, 2014; Borish, 1991). The first Folk High School was created in Denmark by Nikolaj Grundtvig in 1844 as a residential 'school for life' 'where the peasant and the citizen can obtain knowledge and guidance [as a] citizen' (quoted in Moller and

Watson, 1944: 27). Folk High Schools inspired a worldwide network of self-governing residential institutions, including Poconos People's College, Pennsylvania, Waddington People's College in West Virginia and Highlander in the US. Highlander provided education for successive social movements, for labour rights, civil rights, women's liberation and the environment. In Britain the folk high school model informed university settlements and residential colleges in the late nineteenth century (Drews and Fieldhouse, 1996), including Cambridge House, Fircroft, Northern College, Toynbee Hall, Selly Oak, Woodbrooke and other centres for education and social action. Universities settlements started in 1883, giving young people from privileged backgrounds opportunities to serve poor communities, and many still continue. Settlements supported victims of the Spanish Civil War and fascism after 1936, action on homelessness and unemployment in the 1970s and 1980s, and community organizing this century (Brewis, 2014).

The Swedish study circle movement was started in 1912 by the Workers' Educational Association to create an educated citizenry. These self-organized, democratic groups took off among 'workers, farmers and the lower middle class, who had only attended elementary school' (Larsson and Nordvall, 2010: 10). Since the 1970s about 1.5 million people (out of a population of about nine million) took part in some 300,000 study circles every year, learning a range of subjects from art, crafts and music to political issues. Study circles are subsidized by local and national government, covering about half of the costs. Although most subjects studied are not political, the democratic format of study circles promotes a participative culture and encourages people to explore topical issues. Study circles have spread to Australia, Bangladesh, Chile, Estonia, Portugal, Slovenia, Tanzania and many other countries. In the United States, the Study Circles Resource Center was formed in 1989, now called Everyday Democracy, providing resources for communities to address economic and social issues.

LEARN MORE: CIVIC ENGAGEMENT AND PARTICIPATION

Look up the educational opportunities provided by your elected assembly and take part in any that are relevant to your work.

Read *Critical Masses: Social campaigning – a guide for donors and funders*, by Lofgren *et al.* (2008).

For methods of citizen engagement, see:

- Participation Compass http://participationcompass.org/
- Involve (2005) *People and Participation: How to put citizens at the heart of decision-making.* London: Involve. Online. www.involve. org.uk/wp-content/uploads/2011/03/People-and-Participation.pdf
- Everyday Democracy: http://everyday-democracy.org/ recommended-reading-list

Start a study group on a topical issue or practical politics of a subject you are studying.

Chapter 11

Making the case for teaching practical politics

In this chapter you will learn:

- About the politics of establishing new subjects
- Ten steps to curriculum change
- How to create a tipping point for teaching practical politics
- How to deal with opposition

Planning for a new century

A Chinese proverb says, 'If you are planning for a year, sow rice; if you are planning for a decade, plant trees; if you are planning for a century, educate people.'

The vision of this book is that every citizen should be able to learn how to influence what happens. This means learning how the system works, acquiring influencing skills and gaining confidence to act. People can learn this in many different ways, as shown by the previous chapter, but enabling people to learn practical politics throughout the education system is essential for democracy.

Getting any subject on to the curriculum is difficult. A subject as challenging as practical politics may seem impossible. But as Aristotle's 'master subject', practical politics has three big advantages:

1. It can enrich almost any subject or course programme.

2. It is useful throughout life, offering benefits for individuals and society.

3. All democratic societies have a policy commitment to education for democratic citizenship.

Students and teachers should be able develop political skills and democratic practices wherever and whatever they study. But making the case and getting resources to develop effective provision is a challenge. Perhaps the most important lesson from all case studies in this book is to create a tangible project in response to specific needs or opportunities, with clear aims and principles, and then learn and grow with practice.

So how *do* new subjects take off?

It is instructive to see how new subjects have spread or stalled. Over the past 30 years I have worked with many campaigns for curriculum change, including education for citizenship, the environment, family learning and parenting, philosophy for children, self-esteem, study skills and world studies. I have worked with colleagues who helped to establish education for adult literacy, computing, multi-culturalism, racial equality, sex education, vocational skills and women's studies. I have written lesson plans and taught new topics to both children and adults. As a principal lecturer and education officer I also developed curriculum policy and took it through the political process. In the early 1990s I was a local authority education adviser, helping schools adopt the new National Curriculum. I have worked with teachers in schools, adult education and universities to promote new subjects, as well as curriculum authorities, senior civil servants, ministers and professional associations to get high-level support. This has given me first-hand experience of almost every stage of innovation in education, including failures as well as success. Some innovations spread successfully by stealth while high-profile government-backed initiatives were sidelined, diluted or disappeared.

For example, in 1983 the Conservative government launched the Technical and Vocational Education Initiative (TVEI) in England to 'widen and enrich the curriculum' for 14–18 year olds. It was one of Britain's biggest curriculum development programmes, costing more than £900 million (£2 billion at 2016 prices). It was supported by hundreds of curriculum leaders in schools. However, power struggles within government, local authorities and schools sidelined TVEI. It was eclipsed by the more academic National Curriculum after 1990, finally finishing in 1997. Despite support from employers, a strong economic case and substantial funding, TVEI failed. The reasons are many. Gleeson and McLean (1994) concluded that any policy that does not engage with the culture of the school and teaching profession is unlikely to achieve meaningful reform. Although many individual teachers and local education authorities were enthusiastic, the dominance of academic values and 'traditionally low esteem accorded to vocational education' meant it didn't survive when official support ceased (Edwards and Whitty, 1997: 190; see also Pring, 1995). Supporters of vocational education were not well organized, unlike academic subjects with their royal societies, university departments, journals and professional associations to support them, such as biology and geography (Goodson, 2013 [1982]).

One vocational subject that succeeded where others failed was information communications technology (ICT). Computers are so widespread in education we take them for granted, as tools for learning and subjects of study. But computer education is not well established in every country and many other useful subjects struggle for a place in the curriculum. Financial literacy, for example, is actively promoted by consumer groups, citizens' organizations, broadcasters and the financial industry, but is marginal in education, despite obvious benefits. So why was ICT so successful?

ICT benefited from a combination of enthusiastic practitioners in education and the media, financial support from the industry, influential reports and leadership from government, plus a constant stream of new applications that made computing essential for the economy and society. The scale and spread of computer science was achieved by political manoeuvres at every level of education, supported by networks of individuals and organizations who shared experiences and lobbied for funding. However, forty years since the first computer education campaigns, the industry is worried that programming has lost its place in schools, prompting renewed campaigns for computer programming across the curriculum.

Curriculum power struggles

What is taught is the outcome of office politics within institutions, government and sometimes society. Totalitarian rulers can dictate the curriculum, but pluralist societies have more freedom to innovate, although tradition, systems, funding, testing and inspection are powerful constraints.

Political battles over the timetable, recognition and resources take place at every level – in curriculum meetings and governing bodies; through professional associations and subject groups; and decisions by curriculum bodies, exam boards, inspectors and ministers. As society changes disagreement and power struggles over the curriculum are inevitable and necessary. Practical political education will spread if people use political skill to make it happen.

Creating a tipping point

Many excellent innovations in education do not spread widely, while bad practice can persist or be promoted by politicians and pundits persuaded by partial evidence or deeply held convictions. The following table summarizes some common features of successful curriculum movements. The actual sequence depends on opportunities and people's ability to use them.

TEN STEPS TO CURRICULUM CHANGE

1. Teachers, learners and autodidacts pioneer the subject to create communities of practice, often on a voluntary basis using their own resources in the face of scepticism or hostility. They create models of provision and inspire other pioneers.

2. Champions and patrons emerge, who use their influence as managers, funders, academics, commentators, officials or politicians to increase provision and make the case for it within their sphere of influence, sometimes becoming visible public figureheads for the subject.

3. Practitioners, patrons and supporters create various networks or alliances to share and develop practice, gather evidence of its benefits and make the case for it.

4. Major sponsors fund pioneers, networks, curriculum development, research and reports to promote it in a more systematic way.

5. An agency takes the lead to bring different networks together and build a broader base of support to influence policy and fund it, creating a public focus for the campaign through the following three steps:

6. Bring together practitioners, opinion-formers and key individuals representing stakeholders to produce a high-profile report that marshals evidence to show how the subject meets a need and has wider benefits, often expressed through stories, memorable facts and a vivid image or phrase;

7. Seize an opportunity to put the subject onto the political agenda, using the report, a crisis, an anniversary, international year, special event, curriculum review, parliamentary bill or combination of these;

8. Neutralize opposition by addressing their fears and interests where possible, and dividing or marginalizing the rest;

9. Get sufficient political support to mainstream the subject, so that it gets funding, support and recognition as part of education policy at an institutional level;

10. An implementation phase, during which the subject may be mangled, diluted, distorted or high-jacked. Effective practitioners and institutional leaders overcome these dangers to inspire new generations of teachers and students who make it flourish.

Once established the subject needs continuing support to keep momentum or it can fade or be pushed out, so the lead agency, networks and practitioners still have a role.

The first three stages develop experience, institutional support and a base of provision. Pioneer practitioners and brave patrons create new models, such as innocence initiatives, community organizing, service learning or campaign training. Students can organize their own study-action groups or bootcamps. A head of department, principal or official can create space for a new subject to develop and build support. A high-profile report helps supporters find each other and talk with people in power, but it still needs persistent persuasion for curriculum leaders to support it.

Many educational movements, like adult literacy, circle time, co-operative schools or world studies, were spread by practitioners long before they got official support. Even then, government backing for new subjects may not be enough to sustain them, like TVEI. Political and professional effort is necessary to keep subjects fresh and attractive to learners.

Riding the innovation cycle

Everett Rogers (1962) has shown how the spread of successful innovations follows a similar pattern (see Figure 10.1). **Innovators** create a new idea or product, which is taken up by **pioneers** who develop it. Different personality traits can also encourage or inhibit innovation from spreading: innovators are often fierce defenders of their ideas, while pioneers want to make them accessible to as many people as possible, so that innovators and pioneers often fall out, but they can create a winning team by working together. **Early adopters** are people who take up new ideas, but they can prevent an 'early majority' from forming because they want to be different and don't spread the word. Most new ideas never take off: having a brilliant innovation is not enough. It takes an entrepreneur or change agency to promote it.

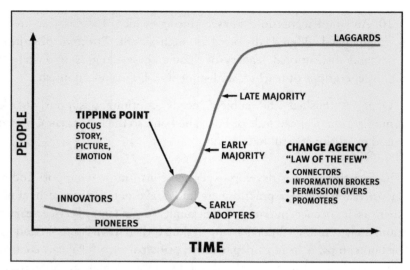

Sharon Dodd
Figure 10.1: The tipping point

In *The Tipping Point*, Malcolm Gladwell (2000) identifies three factors that spread ideas rapidly:

1. **Law of the few**: a small number of key people make a big difference, particularly people with many contacts in *different* networks who create connections between diverse groups and pass on information, and advocates who believe that change is possible and are able to answer objections.

2. **Stickiness** is what gives a message impact, through stories that get people's attention and create understanding.

3. **Context**: recognizing that people are influenced by their situation, fears and hopes, and other people who encourage or discourage the new idea (opinion formers).

These three points can inform any campaign to spread social innovation, including education for practical politics. Gladwell also shows the importance of testing your message and honing it until your target audience hears and responds positively. For more on stickiness, see *Made to Stick* by Chip and Dan Heath (2007).

Your strategy for practical political education
The Tipping Point, Made to Stick and these Ten Steps for Curriculum Change suggest things you can do to help make education for practical politics and

democracy a mainstream subject. Three major lessons from case studies in this book are to:

1. Create a project that meets a clear need, take small steps and build through success, and then let any glory reflect on the wider institution and beyond, not just your project, so that others are invested in your success.

2. Get external funding and allies, or create an independent project so that no one is threatened, and if possible share external funding within your institution to give other people an interest in its success.

3. Get at least one patron with the power to protect your project, and preferably more.

To create high-level cover it is best to present your project in terms of your organization's mission, strategic plans, current policy and official rhetoric. Quote senior politicians, heroes and thinkers from across the political spectrum. If possible, get cross-party support from current political leaders and opinion formers in person. In authoritarian organizations and societies political cover is even more important, since any perceived challenge may lead to dismissal, imprisonment or worse. If the language of democracy and politics is taboo, talk about enterprise, leadership, project management or other acceptable terms to create the space needed to build capacity. It is better to proceed cautiously within established political rhetoric while pushing the boundaries in practice, than to blow rhetorical bubbles and stand still or go backwards. What matters is that people learn how their political system works, who has power and how to influence others, so that they can think and act for themselves on the basis of evidence and insight.

You also need to identify people who could block your project and get their support, or at least their understanding. If possible make a personal connection with likely opponents. They can be surprisingly supportive, if you seek them out, treat them with respect and explain what you are doing in terms they understand. But don't assume that natural allies will be supportive. They may see you as a competitor, or think they should run your project or want it run their way, or fear it may interfere with their plans. In practical politics you can never make assumptions about who are your allies or opponents. Always check them out, if possible in person, and get their support on the record.

Dealing with opposition

Education in practical politics is likely to meet resistance. As in football, it is important to know your opposition, have a strong defence, prepare for challenges, train and persist. Table 11.1 summarizes common obstacles and how to counter them:

Table 11.1: Dealing with obstacles to practical politics

Obstacle	Counter-argument
Higher education is about ideas and analysis, not practice.	Engineering, law, medicine, teaching and business studies are well-established practical subjects where skill matters as much as knowledge.
Education should be politically neutral and above politics.	Agree that education should not promote one political position, but it should enable people to critically evaluate different political positions and articulate their own. This is particularly important in subjects with ideological associations such as economics, business studies and politics. Being 'above politics' does not mean being morally neutral, but to enable people to engage with moral questions effectively. It also means respecting that people have different political positions, and have a right as citizens to learn how to advocate them.
The opposite of the above are advocates of partisan positions who argue that education should take a stand and teach a particular political philosophy or strategy, whether liberalism, Marxism, populism, lobbying, direct action or any other.	Democratic education aims to equip people to think for themselves and use their judgement to act politically. Democracy means trusting people to find the best solution, and arguing the case if you think they are wrong. Partisan education is vulnerable to attack by political opponents, who will also be justified in imposing their view if they control the curriculum. Democratic education should give people more options for political action.

Elites in the press, politics or government who use whatever power or arguments they can to stop education for democracy and public participation.	Free democratic societies need people to be able to speak out about wrong-doing and hold the powerful to account. Social progress is made through political action, even when it is sometimes uncomfortable for those in power. We recognize the benefits of training for competition in sport and business, so why not for politics?
Fear that people doing it may bring the organization into disrepute, come to harm or make mistakes.	Do a risk assessment and minimize harm, set up ethical oversight (see previous chapter) and be prepared for malicious attacks.
Competition from other organizations in civil society.	Where possible create alliances and work together, sharing out the work to increase opportunities for political education.
Indifference and lack of demand, particularly from least power in society.	Generate demand by reaching out in imaginative and accessible ways.

The first and last of these are often the biggest obstacles. People with little power are likely to be suspicious of initiatives from outside. It takes time and commitment to build relationships and develop provision that is appropriate and effective, but many traditions of community organizing show that it is possible. The most important step is to show long-term commitment, developing provision *with* people and organizations in the community.

Education for practical politics cannot avoid contemporary problems or power struggles. Powerful interests may try to stop people teaching advocacy, campaigning, citizenship or political skills at any level. For this reason it is important to acknowledge concerns and address them, while highlighting its benefits. The main arguments against EPP are that it could be partisan and at worst indoctrinate. Its value is more limited if it sides with a particular party, interest or social group. It has to side with citizens and their right to learn, think and act as equals. It is important that political education is pluralistic, questioning and challenging. Promoting one particular doctrine or theory of change will not equip people to deal with the complexity of contemporary politics, in which there are many different political systems and positions. Banning speakers or viewpoints from university campuses denies students the opportunity to develop their ability to argue against people they disagree with. It is bad pedagogy as well as bad politics to teach only one approach, theory or doctrine. If people want to learn particular models of politics in depth, such as community organizing, election campaigning for a particular party or policy advocacy for a cause, they should be able to do so in democratic societies. But public education institutions should be non-partisan, pluralistic and inclusive.

Fear is probably the biggest barrier preventing many individuals and institutions from permitting practical political education. But once you talk it through, address any risks and put an ethical, pluralistic framework in place, the only thing to fear is failure or success, as in any human venture.

LEARN MORE: INFLUENCING SKILLS

Read:

Made to Stick. Chip and Dan Heath (2007)

The Tipping Point. Malcolm Gladwell (2000)

Influence: The psychology of persuasion. Robert Cialdini (2007)

Influencer: The power to change anything. Kerry Patterson *et al.* (2007)

Practice:

Find and take part in a course or workshop on practical politics in your community or online.

Identify groups in your community who could benefit from learning practical politics and work with one of them to develop a workshop or programme that will increase their ability to influence decisions.

Chapter 12

How to create a curriculum for democracy

In this chapter you will learn:

- How to use teachable moments to promote practical politics
- Three key questions for a learning needs analysis
- How to create progression routes
- Twelve core elements for an advanced curriculum in practical politics

The case studies include:

- How the Khan Academy creates change by providing a service.

Case study: How the Khan Academy creates change by providing a service

Salman Khan was a 28-year-old hedge fund analyst in California who started helping his cousin Nadia with her seventh-grade maths homework over the phone, using Yahoo Doodle to illustrate lessons. When other relatives asked for help in 2006, he posted short tutorials on YouTube, calling his channel Khan Academy. His ten-minute lessons got grateful feedback and a worldwide following, so in 2009 he quit his job to do it full-time, saying it was 'the highest social return that one could ever get' (Outlook India, 2010). By 2012 he was running the largest school in the world, with more than ten million students, more than 3,400 lessons and just 37 staff. *Time* magazine named Khan one of the world's 100 most influential people. By April 2015, the Academy offered lessons on more than 6,500 topics, which had been viewed more than 527 million times. It was available in 23 languages, with some videos in 65 languages.

Khan is not is a trained teacher, but uses key pedagogical principles – short visual presentations, everyday language, exercises and fast feedback, with rewards in the form of badges. Topic maps show learners how knowledge fits into a bigger picture and helps them choose what to learn. They progress at their own pace and can become volunteer coaches to help others. Teachers use Khan's lessons to 'flip the classroom' – that is, get pupils to learn at home, at their own pace, to free more time for classroom discussion, problem-solving and peer-support.

Khan wrote:

> *The Academy owned a PC, $20 worth of screen capture software, and an $80 pen tablet; graphs and equations were drawn – often shakily – with the help of a free program called Microsoft Paint. Beyond the videos, I had hacked together some quizzing software running on my $50-per-month web host. The faculty, engineering team, support staff, and administration consisted of exactly one person: me. The budget consisted of my savings … I wanted to restore the excitement – the active participation in learning and the natural high that went with it – that conventional curricula sometimes seemed to bludgeon into submission.*
>
> (2012: 5–6)

Khan started on his own, encouraged by learners, and then attracted support from some of the world's richest men, including Bill Gates, Carlos Slim and Google. He told *Forbes* magazine, 'I could have started a for-profit, venture-backed business' (Noer, 2012). Instead he created a free resource that could be used by children in his parents' countries of origin, Bangladesh and India, as well as America.

'The next bubble to burst is higher education,' according to Jason Fried, one of Khan's funders. 'There's no reason why parents should have to save up a hundred grand to send their kids to college. I like that there are alternative ways of thinking about teaching' (Young, 2010). Khan plans to offer free English language lessons, challenging a US$50 billion global market with more than 1.5 billion learners (BIS, 2013).

Cheap computers, smartphones and internet access could spread education across Africa and Asia faster than any government. In Rwanda the Kepler project aims to bring degree courses for $1,000 a year. Alison. com has more than six million students in 200 countries studying more than 750 vocational courses free of charge.

In the 1940s Oliver Tambo, Nelson Mandela and other young leaders of the South African liberation movement studied law at London University by correspondence. Online learning can help the 'bottom billions' to study, solve problems, challenge political elites and compete or co-operate with people anywhere in the world. A global revolution in education has begun.

Reflections

The Khan Academy does not seem political, but is as political as any pressure group. Its mission is 'to unlock the world's potential. Most people think their intelligence is fixed. The science says it's not.' Khan invites people to 'Join the movement' – 'you only have to learn one thing – you can learn anything.' Its motto is 'A free, world-class education for anyone, anywhere'. He aims to accelerate learning for all: 'With so little effort on my own part, I can empower an unlimited amount of people for all time' (Temple, 2009).

This challenges school systems that test, sort and teach people 'at their level' as if intelligence was fixed. The Academy lets learners control their own learning, selecting what they want to learn, at their own pace. This could be highly individualistic, but the Academy encourages collaboration through peer coaching online and co-operative classrooms, freeing teachers to facilitate learning, discussion and mutual support.

It has the potential to disrupt education systems anywhere people can access the internet. The materials are free under a creative commons licence, threatening the multi-billion textbook business. Khan does not oppose schools, but works with them. Many teachers are joining in, using his materials or creating their own, like Colin Hegarty (HegartyMaths. com), to develop new ways of 'flipping the classroom' to improve learning.

The Khan Academy is a practical project to address a specific need, based on a simple concept with global reach. Its success is based on simplicity, clarity and usefulness, as well as Khan's passionate determination. It is one of many social inventions to address specific needs, like asset-based community development, co-operatives, circles of support, community currencies, mentoring, peer mediation, micro-credit, Transition Towns and many more, which change society below the radar of national politics. My lessons from the Khan Academy are:

- Start small, meet a clearly identified need and use feedback to learn and develop.
- Have a big vision, be bold and commit.
- Communicate your vision and your passion through what you do.
- The internet has enormous potential to disrupt, empower and educate.

The internet is the most powerful means for spreading knowledge since the invention of printing and mass education, which developed over centuries. The online education revolution could do the same within decades. But the internet also connects people horizontally across continents, enabling citizens to organize and influence. As mentioned in chapter 1, the internet is an instrument for global citizenship, as the printing press was for national citizenship. In July 2016 Salman Khan launched a crowd-funding campaign to 'fund videos, articles, and exercises that help people of all ages learn about US government and politics in a fun, engaging, and non-partisan way'. Anyone can use the Academy model of bite-sized online learning to teach practical politics anywhere in the world.

Stepping stones on a learning journey for democracy

The biggest challenge is not creating a curriculum for democracy – there are many excellent ones, as well as materials for practical political education in almost any context from rural development to boardroom battles. The challenge is to get support from education providers and to increase demand from people who will benefit most. People who are disaffected by politics and feel they have no power are unlikely to be motivated to learn how to use it.

In a democracy all education institutions, local authorities, public libraries, museums, health services, prison services, the media and elected assemblies should provide some education in practical democracy as part of their social purpose. In many institutions this is difficult, but it can be done by stealth with a 'Trojan mouse' strategy. This means starting a small project within the institutions' comfort zone, building trusted relationships and using 'teachable moments' to develop provision, as described below.

Education for practical politics is done under many labels, including community arts, crime prevention, economic regeneration, job creation, family learning, literacy, patient participation and story-telling. Everything involves politics, so anything can be a springboard for people to ask questions, think critically, understand power structures and become confident citizens.

The following questions assume you want to develop a political education project within an existing institution, whether it is a college, school, non-profit, citizens' group or media platform, but similar questions apply if you are outside any institution.

In either case you can start in one of three ways:

1. **Democratize the institution:** develop democratic skills and experience through participation in the institution itself, such as co-operative schools or a community association.

2. **Identify a constituency:** people for whom learning how to influence decisions will make a difference, such community members, as for Citizens UK, parents, students or other group.

3. **Identify a need,** area of concern, problem or issue, such as road safety, FGM, miscarriages of justice, debt or access to knowledge.

Often it is easiest to use an institution as a base, accepting the fact that it is bureaucratic, hierarchical and undemocratic, to develop a project within your area of responsibility. Sometimes, however, you can achieve more by democratizing the institution itself, developing the way it recruits and welcomes new members, and making decision-making more open, inclusive and accountable, so that people learn by being part of it.

Learning needs analysis

Whether you focus on a constituency, issue or the institution, it is a practical political education project. The next step is to find out what you and others need to learn. Your project is likely to change in the process. You may start with the idea of running a citizenship class for parents and discover that what is wanted is democratic change of the school, or you want to run an investigative journalism course for environmentalists and discover they need to learn company law and advocacy. An open mind is essential for practical politics.

The following questions can help you understand what is needed in almost any context:

Why is it needed?

a) What are the problems you want to address?

b) Who are the potential learners/participants and what are their priorities?

c) How would the project fit the mission, values and purpose of the institution?

d) How could your project make a difference for participants?

e) Who else could benefit from or support the project?

f) Who could see it as a threat?

Your institution, potential participants or other partners may not see the need for the project, so you need to talk with people and develop it in conversation, so that you are really clear about how it meets people's needs and helps them solve problems. As with many innovations, people may not know they need it until they see it or do it, so start from where *they* are and build bridges to it. Do not assume support from anyone, including people you think of as natural allies. Talk it through with them and get their support, in person if possible. They may see it as competition, or be put out that they didn't come up with it or oppose it for their own internal political reasons.

Who are the learners? What are their strengths? What do they want and need?

When you know who you want to take part in your project, learn more about them as people, what they want, the challenges and issues they face in their lives, the resources and opportunities open to them, the experiences they bring and hopes they have. This can be done through the recruitment process and should always be part of the opening sessions, but course organizers need to have deeper knowledge before they begin, and if necessary learn more about their concerns.

What issues are likely to come up?

Any programme in practical politics can come across controversial issues. Organizers need to be ready and willing to address issues they had not considered and develop new activities, tactics and strategies to support learners. They need to be aware of possible conflict or controversy, how to respond and their boundaries. Always be clear about the distinction between teaching, learning and doing practical politics. The teacher's responsibility is to lead and facilitate learning, with a duty of care for learners' safety. Learners are responsible for how they use their knowledge and any political action they choose to take. This requires judgement and a risk assessment. If the risk is low and the authorities in your institution are weak or unlikely to be supportive, it may be best to tell no one except allies or it will never start. If there is any risk of controversy, brief allies inside and outside the institution, so that if it is attacked your defence is ready. If possible, prepare anyone in authority who could stop the programme if it does become controversial so that they are able to defend the project in public. Naturally, this is part of the curriculum.

Progression routes in practical politics

Whatever your starting point, everyone is a learner. However knowledgeable and experienced you are, there is always more to learn. You may be mistaken or the world may have changed in the last ten minutes. Political education is always a dialogue between people and with the evidence. The next steps are about creating progression routes, from your learning needs analysis and teachable moments to an advanced programme.

Teachable moments

These are opportunities to raise awareness and learn about politics in any context. Whenever someone:

- asks a question or makes an open-ended comment about an issue or conflict, you can stimulate curiosity, suggest a line of inquiry or offer more information
- says it is impossible to change something, they are powerless or afraid, you can find out why, explore if they really want to change it, suggest

change is possible if people really want it and are willing to work for it (or support others working for it)

- notices a power dynamics or conflict in any situation.

Moments like these arise in everyday conversation, the classroom and on social media. They are a chance to explore an issue, understand power dynamics, find small steps to make a difference and encourage people to want more. When people want to do something constructive about an issue, the following questions can help them start:

- What is the outcome you want?
- Who has the power to make it happen?
- Who else is working on the issue?
- What can you tell me about the issue?
- What small step could you do now?

If you think their solution or issue is mistaken, focus on their positive intention and use questions to help them go more deeply into the issue and find alternatives. Similarly, when people say something prejudiced or ignorant, encourage learning by asking questions such as:

- What's the evidence for that?
- Have you double checked the evidence and looked at other sources?
- Have you considered a counter example?

Teachable moments get people to think and become better at doing politics. This differs from many political arguments, which often confirm people's views without either side learning anything new. A democratic political educator encourages people to think more deeply, look at evidence on all sides of an argument and take effective action.

Entry level: Tasters, tempters and triggers

Perhaps the biggest need is for short activities that entice people to take part – tasters, one-off workshops, talks, stalls in the street, pop-up shops, webinars, videos or other activities that encourage citizens to develop and use their power effectively. Bite the Ballot (UK), Operation Black Vote and Rock the Vote (US) use music, video, social media, celebrities and fun to get people to see the point of politics and register to vote. The Workers' Educational Association, Patchwork Foundation, Sheila McKechnie Foundation and many projects provide non-partisan entry points.

The following events create opportunities to organize learning activities for political engagement:

- Any election, from school board to president, about the choices facing voters.
- A controversy, such as banking, climate change, fracking, homelessness, immigration or student fees.
- A public consultation.
- A film or series on television, radio or other medium that raises political issues.
- Anniversaries of historical events.
- A community festival, fair, conference, or anywhere people gather.

The aim is to encourage people to think for themselves, understand the issues and power structures, see different sides and find the best way to have their say if they want to.

Short courses or modules

Almost any subject, issue or institution can benefit from lessons in how to advocate, campaign or influence people. In most cases this means discussing questions about social purpose, values, interests, funding and institutional dynamics, not party politics. This is about understanding subjects in more depth, not reducing them to a cypher in a political struggle. Schools can run short courses for parents on how it makes decisions, its current policies and how to have a say. Local authorities can run workshops, webinars or videos on how it works, what elected representatives do, how to influence them and how to stand for election.

Courses in practical politics have been developed under names such as advocacy, campaigning, influencing skills, leadership, public policy and political communication. Most are outside the formal education sector for businesses, non-profits or professional development. Once you start looking, you will see where and how a short course in practical politics can enhance any discipline.

Advanced courses

Like any applied discipline, politics needs advanced programmes rooted in practice, dealing with real problems to develop political craft and deep knowledge of issues and power structures. This is itself a practical political challenge, because it is much easier to create a rigorous, intellectually stimulating but safe course that addresses problems in the abstract without the risks of taking action. It is also easier to set up service learning to soothe social wounds and institutional consciences without addressing causes. A good advanced course includes both practical challenges with fearless pursuit of knowledge.

Twelve elements of a curriculum for action

Figure 11.1 summarizes the elements of a curriculum for effective political action. How you combine these depends on the context and needs of participants, so I offer them as an inspiration, not a syllabus. They are based on my experience of both doing practical politics at every level, from the very local to global, and of running campaign training. They also draw on programmes such as community organizer training, the Young Foundation's *Uprising, Training for Transformation* and Ian Chandler's campaign training, from Alexander, *Learning Power* (2006).

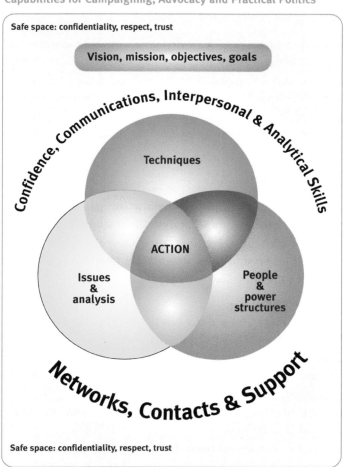

Sharon Dodd

Figure 11.1: Capabilities for practical politics

To start with, organizers need to create a safe space where participants can share fears, hopes and thoughts without being judged. This is done by creating ground rules and a democratic learning community in which people can develop confidence as well as interpersonal and communication skills. This is also where participants share experiences, clarify values and sharpen their political objectives. Every classroom can become a safe space to explore all sides of an issue. The spheres show three areas of knowledge:

1. **problems** or issues participants are addressing

2. people and **power structures** that make decisions about the issue

3. **methods:** strategy, tactics and techniques of advocacy campaigning, including theories of change and communication methods.

Around the three spheres of knowledge are the core abilities for politics – confidence, communication, interpersonal and analytical skills, as well as the ability to network, make contacts and build support. But above all is the need to develop a clear vision, values and goals to guide action. Action is at the centre, because effective action is the only real test of education in practical politics. The following paragraphs describe each of these elements under three headings:

Experiential learning

1. **Create a democratic learning community:** people learn about power through relationships and what they do, which has more lasting influence than course content. A learning community would involve participants in drawing up ground-rules, negotiating the curriculum, co-facilitating activities and peer-evaluation.

2. **Draw on personal experience:** share experiences of powerlessness and power, and reflect on political activities they have been involved in – What was it about? Why did you get involved? What did you do? Who did what? What happened? What was the outcome? What influenced the results and how? The 1970s women's movement created 'consciousness-raising groups' to explore personal experience of patriarchy. In *The Pedagogy of Freedom,* Paulo Freire talks about the importance of talking with students about the concrete reality of their lives to awaken critical consciousness (Freire, 1998: 36). Connecting diverse personal experiences can also reveal a bigger picture about social patterns and influences.

3. **Use stories and case studies:** analyse successful and unsuccessful political action and campaigns. Build up a database of case studies for each generation of learners to use (see, for example, www.practicalpolitics. global). Use political art, drama, films, novels and songs.

4. **Project learning:** develop investigations, projects, placements and service learning opportunities. The main test of practical politics is whether it brings about the desired result.

Knowledge

5. **Develop values and principles:** values address fundamental questions as to *why* do something, while principles are about *how* you do it, such as the Nolan principles of public life.

6. **Understand theories of change:** every institution, party or campaign has assumptions about how change happens, so you need to explore different change models. A theory is a hypothesis to be tested: applying the same theory to all circumstances is like prescribing one cure for all ills, whether it is direct action, lobbying, unfettered markets or workers revolution. For a summary of different theories see *Pathways for Change: 10 theories to inform advocacy and policy change efforts* (Stachawiak, 2013). Exploring different theories of change enables learners to become more flexible and effective change agents.

7. **Analyse the problem (domain knowledge):** expertise gives campaigners credibility and detailed technical knowledge that can be decisive at critical moments. Knowing too much can also make it difficult to focus on the few simple messages needed for campaigning. In *How to Win Campaigns*, Chris Rose (Rose, 2010: 23) argues that education and campaigning are opposites. Learning about an issue leads to greater complexity and indecision, while campaigning needs to narrow the focus. When a business launches a campaign to promote a new product, it does not hold seminars on all the alternatives, but relentlessly focuses on its benefits.

    Activists need to respect evidence and work closely with experts. The art of politics is about asking the right questions, identifying who has the power, developing effective messages and influencing people to achieve the outcome you want. Seeing the issue from the outside can be a great advantage, but getting facts wrong can destroy a campaign, or fail to produce the results you want if it succeeds. Key skills for practical politics therefore include rapid research, using experts effectively and asking questions. Asking questions can also get powerful individuals or agencies to address a problem or start the change process.

8. **Understand the power structures and processes:** this is often more important than knowledge of the issue itself: who are the key decision-makers? What keeps them awake at night? What are their underlying beliefs? Who advises them? What are the external influences on their decisions, such as consumers, competitors, history, faith, financial markets, law, relatives, regulators, reputation, voters, technology, the media or other stakeholders? All these need to be identified for their potential to influence decisions.

It is also important to understand how people see issues, the unconscious mental frames that shape perceptions, as developed by the FrameWorks Institute and George Lakoff in *Don't Think of an Elephant* (2004), *The Political Mind* (2009) and other works.

Skills

9. **Influencing skills** include communication, asking questions, decision-maker dialogue, organizing, coalition building, negotiating, using the media, lobbying, stunts and non-violent direct action are just some of the methods students of EPP could practise.

10. **Social media and the internet:** to understand and evaluate the range of online tools available, and learn how to develop new tools to meet particular needs.

11. **Campaign strategy and tactics** means putting these elements together to achieve an outcome. A campaign strategy is the equivalent of a business plan, which sets out what you want to achieve, why and how; the problem you want to address, your solution and critical evidence about it; and who can help or hinder (stakeholders), what actions you plan to take, the risks involved and other factors, while allowing for spontaneity to seize opportunities when they arise.

12. **Evaluation:** learn to evaluate every action, encounter and campaign so that you learn and grow.

Chris Rose describes campaigning as a conversation with society (Rose, 2010: 1), which follows a planned sequence of communications, from raising awareness to proposing solutions and a call to action (20) to creating a dialogue with the public about the issue and how to deal with it (see Figure 11.2). This theory of change may not be applicable in all cases:

not all issues have an enemy, or sometimes the enemy is so big and powerful it is better not to rouse them and create a distraction or roundabout route instead. But the concept of campaigning as a public conversation is useful.

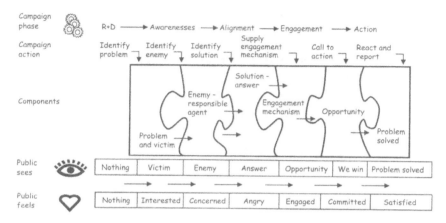

Figure 11.2: Rose's campaign strategy

Not every campaign needs a victim or an enemy. Targeting an enemy draws their fire and may create unnecessary battles. Attack can strengthen the opposition to your cause. Sometimes it is much simpler to focus on the solution and its benefits, taking attention away from the problem altogether (Jackson and McKergow, 2002). Big difficult problems like climate change, female genital mutilation or over-fishing may have complex solutions that can't be solved by demonizing those who cause harm because they are part of the solution.

But sometimes individuals or organizations actively resist the change you want, in which case you need a strategy to defeat or get round them. Even if you choose not to identify an enemy, you need to be prepared for attack from any quarter, including people on your own side. The 2016 UK referendum on membership of the European Union was a dramatic demonstration of erstwhile allies becoming adversaries overnight. In politics you should never make assumptions or take anything for granted.

LEARN MORE: CAMPAIGNING AND THEORIES OF CHANGE

Find an opportunity to develop education for practical politics and draw up a plan to make it happen, drawing on the following resources for reference (alternatively, create a campaign plan for an issue you care about):

- *How to Win Campaigns.* (Rose, 2010)
- *Pathways for Change: 10 theories to inform advocacy and policy change efforts.* (Stachawiak, 2013)
- Albert Bandura's social learning theory (Bandura, 1977), particularly in the applications described in *Influencer: The new science of leading change* (Grenny *et al.*, 2013)
- *The Tipping Point* (Gladwell, 2000), an application of Rogers's theory of diffusion of innovations (Rogers, 1962)
- *Switch: How to change things when change is hard* by Chip and Dan Heath (2010).

Practise by volunteering with a successful campaigning organization.

Conclusion: Next steps

The 2012 London Olympics are remembered for involving thousands of volunteers in a nationwide torch relay and stewarding events; for the opening ceremony's eccentric, exuberant celebration of British life and for the diversity of athletes who won medals in the Paralympics and Olympiad. In 2014 the Scottish independence referendum also achieved unparalleled participation, with 97 per cent voter registration, 85 per cent turnout and intense political debate, as well as the promise of greater devolution of power.

These two events sought to break out of the elite ghettos of premier league sport and politics respectively. They were committed to inclusion, diversity and excellence in everyone. Participation in sport or politics depends on encouragement and support for people to take part. There were winners and losers in both events, but at another level society gained and many of those who lost learnt something of value.

Bernard Crick dismissed the 'common-tongue' idea that politics takes place in 'any old castle called "government"' (1982: 162). This book, however, has argued that every decision-making arena is a 'polity' where conflicting interests are resolved, whether it is the International Olympic Committee, FIFA or a referendum on nationhood. Open, democratic political systems at scale are relatively new and rare in human history. Even in the West most practical politics takes place behind closed doors, among politicians, officials and lobbyists who know how the system works. The 'master science' of politics is open to all, but few have the opportunity to learn how to take part.

The arts of persuasion, influencing and organizing are taught in business schools to help people compete in the market, but not in ordinary schools to help people take part in democracy. As a result, commerce is much stronger, more productive and effective than democracy. The market offers abundant diversity, disruptive innovation and competition, but in politics the main choice is between a few tarnished brands offering unbelievable promises at election times. Yet politics, like markets, never sleep. Someone is always organizing to gain advantage in the ceaseless tussle between competing interests, only most people are barely aware it's happening.

This book, like Bernard Crick's celebrated *Defence of Politics*, 'simply seeks to help in the task of restoring confidence in the virtues of politics as a great and civilizing human activity' (1962: 15). I have disagreed with Crick about the scope of politics, because I see it everywhere there are conflicts of interest and differences in power, but I agree that politics is 'something with a life and character of its own. Politics is not religion, ethics, law, science, history, or economics' (15). It 'arises from accepting the fact of the simultaneous existence of different groups, hence different interests and different traditions' (18). But it is now clearer than in 1962 that politics inside government departments, quangos and other offices is at least as important as parties; that international rules of trade, transport, finance and communications are as much part of domestic politics as national government; and that Google, Shell, Greenpeace and *al-Qaida* are engaged in politics no less than parties, and they may have more impact on how we are governed than any party.

Like Crick, I agree with Aristotle that politics is the 'master science'. This means we cannot ignore Charter 77, *Solidarność* or pro-democracy demonstrators in Hong Kong just because they were not part of open political systems. Both they and their Communist adversaries were intensely engaged in politics. Politics takes great skill and courage in a closed political system, so people from authoritarian societies should be able to learn politics arts appropriate to their circumstances. Likewise company employees seeking to introduce the living wage, a works council or sustainable supply chain, are engaged in politics, just as much as the boss who insists that shareholder value is the only thing that matters, or the politician who pursues similar causes in parliament. All are involved in political processes.

'Politics are' Crick wrote, 'the market place and the price mechanism of all social demands – though there is no guarantee that a just price will be struck; and there is nothing spontaneous about politics – it depends on deliberate and continuous individual activity' (24). The problem is, for most people the marketplace appears closed most of the time, or at best a bear pit behind a glass barrier. In democratic societies the majority are invited to take part in elections and largely ignored most of the time. But politics takes place all year round, often in circumstances more like a corporate hierarchy than the ideal of an open political system. Politics is a complex activity, which, I have argued, can be learned through a mixture of experience and study, but more experience than study, because it is indeed more like sport or business than history, where proof of any model is in the result, not a text. As Crick wrote, 'neither the activity nor the study [of politics] can exist apart from each other' (164). He concluded his book with the words 'Only political solutions can meet whole world problems' (288).

Universities develop advanced skills and knowledge about whole world problems. They are the dominant institutions in education, and have greater freedom than any other part of education. Politics is a discipline relevant to all areas of knowledge and all aspects of society. In a democracy, everyone needs political skills and knowledge to take part as equal citizens. Universities could take a lead in making education for practical politics available to all. In particular, the education of school teachers should include an element of practical politics so that they can help all pupils take confident steps on their journey to democratic citizenship.

To ensure that this does not widen the participation gap by training an elite who leave the majority behind, this should include a large element of service learning, in which students develop political abilities alongside people with less power, to strengthen their influence at the same time. In this way everyone can benefit from education for practical politics.

References

Abelson, D.E. (2002) *Do Think Tanks Matter? Assessing the impact of public policy institutes*. Montreal: McGill-Queens University Press.

Abouharb, M. Rodwan and Cingranelli, David (2007) *Human Rights and Structural Adjustment*. Cambridge: Cambridge University Press.

Acemoglu, D. and Robinson, J.A. (2008) 'Persistence of power, elites and institutions'. *American Economic Review,* 98 (1), 267–93.

— (2012) *Why Nations Fail: The origins of power, prosperity, and poverty*. New York: Crown.

Ainley, J., Schulz, W. and Friedman, T. (eds) (2013) *ICCS 2009 Encyclopaedia: Approaches to civic and citizenship education around the world*. Amsterdam: International Association for the Evaluation of Educational Achievement. Online. www.iea.nl/fileadmin/user_upload/Publications/Electronic_versions/ICCS_2009_Encyclopedia.pdf (accessed 11 August 2016).

Alexander, R. (2009) 'Plowden, truth and myth: A warning'. Lecture presented at the University of Cambridge, 15 May. Online. www.robinalexander.org.uk/wp-content/uploads/2012/05/Plowden-truth-and-myth.pdf (accessed 11 August 2016).

Alexander, T. (1997) *Family Learning: The foundation of effective education*. London: Demos.

— (2001) *Citizenship Schools: A practical guide to education for citizenship and personal development*. London: Campaign for Learning.

— (2006) *Learning Power: A contribution to the national skills strategy*. London: Campaign for Learning/Scarman Trust. Online. http://docplayer.net/13867892-Learning-power-a-contribution-to-the-national-skills-strategy-titus-alexander-director-for-learning-the-scarman-trust.html (accessed 11 August 2016).

— (2016) 'Institutions as Social Theory', unpublished MS.

Alkire, S. (2008) 'Concepts and Measures of Agency'. *OPHI Working Papers*. Oxford: Queen Elizabeth House, University of Oxford.

Andres, G.J. (1985) 'Business involvement in campaign finance: Factors influencing the decision to form a Corporate PAC'. *Political Science and Politics,* 18: 213–20.

Andrews, K. and Edwards, B. (2004) 'Advocacy organizations in the US political process'. *Annual Review of Sociology,* 30: 479–506.

Ansolabehere, S., De Figueiredo, J.M. and Snyder, J.M. (2003) 'Why is there so little money in politics?' *Journal of Economic Perspectives,* 17 (1), 105–30.

Aristotle (2000) *Nicomachean Ethics*. Trans. Crisp, R. Cambridge: Cambridge University Press.

Arnold-Baker, C. (1967) *The 5000 and the Power Tangle*. London: John Murray.

Arquilla, J. and Ronfeldt, D. (1999) 'The emergence of noopolitik: Toward an american information strategy'. Santa Monica: RAND Corporation. Online. www.rand.org/pubs/monograph_reports/MR1033 (accessed 14 April 2016).

Arthur, C. (2012) 'Apple's Tim Cook shows ruthless streak in firing maps and retail executives'. *The Guardian,* 30 October. Online. www.theguardian.com/technology/2012/oct/30/apple-tim-cook-ruthless-streak (accessed 23 September 2014).

Audsley, J., Chitty, C., O'Connell, J., Watson, D. and Wills, J. (2013) *Citizen Schools: Learning to rebuild democracy.* London: IPPR.

Bagehot, W. (1867) *The English Constitution.* London: Chapman and Hall.

Baha'i (1985) 'The Universal House of Justice'. *Baha'i Library.* Online. www.bahai.org/library/authoritative-texts/the-universal-house-of-justice/messages/19851001_001/19851001_001.pdf (accessed 11 August 2016).

Bandura, A. (1977) *Social Learning Theory.* Alexandria, VA: Prentice Hall.

— (1997) *Self-efficacy: The exercise of control.* New York: Worth Publishers.

Batty, E. and Flint, J. (2010) 'Self-esteem, comparative poverty and neighbourhoods'. *Research Paper No. 7,* Centre for Regional Economic and Social Research, Sheffield Hallam University. Online. http://research.shu.ac.uk/cresr/living-through-change/documents/RP7_SelfEsteem.pdf (accessed 11 August 2016).

Baumgartner, F.R., Berry, J.M., Hojnacki, M., Kimball, D.C. and Leech, B.L. (2009) *Lobbying and Policy Change: Who wins, who loses, and why.* Chicago: University of Chicago Press.

BBC (2012) 'Jimmy Savile abuse allegations: Timeline'. Online. www.bbc.co.uk/news/uk-19921658 (accessed 11 August 2016).

Benabou, R. (2000) 'Unequal Societies: Income distribution and the social contract'. *American Economic Review,* 90 (1), 96–129.

Bennett, N. (1976) *Teaching Styles and Pupil Progress.* London: Open Books.

Berman, S. (1997) 'Civil society and the collapse of the Weimar Republic'. *World Politics,* 49 (3), 401–29. Cambridge University Press.

Bernays, E.L. (1928) 'Manipulating public opinion: The why and the how'. *American Journal of Sociology,* 33 (6), 958–71.

— (1928) *Propaganda.* New York: Routledge; Brooklyn: IG Publishing.

— (1992) 'The future of public relations'. Talk at the Association for Education in Journalism and Mass Communication (AEJMC) Convention. Online. http://prvisionaries.com/bernays/bernays_1990.html (accessed 11 August 2016).

Bevir, M. (2013) *A Theory of Governance.* Berkeley: University of California Press.

Birchall, J. (1997) *The International Co-operative Movement.* Manchester: Manchester University Press.

Blair, T. (2010) *A Journey: My political life.* London: Random House; Hutchinson.

Blyth, M. (2013) *Austerity: The history of a dangerous idea.* Oxford: Oxford University Press.

Boal, A. (1979) *Theatre of the Oppressed.* London: Pluto Press.

— (1998) *Legislative Theatre: Using performance to make politics.* London: Routledge.

Bode, B. (2007) *Power Analysis in the Context of Rights-Based Programming.* CARE Bangladesh.

Bogdanor, V. (1995) *The Monarchy and the Constitution.* Oxford: Oxford University Press.

Bok, D. (2004) *Universities in the Marketplace: The commercialization of higher education*. Princeton, NJ: Princeton University Press.

Bonica, A., McCarty, N., Poole, K.T. and Rosenthal, H. (2013) 'Why hasn't democracy slowed rising inequality?' *Journal of Economic Perspectives*, 27 (3), 103–24.

Boris, E. and Krehely, J. (2002) 'Civic participation and advocacy'. In Salamon, L. (ed.) *The State of Nonprofit America*. Washington, DC: Brookings, 299–330.

Borish, S.M. (1991) *The Land of the Living: The Danish folk high schools and Denmark's non-violent path to modernization*. Nevada City, CA: Blue Dolphin (includes substantial bibliography).

Bounfour, A. (2000) *The Management of Intangibles: The organization's most valuable assets*. London: Routledge.

Bourdieu, P. (1977) [1972] *Outline of a Theory of Practice*. Cambridge: Cambridge University Press, trans.

— (1988) *Homo Academicus*, Cambridge: Polity Press.

— (1996) *The State Nobility: Elite schools in the field of power*. Cambridge: Polity Press.

Boyle, D. (2012) *The Human Element: Ten new rules to kickstart our failing organizations*. London; New York: Earthscan.

Brennan, J., King, R. and Lebeau, Y. (2004) *The Role of Universities in the Transformation of Societies: An international research project, synthesis report*. London: Association of Commonwealth Universities.

Breton, G. and Lambert, M. (2003) *Universities and Globalization: Private linkages, public trust*. Paris: UNESCO; Université Laval.

Brewis, G. (2014) *A Social History of Student Volunteering: Britain and beyond, 1880–1980*. New York: Palgrave Macmillan.

Brown, R. (2010) 'Situating social inequality and collective action in cognitive analytic therapy'. *Reformulation*, Winter, 28–34.

Butin, D.W. (2010) *Service-learning in Theory and Practice: The future of community engagement in higher education*. New York: Palgrave Macmillan.

Cable, V. (2010) *The Storm: The world economic crisis and what it means*. London: Atlantic.

Calhoun, C. (1994) *Social Theory and the Politics of Identity*. Oxford: Blackwell.

Callaghan, J. (1976) 'A rational debate based on the facts'. Talk given at Ruskin College, October. Online. www.educationengland.org.uk/documents/speeches/1976ruskin.html (accessed 15 April 2016).

Campbell, A. (2007) *The Blair Years*. London: Hutchinson.

— (2010) *Diaries, Vol. 1: Prelude to power 1994–1997*. London: Hutchinson.

— (2011) *Diaries, Vol. 2: Power and the people 1997–1999*. London: Hutchinson.

— (2012) *Diaries, Vol. 3: Power and responsibility 1999–2001*. London: Hutchinson.

Campbell, J.L., Hall, J.A. and Pedersen, O.K. (2006) *National Identity and the Varieties of Capitalism: The Danish experience*. Montreal: McGill-Queens University Press; Copenhagen: DJØF Publishing.

Carswell, D. (2012) *The End of Politics and the Birth of Democracy*. London: Biteback.

Castells, M. (2001) 'Universities as dynamic systems of contradictory functions'. In Muller, J., Cloete, N., and Badat, S. (eds) *Challenges of Globalisation: South African debates with Manuel Castells*. Cape Town: Maskew Miller Longman, 206–23.

Cave, T. and Rowell, A. (2014) *A Quiet Word: Lobbying, crony capitalism and broken politics in Britain*. London: Bodley Head.

Center on Congress (2015) 'Culture of political "eye-poking" on Capitol Hill yields poor ratings for Congress in center survey'. Bloomington, IN: Indiana University. Online. www.centeroncongress.org/eye-poking-yields-poor-ratings (accessed 25 April 2015).

Chakrabarti, S. (2014) 'How handpicked experts like Arvind Panagariya, Ravi Mantha are helping Narendra Modi fine-tune his 2014 poll strategy'. *ET Bureau*. Online. http://articles.economictimes.indiatimes.com/2014-02-19/news/47490223_1_narendra-modi-team-modi-big-speech (accessed 16 August 2014).

Chambers, R. (1983) *Rural Development: Putting the last first*. London: Longman.
— (1997) *Whose Reality Counts? Putting the first last*. London: Intermediate Technology Publications.

Chandler, A.D. (1977) *The Visible Hand: The managerial revolution in American business*. Cambridge, MA: Harvard University Press.

Chandler, A.D., Amatori, F., and Hikino, T. (eds) (1997) *Big Business and the Wealth of Nations*. Cambridge: Cambridge University Press.

Chenoweth, E. and Stephan, M.J. (2011) *Why Civil Resistance Works: The strategic logic of nonviolent conflict*. New York: Columbia University Press.

Cialdini, R. (1984) *Influence: The psychology of persuasion*. New York: Collins, revised ed., 2007.

Cipolle, S.B. (2010) *Service-learning and Social Justice: Engaging students in social change*. London: Rowman and Littlefield.

Colby, A., Beaumont, E., Ehrlich, T. and Corngold, J. (2007) *Educating for Democracy: Preparing undergraduates for responsible political engagement*. San Francisco, CA: Jossey-Bass.

Collins, J. (2001) *Good to Great: Why some companies make the leap … and others don't*. London: Random House Business.

Collins, J. and Porras, J.I. (1994) *Built to Last: Successful habits of visionary companies*. New York: Harper Business Essentials.

Council of Europe (2010) 'Charter on Education for Democratic Citizenship and Human Rights Education', Recommendation CM/Rec (2010) 7, 11 May 2010, Strasbourg: Council of Europe Publishing. Online. www.coe.int/en/web/edc/charter-on-education-for-democratic-citizenship-and-human-rights-education (accessed 11 August 2016).

Crawford, N., Lutz, C., Mazzarino, A.C. (2015) *The Cost of War*. Watson Institute for International Studies, Brown University. Online. http://watson.brown.edu/costsofwar/about (accessed 11 August 2016).

Crick, B. (1982) [1962] *In Defence of Politics*, 2nd ed., London: Pelican.

— (1998) 'Education for citizenship and the teaching of democracy in schools: Final report of the Advisory Group on the Teaching of Citizenship and Democracy in schools'. London: Qualifications and Curriculum Authority. Online. www.educationengland.org.uk/documents/pdfs/1998-crick-report-citizenship.pdf (accessed 11 August 2016).

— (2000) *Essays on Citizenship*. London: Continuum.

— (2013) [2000] *In Defence of Politics*, 5th ed., London: Bloomsbury.

Crutchfield, Leslie and McLeod Grant, Heather (2008) *Forces for Good: The six practices of high-impact non-profits*. Hoboken, NJ: Wiley.

Culpepper, P.D. (2011) *Quiet Politics and Business Power: Corporate control in Europe and Japan*. Cambridge: Cambridge University Press.

Davidson, R.H. and Oleszek, W.J. (2013) *Congress and its Members*. Washington, DC: CQ Press.

Dávila, J.D. (ed.) (2013) 'Urban mobility and poverty: Lessons from Medellín and Soacha, Colombia'. *Development Planning Unit*, UCL and Universidad Nacional de Colombia. Online. www.bartlett.ucl.ac.uk/dpu/metrocables/book/Davila_2013_UrbanMobility_Poverty_Eng.pdf (accessed 11 August 2016).

De Soto, H. (2003) *The Mystery of Capital: Why capitalism triumphs in the West and fails everywhere else*. New York: Basic Books.

Deace, S. (2014) *Rules for Patriots: How conservatives can win again*. New York: Post Hill Press.

Delanty, G. (2001) *Challenging Knowledge: The university in a knowledge society*. Buckingham: Open University Press.

Deming, W.E. (1993) *The New Economics*. Cambridge, MA: MIT Press.

Democratic Audit (2015) 'Quangos and quangocrats'. Online. www.democraticaudit.com/?page_id=616 (accessed 14 April 2016).

Department for Business, Innovation & Skills (BIS) (2013) 'International education – global growth and prosperity: An accompanying analytical narrative'. HMSO, Department for Business, Innovation and Skills, BIS/13/1082. Online. www.gov.uk/government/uploads/system/uploads/attachment_data/file/340601/bis-13-1082-international-education-accompanying-analytical-narrative-revised.pdf (accessed 20 August 2015).

Department for International Development (DFID) (2009) 'Political economic analysis: How to note'. Online. www.odi.org/sites/odi.org.uk/files/odi-assets/events-documents/3501.pdf (accessed 15 April 2016).

— (2013) 'UK to help end female genital mutilation'. Online. www.gov.uk/government/news/uk-to-help-end-female-genital-mutilation. See also: Policy: www.gov.uk/government/policies/improving-the-lives-of-girls-and-women-in-the-worlds-poorest-countries (accessed 10 February 2015).

Desforges, C. (2003) *The Impact of Parental Involvement, Parental Support and Family Education on Pupil Achievements and Adjustment*. London: Department for Education and Science.

Desmond, R. (2015) *The Real Deal: The autobiography of Britain's most controversial media mogul*. London: Random House.

Devlin, M. and Chaskel, S. 'From fear to hope in Colombia: Sergio Fajardo and Medellín, 2004–2007'. *Innovations for Successful Societies*, Princeton University. Online. www.princeton.edu/successfulsocieties (accessed 25 May 2015).

Dewey, J. (1900) *School and Society*, Chicago, IL: University of Chicago Press.

— (1916) *Democracy and Education: An introduction to the philosophy of education*. New York: Macmillan.

— (1938) *Experience and Education*. New York: Kappa Delta Pi, Touchstone ed., 1997.

Diers, J. (2004) *Neighborhood Power: Building community the Seattle way*. Seattle, WA: Washington University Press.

Domhoff, G.W. (2012) 'How to do Power Structure Research'. Online. www2. ucsc.edu/whorulesamerica/methods/how_to_do_power_structure_research.html (accessed 17 April 2016).

— (2013) [1967] *Who Rules America? The triumph of the corporate rich*, 7th ed., New York: McGraw-Hill Education.

— (2016) *Who rules America? Power, politics, and social change*. Online. www2. ucsc.edu/whorulesamerica/ (accessed 17 April 2016).

Donaldson, L. (2008) 'Developing a progressive advocacy program within a human services agency'. *Administration in Social Work*, 32 (2), 25–47

Drews, W. and Fieldhouse, R. (1996) 'Residential colleges and non-residential settlements and centres'. In Fieldhouse, R. and associates, *A History of Modern British Adult Education*. Leicester: NIACE.

Driscoll, A. (2006) 'The benchmarking potential of the new Carnegie classification: Community engagement'. Carnegie Foundation for the Advancement of Teaching. In Holland, B. and Meeropol, J. (eds) *A More Perfect Vision: The future of campus engagement*. Providence, RI: Campus Compact.

Drucker, P. (1946) *Concept of the Corporation*. New York: John Day.

Drucker, P. (1954) *The Practice of Management*. New York: Harper and Brothers.

— (1959) *Landmarks of Tomorrow*. New York: Harper and Brothers.

— (1969) *The Age of Discontinuity*. New York: Harper and Row.

Drucker, P. (1973) *Management: Tasks, responsibilities, practices*. New York: Harper and Row.

Drucker, P. (1989a) 'Sell the mailroom'. *Wall Street Journal*, 25 July 1989, reprinted 15 November 2005. Online. www.wsj.com/articles/SB113202230063197204 (accessed 26 July 2015).

Drucker, P. (1989b) 'What business can learn from nonprofits'. *Harvard Business Review*, July. Online. https://hbr.org/1989/07/what-business-can-learn-from-nonprofits (accessed 11 August 2016).

Drucker, P. (2001) *The Essential Drucker*. New York: Harper Business.

Durnev, A. (2010) 'The real effects of political uncertainty: Elections, capital allocation, and performance'. *Working Paper*, Paris, December 2010 Finance Meeting EUROFIDAI–AFFI. Online. www.law.northwestern.edu/research-faculty/colloquium/law-economics/documents/Spring%202013%20Durnev%20REAL%20EFFECTS%20OF%20POLITICAL%20UNCERTAINTY.pdf (accessed 6 June 2016).

Ebenstein, A. (2010) 'The "missing girls" of China and the unintended consequences of the one child policy'. *Journal of Human Resources*, 45 (1), 87–115.

Economist, The (2010) 'Gendercide: The worldwide war on baby girls, technology, declining fertility and ancient prejudice are combining to unbalance societies'. 4 March 2010. Online. www.economist.com/node/15636231 (accessed 16 April 2016).

— (2015) 'The marriage squeeze in India and China'. 18 April 2015. Online. www.economist.com/news/asia/21648715-distorted-sex-ratios-birth-generation-ago-are-changing-marriage-and-damaging-societies-asias (accessed 16 April 2016).

Edelman (2013) *Trust Barometer,* slide 10. Online. www.slideshare.net/EdelmanInsights/global-deck-2013-edelman-trust-barometer-16086761 (accessed 11 August 2016).

— (2014) *Trust Barometer.* Online. www.slideshare.net/fullscreen/EdelmanInsights/2014-edelman-trust-barometer/1 (accessed 11 August 2016).

Edmonds, T., Jarrett, T. and Woodhouse, J. (2010) 'The credit crisis: A timeline'. House of Commons, Standard Note: SN/BT/4991.

Edwards, T. and Whitty, G. (1997) 'Marketing quality: Traditional and modern versions of educational excellence'. In Glatter, R. *et al.* (eds) *Choice and Diversity in Schooling: Perspectives and Prospects.* London: Routledge, 29–43.

Eichhorn, J., Kenealy, D., Parry, R., Paterson, L. and Remond, A. (2015) 'Elite and mass attitudes on how the UK and its parts are governed: England and the process of constitutional change'. Academy of Government: Online. www.aog.ed.ac.uk/news/last_3_months6/new_research_on_attitudes_to_uk_constitutional_change_released (accessed 16 April 2016).

Ellis, H. (2013) 'Efficiency and counter-revolution: Connecting university and civil service reform in the 1850s'. *History of Education: Journal of the History of Education Society,* 42 (1), 23–44.

Elsner, W. and Hanappi, G. (2008) *Varieties of Capitalism and New Institutional Deals: Regulation, regulation and the new economy.* Cheltenham: Edward Elgar.

Ethical Consumer (2014) *Internet Report.* Online. www.ethicalconsumer.org/ethicalreports/internetreport/taxavoidance.aspx (accessed 16 April 2016).

Eurydice (2012) *Citizenship Education in Europe.* Brussels: Eurydice.

Evans, R. (2013) *Infiltration: The secret world of police surveillance.* London: Guardian Books.

Eyler, J. and Giles Jr., D.E. (1999) *Where's the Learning in Service-Learning?* San Francisco, CA: Jossey-Bass.

Eyler, J., Giles Jr., D.E., Stenson, C.M. and Gray, C.J. (2001) *At a Glance: What we know about the effects of service-learning on college students, faculty, institutions and communities, 1993–2000,* 3rd ed., Nashville, TN: Vanderbilt University.

Falconer, C. (2003) 'Department for Constitutional Affairs: Justice, rights and democracy' speech to the Institute for Public Policy Research, London, 3 December. See also: Falconer, C. 'Constitutional Reform speech', University College, London, 8 December.

Fatás, A. and Mihov, I. (2009a) 'Another challenge to China's growth'. *Harvard Business Review,* March 2009. Online. https://hbr.org/2009/03/another-challenge-to-chinas-growth (accessed 11 August 2016).

Fatás, A. and Mihov, I. (2009b) 'The 4 I's of economic growth'. *INSEAD Business School.* Online. http://faculty.insead.edu/fatas/wall/wall.pdf (accessed 16 April 2016).

Faulkner, R.O. (1973) 'The instruction of Merikare'. In Simpson, W.K. (ed.) *The Literature of Ancient Egypt*. New Haven, CT and London: Yale University Press, 180–92. Online. www.reshafim.org.il/ad/egypt/merikare_papyrus.htm (accessed 16 April 2016).

Federal Deposit Insurance Corporation (FDIC) (2015) *Failed Bank List*. Federal Deposit Insurance Corporation. Online. www.fdic.gov/bank/individual/failed/banklist.html (accessed 16 April 2016).

Feinstein, L. (2007) *Education and the Family: Passing success across the generations*. London: Routledge. Online. http://cep.lse.ac.uk/centrepiece/v08i2/feinstein.pdf (accessed 16 April 2016).

Fijnaut, C.J.C.F. (ed.) (1995) *Undercover Police Surveillance in Comparative Perspective*. Leiden, Netherlands: Brill Academic.

Financial Times (2014) 'More evidence of low tax payments by US tech groups' by Vanessa Houlder and Jim Pickard. Online. www.ft.com/cms/s/0/28e15a82-7230-11e3-9c5c-00144feabdc0.html#axzz4H27LHOAV (accessed 11 August 2016).

— (2015) '"Mythical" Lynton Crosby is master of "wedge politics" in Australia' by Jamie Smith, 13 March. Online. www.ft.com/cms/s/0/ebfeecb0-c8c8-11e4-b43b-00144feab7de.html#axzz3datfXKXK (accessed 16 April 2016).

Flinders, M. and Buller, J. (2004) 'Depoliticisation, democracy and arena-shifting'. Paper to SCANCOR/SOG conference.

— (2006) 'Depoliticization, democracy and arena-shifting'. In Lægreid, P. and Christensen, T. (eds) *Autonomy and Regulation: Coping with agencies in the modern state*. London: Edward Elgar.

Flinders, M. and Smith, M.J. (eds) (1998) *Quangos, Accountability and Reform: The politics of quasi-government*. Basingstoke: Palgrave Macmillan.

Forbes (2014) 'The largest US charities' by William P. Barrett. 12 October.

Ford, M. (2015) *Rise of the Robots: Technology and the threat of a jobless future*. New York: Basic Books.

Forsyth, P. (2006) *Manage Your Boss*. Singapore: Marshall Cavendish Business.

Foster, R.N. and Kaplan, S. (2001) *Creative Destruction: Why companies that are built to last underperform the market – and how to successfully transform them*. New York: Penguin Random House.

Foster, S. (2010) *Political Communication*. Edinburgh: Edinburgh University Press.

Freedom House (2014) 'Freedom in the world 2014'. Washington, DC: Freedom House. Online. https://freedomhouse.org/report/freedom-world/freedom-world-2014#.VN26nhtybIU (accessed 11 July 2016).

— (2015) 'Discarding democracy: Return to the iron fist, freedom in the world 2015'. Washington, DC: Freedom House. Online. https://freedomhouse.org/report/freedom-world/freedom-world-2015#.VRh0GRt0zIU (accessed 11 August 2016).

Freire, P. (1998) *Pedagogy of Freedom: Ethics, democracy and civic courage*. Lanham, MD: Rowman and Littlefield.

Fukuyama, F. (2006) *After the Neocons: America at the crossroads*. New Haven, CT: Yale University Press.

Fullan, M. (1992) *Successful School Improvement: The implementation perspective and beyond*. Buckingham and Philadelphia, PA: Open University Press.

— (2001) *Leading in a Culture of Change*. San Francisco, CA: Jossey-Bass.

— (2006) 'Change theory: A force for school improvement'. *Seminar Series Paper No. 157.* Victoria: Centre for Strategic Education. Online. www.michaelfullan.com/media/13396072630.pdf (accessed 14 March 2016).

— (2012) [1993] *Change Forces: Probing the depths of educational reform.* London and New York: Routledge.

Galbraith, J.K. (1952) *American Capitalism: The concept of countervailing power.* London: Hamish Hamilton.

— (1983) *The Anatomy of Power.* Boston, MA: Houghton Mifflin.

Galil, G. (ed.) (2015) *Political Trust and Disenchantment with Politics: International perspectives.* Leiden, Netherlands: Brill Academic.

Galton, M.J., Simon, B., and Croll, P. (1980) *Inside the Primary Classroom.* London: Routledge and Kegan Paul.

Gartenstein-Ross, D. (2011) *Bin Laden's Legacy: Why we're still losing the War on Terror.* Hoboken, NJ: Wiley.

— (2014a) 'Interpreting Al Qaeda'. *Foreign Policy,* 6 January.

— (2014b) 'Thank you for bombing: Why al Qaeda might be the biggest winner of America's airstrikes on the Islamic State'. *Foreign Policy,* 23 September.

Gasiorowski, M.J. and Byrne, M. (eds) (2004) *Mohammad Mosaddeq and the 1953 Coup in Iran.* New York: Syracuse University Press.

Gatto, J.T. (1992) *Dumbing Us Down: The hidden curriculum of compulsory schooling.* Philadelphia, PA: New Society Publishers, 10th Anniversary ed., 2002.

Gaventa, J. (2006) 'Finding spaces for change'. *IDS Bulletin,* 37, 6 November. Brighton: Institute of Development Studies.

Gaventa, J. and McGee, R. (2011) 'Shifting power? Assessing the impact of transparency and accountability initiatives'. *IDS Working Paper 383.* Brighton: Institute of Development Studies. Online. www.ids.ac.uk/files/dmfile/Wp383.pdf (accessed 16 April 2016).

Geiger, R. (2004) *Knowledge and Money: Research universities and the paradox of the marketplace.* Palo Alto, CA: Stanford University Press.

Ghosh, P. (2013) 'Talk is not cheap: Why do ex-politicians earn huge money from making speeches?' *International Business Times,* 18 December 2013. Online. www.ibtimes.com/talk-not-cheap-why-do-ex-politicians-earn-huge-money-making-speeches-1512632 (accessed 4 October 2014).

Gilens, M. and Page, B.I. (2014) 'Testing theories of American politics: Elites, interest groups, and average citizens'. *Perspectives on Politics,* 12 (3), 564–81.

Ginwright, S., Noguera, P. and Cammarota, J. (eds) (2006) *Beyond Resistance! Youth activism and community change: New democratic possibilities for practice and policy for America's youth.* Abingdon: Routledge.

Gladwell, M. (2000) *The Tipping Point: How little things can make a big difference.* London: Little, Brown.

Glasser, W. (1990) *The Quality School: Managing students without coercion.* New York: Harper Collins.

Gleeson, D. and McLean, M. (1994) 'Whatever happened to TVEI?: TVEI, curriculum and schooling'. *Journal of Education Policy,* 9 (3), 233–44.

Goldman, R.M. (2002) 'The future catches up', *Writers Club Press,* Lincoln, from [1959] 'Passive but powerful', in *National Civic Review,* 48 (5), 231–6.

Goodson, Ivor F. (2013) [1982] *School Subjects and Curriculum Change*. London: Falmer Press.

Goren, P. (2005) 'Party identification and core political values'. *American Journal of Political Science*, 49 (4) 882–97.

Gould, P. (1998) *The Unfinished Revolution*. London: Little, Brown.

Gray, R., with Bebbington, J. and Walters, D. (2007) [1993] *Accounting for the Environment*, 2nd ed., London: Paul Chapman Publishing.

Green, D., Palmquist, B. and Schickler, E. (2002) *Partisan Hearts and Minds: Political parties and the social identities of voters*. New Haven, CT: Yale University Press.

Greenspan, A. (2007) TAGES-ANZEIGER 7 September 2007, quoted in Poggi, G. (2014) *Varieties of Political Experience: Power phenomena in modern society*. ECPR Press, University of Essex, p.104.

Greenwald, G. (2015) *No Place to Hide: Edward Snowden, the NSA and the Surveillance State*. London: Penguin.

Grenier, P. (2003) 'Jubilee 2000: Laying the foundations for a social movement'. In Clark, J. (ed.) *Globalizing Civic Engagement: Civil society and transnational action*. London: Earthscan.

Grenny, J., Patterson, K., Maxfield, D., McMillan, R. and Switzler, A. (2013) *Influencer: The new science of leading change*. New York: McGraw-Hill.

Grimson, A. (2012) 'Lynton Crosby, David Cameron and the old dog whistle test', *New Statesman*, 13 November. Online. www.newstatesman.com/politics/politics/2012/11/lynton-crosby-david-cameron-and-old-dog-whistle-test (accessed 11 August 2016).

Hailsham, Lord (1976) 'Elective dictatorship'. *The Listener*, 21 October, 496–500.

Haines, A. and Donald, A. (eds) (1998) *Getting Research Findings into Practice*. London: BMJ Books.

Hall, P.A. and Soskice, D. (2001) *Varieties of Capitalism: The institutional foundations of comparative advantage*. Oxford: Oxford University Press.

Hall, R.L. and Deardorff, A.V. (2006) 'Lobbying as legislative subsidy'. *American Political Science Review*, 100 (1), 69–84.

Halpin, D.R. (2010) *Groups, Representation and Democracy: Between promise and practice*. Manchester: Manchester University Press.

Hammer, M. and Champy, J. (2006) *Reengineering the Corporation: A manifesto for business revolution*. New York: Harper Business Essentials.

Handy, C. (1986) *Understanding Schools as Organisations*. London: Penguin.

Hanisch, C. [1969] (2000) 'The personal is political'. In Crow, B.A. (ed.) *Radical Feminism: A documentary reader*. New York: NYU Press, 113–17. Online. www.carolhanisch.org/CHwritings/PIP.html

Hannam, D. (2001a) 'Attitudes, attainment, attendance and exclusion in secondary schools that take student participation seriously: A pilot study'. Paper presented to Seminar 3 of the Economic and Social Research Council (ESRC) Consulting Pupils about Teaching and Learning Project 'Pupil Voice and Democracy', University of Cambridge, 15 October.

— (2001b) 'A pilot study to evaluate the impact of the student participation aspects of the citizenship order on standards of education in secondary schools', Report for Prof Bernard Crick, Ministerial Adviser for Citizenship Education at the Department for Education and Employment (DfEE), London: CSV.

Hansell, S. and Muehring, K. (1992) 'Why derivatives rattle the regulators'. *Institutional Investor*, September.

Harding, L. (2014) *The Snowden Files: The inside story of the world's most wanted man*. London: Guardian Books.

Harris, P. and Fleisher, C.S. (eds) (2005) *The Handbook of Public Affairs*. London: Sage.

Harrison, F. (2005) *Boom Bust: House prices, banking and the depression of 2010*. London: Shepheard-Walwyn.

Hausmann, R., Hidalgo, C.A., Bustios, S., Coscia, M., Simoes, A. and Yildirim, M. (2014) *The Atlas of Economic Complexity: Mapping pathways to prosperity*. Cambridge, MA: MIT Press.

Hay, C. (2007) *Why We Hate Politics*. Cambridge: Polity Press.

— (ed.) (2010) *New Directions in Political Science: Responding to the challenge of an independent world*. Basingstoke: Palgrave Macmillan.

Heath, C. and Heath, D. (2007) *Made to Stick: Why some ideas take hold and others come unstuck*. London: Random House.

— (2010) *Switch: How to change things when change is hard*. London: Random House Business.

Helpman, E. (2004) *The Mystery of Economic Growth*. Cambridge, MA: Belknap Press of Harvard University.

— (2008) *Institutions and Economic Performance*. Cambridge, MA: Harvard University Press.

Helpman, E. and Grossman, G.M. (1991) *Innovation and Growth in the Global Economy*. Cambridge, MA: MIT Press.

Henderson, A.T. and Mapp, K.L. (eds) (2002) 'A new wave of evidence: The impact of school, family, and community connections on student achievement'. *National Center for Family and Community Connections with Schools*, SEDL, Austin, TX. Online. www.sedl.org/connections/resources/evidence.pdf (accessed 11 August 2016).

Herman, E.S. and Chomsky, N. (2002) *Manufacturing Consent: The political economy of the mass media*. New York: Pantheon.

Hestbaek, C. (2014a) *Closing in on Change: Measuring the impact of campaigning*. London: New Philanthropy Capital. Online. www.thinknpc.org/publications/closing-in-on-change/ (accessed 11 August 2016).

Hestbaek, C. (2014b) *Campaigning for Social Change: The role of trustees*. London: New Philanthropy Capital.

Higgins, C. (2014) 'The BBC Report'. *The Guardian*, 15 May–20 August. www.theguardian.com/media/series/the-bbc-report (accessed 23 September 2014).

— (2015) *This New Noise: The extraordinary birth and troubled life of the BBC*. London: Guardian Books.

HOGRC (2008) THE FINANCIAL CRISIS AND THE ROLE OF FEDERAL REGULATORS: HEARING, Serial No. 110–209. Online. www.gpo.gov/fdsys/pkg/CHRG-110hhrg55764/html/CHRG-110hhrg55764.htm video: www.washingtonpost.com/wp-dyn/content/video/2008/10/23/VI2008102301451.html (accessed 26 July 2015).

Holt, J. (1990) *Learning all the Time*. Cambridge, MA: Da Capo Press.

— (1995) [1964] *How Children Learn*. Cambridge, MA: Da Capo Press.

Hope, A. and Timmel, S. (1984) *Training for Transformation: A handbook for community workers*, Vols 1–3. Zimbabwe: Mambo Press (revised 1995).

— (1999) *Training for Transformation: A handbook for community workers*, Vol. 4. ITDG/Practical Action (revised 1995).

— (eds) (2014) *Training for Transformation in Practice*. London: Practical Action.

Hopper, K. and Hopper, W. (2009) *The Puritan Gift*. London: IB Tauris.

Houser, J.H.W. (2014) 'Community- and school-sponsored program participation and academic achievement in a full-service community school'. *Education and Urban Society*, 7 May. doi: 10.1177/0013124514533792

Humphreys, M., Sachs J.D. and Stiglitz, J.E. (eds) (2007) *Escaping the Resource Curse*. New York: Columbia University Press.

Hurd, I. (2010) *International Organizations: Politics, law, practice*. Cambridge: Cambridge University Press.

Hyden, G. (2005) 'Why do things happen the way they do? A power analysis of Tanzania'. Online. http://xa.yimg.com/kq/groups/20674633/1114493356/name/Goran+Hyden_Power+Analysis_Tanzania.pdf (accessed 11 August 2016).

ICA (2014) *World Co-operative Monitor*. Belgium: International Co-operative Alliance. Online. http://monitor.coop/ (accessed 11 August 2016).

— (2015) *Co-operative Facts and Figures*. Belgium: International Co-operative Alliance. Online. http://ica.coop/en/whats-co-op/co-operative-facts-figures (accessed 11 August 2016).

IDEA (2015) Voter Turnout Database. Online. www.idea.int/vt/viewdata.cfm (accessed 11 August 2016).

infed.org (2014) 'The development of folk high schools: Pedagogy for change'. Online. www.infed.org/schooling/b-folk.htm (accessed 11 August 2016).

Involve (2005) *People and Participation: How to put citizens at the heart of decision-making*, London: Involve. Online. www.involve.org.uk/wp-content/uploads/2011/03/People-and-Participation.pdf (accessed 16 April 2016).

Jackson, N.J. (2016) *Exploring Learning Ecologies*. Bloomington, IN: AuthorHouse.

— (ed.) (2011) *Learning for a Complex World: A lifewide concept of learning, education and personal development*. Bloomington, IN: AuthorHouse.

Jackson, P.W. (1991) [1968] *Life in Classrooms*. New York: Teachers' College Press.

Jackson, P.Z. and McKergow, M. (2002) *The Solution Focus: The SIMPLE way to positive change*. London: Nicholas Brearley.

Jacoby, B. (ed.) (2009) *Civic Engagement in Higher Education: Concepts and practices*. San Francisco, CA: Jossey-Bass/Wiley.

James, O. (2013) *Office Politics: How to thrive in a world of lying, backstabbing and dirty tricks*. London: Vermillion; Penguin.

Jameson, N. and Chapleau, S. (2011) *Engaging Citizens to Secure our Democracy*. London: Citizens UK.

Jefferys, K. (2012) *Sport and Politics in Modern Britain: The road to 2012*. Basingstoke: Palgrave Macmillan.

Jost, J.T., Banaji, M.R. and Nosek, B.A. (2004) 'A decade of system justification theory: Accumulated evidence of conscious and unconscious bolstering of the status quo'. *Political Psychology*, 25 (6), 881–919.

Kairys , D. (ed.) (1998) *The Politics of Law: A progressive critique*. New York: Basic Books.

Karri, S. (2009) 'Indian politics is a family affair'. *The Guardian*, 13 June. Online. www.theguardian.com/commentisfree/2009/jun/13/india-family-politics (accessed 11 August 2016).

Kathi, P.C. and Cooper, T.L. (2005) 'Neighborhood councils and city agencies: A model of collaborative coproduction'. *National Civic Review*, 94 (1), 43–53.

Keane, J. (2009) *The Life and Death of Democracy*. London: Simon and Schuster.

Keating, A., Kerr, D., Benton, T., Mundy, E. and Lopes, J. (2010) *Citizenship Education in England 2001 to 2010: Young people's practices and prospects for the future: The eighth and final report from the Citizenship Education Longitudinal Study*. Research Report DFE-RR059, London: DfE. Online. www.gov.uk/government/uploads/system/uploads/attachment_data/file/181797/DFE-RR059.pdf (accessed 11 August 2016).

Kelly, C. (2011) *Political Party Finance: Ending the big donor culture, Thirteenth Report of the Committee on Standards in Public Life*. London: The Stationery Office. Online. www.gov.uk/government/publications/thirteenth-report-of-the-committee-on-standards-in-public-life (accessed 17 April 2016).

Kennedy, H. (2006) *Power to the People: An independent inquiry into Britain's democracy*. Online. www.jrrt.org.uk/sites/jrrt.org.uk/files/documents/PowertothePeople_001.pdf (accessed 11 August 2016).

Kennedy, Kerry J., Fairbrother, Gregory and Zhao, Zhenzhou (eds) (2014) *Citizenship Education in China: Preparing citizens for the 'Chinese Century'?* New York: Routledge.

Kennedy, K.J., Fairbrother, G. and Zhao, Z. (eds) (2013) *Citizenship Education in China: Preparing citizens for the Chinese century?* New York: Routledge.

Khan, Salman (2012) *The One World Schoolhouse: Education reimagined*. New York: Twelve/Hachette Book Group.

Kibbe, M.B. (2013) *Rules for Patriots*. Washington, DC: Freedom Works. Online. http://rulesforpatriots.fwsites.org/wp-content/uploads/sites/26/2013/05/028_rules_for_patriots_book.pdf (accessed 11 August 2016).

Kimberlin, S.E. (2010) 'Advocacy by nonprofits: Roles and practices of core advocacy organizations and direct service agencies'. *Journal of Policy Practice*, 9, 164–82.

King, A. and Crewe, I. (2013) *The Blunders of our Governments*. London: Oneworld.

Kleiner, A. (1996) *The Art of Heretics*. London: Nicholas Brealey.

— (2003) *Who Really Matters: The Core Group theory of power, privilege and success*. New York: Currency; Doubleday.

Konadu-Agyemang, K. (2001) *IMF and World Bank Sponsored Structural Adjustment Programs in Africa: Ghana's experience, 1983–1999*. Aldershot: Ashgate.

Kornbluh, P. (1973) 'Chile and the United States: Declassified documents relating to the military coup, September 11, 1973'. National Security Archive Electronic Briefing Book No. 8 http://nsarchive.gwu.edu/NSAEBB/NSAEBB8/nsaebb8i.htm (accessed 29 August 2014).

Krugman, P. (2013) *End this Depression Now!* New York: Norton.

Kuh, G.D. (2007) 'Success in college'. In Lingenfelter, P. (ed.) *More Student Success: A systemic solution.* Boulder, CO: State Higher Education Executive Officers.

Kuznets, S. (1962) 'How to judge quality'. *The New Republic,* 20 October.

Lakoff, G. (2004) *Don't Think of an Elephant: Know your values and frame the debate.* White River Junction, VT: Chelsea Green.

— (2009) *The Political Mind: A cognitive scientist's guide to your brain and its politics.* New York: Penguin.

Lambert, T. (1996) *The Power of Influence: Intensive influencing skills at work.* London: Nicholas Brealey.

Lanier, Jaron (2013) *Who Owns the Future?* London: Penguin.

Lardy, N. (2014) *Markets over Mao: The rise of private business in China.* Washington, DC: Peterson Institute for International Economics.

Larsson, S. and Nordvall, H. (2010) 'Study circles in Sweden: An overview with a bibliography of international literature.' Linköping University Electronic Press. Online. http://liu.diva-portal.org/smash/resultList.jsf?aq=%5B%5B%7B%22f reetext%22%3A%22Study+Circles+in+Sweden%3A+An+Overview+with+a+ Bibliography+of+International+Literature%22%7D%5D%5D&aq2=%5B% 5B%5D%5D&sf=all&aqe=%5B%5D&searchType=RESEARCH&query= &sortOrder=title_sort_asc&onlyFullText=false&noOfRows=50&language=sv &dswid=-2623 (accessed 11 October 2015).

Lasswell, H.D. (1936) *Politics: Who gets what, when, how.* New York: McGraw-Hill (reprinted Meridian World, 1958).

LeBor, A. (2013) *Tower of Basel: The shadowy history of the secret bank that runs the world.* New York: Public Affairs.

Lees-Marshment, J. (2001) *Political Marketing and British Political Parties: The party's just begun.* Manchester: Manchester University Press.

Leithwood, K., Seashore Louis, K., Anderson, S. and Wahlstrom, K. (2004) 'Review of research: How leadership influences student learning'. The Wallace Foundation. Online. www.wallacefoundation.org/knowledge-center/Documents/ How-Leadership-Influences-Student-Learning.pdf (accessed 9 June 2016).

Lenin, V.I. (1914) 'The Taylor System: Man's enslavement by the machine'. *Put Pravdy,* 35, 13 March. In Lenin, V.I. (1972) *Collected Works.* Moscow: Progress Publishers, Vol. 20, 152–4.

— (1920) 'Speech delivered at an all-Russia conference of political education workers of Gubernia and Uyezd Education Departments'. Online. www. marxists.org/archive/lenin/works/1920/nov/03.htm (accessed 11 August 2016).

Leydesdorff, L. (2006) *The Knowledge-Based Economy: Modeled, measured, simulated.* Boca Raton, FL: Universal Publishers.

Lofgren, G., Lumley., T. and O'Boyle, A. (2008) *Critical Masses, Social Campaigning: A guide for donors and funders.* London: New Philanthropy Capital.

Luce, S. (2004) *Fighting for a Living Wage.* Ithaca, NY: Cornell University Press.

Lukes, S. (2005) [1974] *Power: A radical view.* Basingstoke: Palgrave Macmillan.

Lutz, C. (2013) *US and Coalition Casualties in Iraq and Afghanistan.* Watson Institute for International Studies, Brown University. 21 February. Online. http:// watson.brown.edu/costsofwar/files/cow/imce/papers/2013/USandCoalition.pdf (accessed 11 August 2016).

Mail Online (2013) 'Revealed: One in four of the UK's top companies pay no tax while we give THEM millions in credits' by Alex Hawkes and Simon Watkins for *The Mail on Sunday*, 3 March. Online. www.dailymail.co.uk/news/article-2287216/Revealed-One-UKs-companies-pay-tax.html#ixzz3vYoLCxnE (accessed 11 August 2016).

Mair, P. (2013) *Ruling the Void: The hollowing of Western democracy*. London: Verso.

Mallaby, S. (2010). *More Money than God: Hedge funds and the making of a new elite*. London: Penguin.

Mao Tse-tung (1938) 'Problems of War and Strategy: The War History of the Kuomintang' in *Selected Works Vol. II*. Online. www.marxists.org/reference/archive/mao/selected-works/volume-2/mswv2_12.htm (accessed 11 August 2016).

Marshall, S., Ramsay, I.M. and Mitchell, R.J. (eds) (2008) *Varieties of Capitalism, Corporate Governance and Employees*. Melbourne: Melbourne University Press.

Marx, G.T. (1989) *Undercover: Police surveillance in America*. Berkeley, CA: University of California Press.

Marx, K. and Engels, F. [1848] *Manifesto of the Communist Party*. Marxist Internet Archive. Online. www.marxists.org/archive/marx/works/download/pdf/Manifesto.pdf (accessed 11 August 2016).

Mazower, M. (1998) *Dark Continent: Europe's Twentieth Century*. London: Allen Lane.

McAlpine, A. (2000) *The New Machiavelli: The art of politics in business*. New York: Wiley.

McBride, D. (2013) *Power Trip: A decade of policy, plots and spin*. London: Biteback.

McDonald, D. (2013) 'The CEO factory: Ex-McKinsey consultants get hired to run the biggest companies'. *Observer*, 9 October. Online. http://observer.com/2013/09/the-ceo-factory-ex-mckinsey-consultants-get-hired-to-run-the-biggest-companies/ (accessed 9 June 2016).

— (2014) *The Firm: The inside story of McKinsey: the world's most controversial management consultancy*. London: Oneworld.

McGann, J.G. (2015) '2015 global go to think tanks index report'. University of Pennsylvania Think Tanks and Civil Societies Program. Online. http://repository.upenn.edu/do/search/?q=2015%20Global%20Go%20To%20Think%20Tanks%20Index%20Report&start=0&context=1700249 (accessed 9 June 2016).

McGuire, W. (2002) *A Guide to the End of the World: Everything you never wanted to know*. Oxford: Oxford University Press.

McKnight, J. and Kretzmann, J. (1993) *Building Communities from the Inside Out: A path towards finding and mobilizing a community's assets*. Chicago: Asset Based Community Development Institute.

Meadows, D.H. (2009) *Thinking in Systems: A primer*. London: Earthscan.

Merin, C., Nikolov, A. and Vidler, A. (2013) *Local Government Handbook: How to create an innovative city*. Knowledge@Wharton, University of Pennsylvania. Online. http://knowledge.wharton.upenn.edu/article/local-government-handbook-create-innovative-city/ (accessed 25 May 2015).

Mills, C.W. (1956) *The Power Elite*. New York: Oxford University Press.

Mindell, D. (2015) *Our Robots, Ourselves: Robotics and the myths of autonomy.* London: Penguin.

Mjøset, L. (ed.) (2011) *The Nordic Varieties of Capitalism.* Bingley: Emerald.

Moller, J.C. and Watson, K. (1944) *Education in Democracy: The folk high schools of Denmark.* London: Faber and Faber.

Mone, M.A., Baker, D.D. and Jeffries, F. (1995) 'Predictive validity and time dependency of self efficacy, self-esteem, personal goals, and academic performance'. *Educational and Psychological Measurement,* 55 (5), 716–727.

Montgomerie, T. (2015) 'Crosbyisation: Tim Montgomerie responds to criticism from Lynton Crosby, David Cameron's chief election strategist'. The Good Right blog. Online. http://immersive.sh/thegoodright/3gmCW-N_8 (accessed 11 August 2016).

Moore, C. (2015) *Greg Dyke: My part in his downfall: Days and awaydays in BBC News 2001–2004.* London: Universe Press.

Morgan, P. (2005) *The Insider: The private diaries of a scandalous decade.* London: Ebury Press.

Morgan, W. and Strebb, M. (2001) 'Building citizenship: How student voice in service-learning develops civic values'. *Social Science Quarterly,* 82 (1), 154–69.

Mosey, R. (2015) *Getting Out Alive: News, sport and politics at the BBC.* London: Biteback.

Mulgan, G. (2009) *The Art of Public Strategy: Mobilising power and knowledge for the common good.* Oxford: Oxford University Press.

National Audit Office (NAO) Memorandum (2013) 'The role of major contractors in the delivery of public services'. London: National Audit Office. Online. www.nao.org.uk/wp-content/uploads/2013/11/10296-001-BOOK-ES.pdf (accessed 17 April 2016).

Nelson, A.R. and Wei, I.P. (eds) (2012) *The Global University: Past, present, and future perspectives.* Basingstoke: Palgrave Macmillan.

Neshkova, M.I. and Guo, H.D. (2012) 'Public participation and organizational performance: Evidence from state agencies'. *Journal of Public Administration Research and Theory,* 22 (2), 267–88. doi: 10.1093/jopart/mur038

Niikko, A. (2006) 'Finnish daycare: Caring, education and instruction'. In Einarsdottir, J. and Wagner, J.T. (eds) *Nordic Childhoods and Early Education: Philosophy, research, policy and practice in Denmark, Finland, Iceland, Norway, and Sweden.* Greenwich, CT: Information Age Publishing, 141.

Noer, M. (2012) 'One man, one computer, 10 million students: How Khan Academy is reinventing education'. *Forbes,* 19 November. Online. www.forbes.com/sites/michaelnoer/2012/11/02/one-man-one-computer-10-million-students-how-khan-academy-is-reinventing-education/ (accessed 17 August 2015) (requires subscription).

Normington, D. (2014) 'The blunders of our governments'. *Civil Service Quarterly Blog,* 15 July. Online. https://quarterly.blog.gov.uk/2014/07/15/the-blunders-of-our-governments-review-by-sir-david-normington-gcb/ (accessed 25 April 2015).

Norris, P. (2011) *Democratic Deficit: Critical citizens revisited.* New York: Cambridge University Press.

NYT (1988) 'Judge drops murder charges in the Hurricane Carter case'. *The New York Times*, 27 February. Online. www.nytimes.com/1988/02/27/nyregion/judge-drops-murder-charges-in-the-hurricane-carter-case.html (accessed 27 February 2016).

O'Neill, T. and Hymel, G. (1994) *All Politics is Local and Other Rules of the Game*. New York: Times Books; Random House.

Obama, B. (2007) *The Audacity of Hope*. Edinburgh: Canongate.

Office of Tony Blair (2013) *Financial Statements*. Online. www.tonyblairoffice.org/pages/annual-financial-statements/ (accessed 11 August 2016).

Organisation for Economic Co-operation and Development (OECD) (2011) *OECD Better Life Index*. Online. oecdbetterlifeindex.org (accessed 11 August 2016).

— (2014) 'How many young people enter tertiary education?' In *Education at a Glance 2014*, Online. www.oecd.org/edu/Education-at-a-Glance-2014.pdf (accessed 11 August 2016).

Orr M. (ed.) (2007) *Transforming the City: Community organising and the challenge of political change*. Lawrence, KS: University of Kansas Press.

Osborne, D. and Gaebler, T. (1993) *Reinventing Government: How the entrepreneurial spirit is transforming the public sector*. New York: Plume; Penguin.

Outlook India (2010) 'Bookmark: The prof who keeps his shirt on' by Ashish Kumar Sen On, *Outlook India*, 28 June. Online. www.outlookindia.com/article/bookmark-the-prof-who-keeps-his-shirt-on-/265875 (accessed 17 August 2015).

Owen, J. (2007) *Power at Work: The art of making things happen*. Harlow: Pearson Education

Pattberg, P. (2004) 'The institutionalisation of private governance: Conceptualising an emerging trend in global environmental politics'. *Global Governance Working Paper No. 9*. Potsdam, Amsterdam, Berlin, Oldenburg: The Global Governance Project. Online. www.glogov.org/images/doc/WP9.pdf (accessed 11 August 2016).

Patterson, K., Grenny, J., Maxfield, D., McMillan, R. and Switzler, A. (2007) *Influencer: The power to change anything*. New York, London: McGraw-Hill.

Paytas, J., Gradeck, R. and Andrews, L. (2004) *Universities and the Development of Industry Clusters*. Pittsburgh, PA: Center for Economic Development, Carnegie Mellon University.

Pearpoint, J. (1990) *From Behind the Piano: The building of Judith Snow's unique circle of friends*. Toronto: Inclusion Press.

Peters, Thomas J. (2001) 'Tom Peters's True Confessions'. *Fast Company*, 53. Online. www.fastcompany.com/44077/tom-peterss-true-confessions (accessed 11 August 2016).

Peters, J.D. and Simonson, P. (2004) *Mass Communication and American Social Thought: Key texts, 1919–1968*. Lanham, MD: Rowman and Littlefield.

Peters, T.J. and Waterman Jr., R.H. (1982) *In Search of Excellence: Lessons from America's best-run companies*. New York: Harper and Row.

Petersen, M.B., Giessing A. and Nielsen, J. (2015) 'Physiological responses and partisan bias: Beyond self-reported measures of party identification'. *PLoS ONE*, 10 (5), e0126922. doi:10.1371/journal.pone.0126922.

Pettifor, A. (2013) *Just Money: How society can break the despotic power of finance*. London: PRIME.

Plowden Report (1967) *Children and Their Primary Schools*. London: Department of Education and Science, HMSO.

PNAC [Project for the New American Century] (1970) *Project for the New American Century*. See copy at Library of Congress. Online. www.loc.gov/item/lcwa00010308/ (accessed 14 June 2016).

— (2000) *Rebuilding America's Defences*. Online. http://pnac.info/RebuildingAmericasDefenses.pdf (accessed 14 June 2016).

Polanyi, K. (1944) *The Great Transformation*. New York: Farrar and Rinehart.

Porter, M.E. (1998) *On Competition*. Boston: Harvard Business School Press.

Postman, N. and Weingartner, C. (1971) *Teaching As a Subversive Activity*. New York: Bantam Doubleday Dell.

Powercube (2011) Institute of Development Studies. Online. www.powercube.net/ (accessed 11 August 2016).

PR Week (2013) *PR Census 2013*. Online. www.prweek.com/article/1225129/pr-census-2013 (accessed 11 August 2016).

Priest, D.M. and St John, E.P. (eds) (2006) *Privatization and Public Universities*. Bloomington, IN: Indiana University Press.

Pring, R. (1995) *Closing the Gap: Liberal education and vocational preparation*. London: Hodder and Stoughton.

Protess, D. and Warden, R. (1998) *A Promise of Justice*. New York: Hyperion.

Public Administration Select Committee (2012) 'Strategic thinking in government: Without national strategy'. HC 1625, 24 April, p.39. Online. www.publications.parliament.uk/pa/cm201012/cmselect/cmpubadm/1625/1625.pdf (accessed 11 August 2016).

Rajan, R. (2010) *Fault Lines: Hidden fractures still threaten the world economy*. Princeton, NJ: Princeton University Press.

Readings, B. (1996) *The University in Ruins*. Cambridge, MA: Harvard University Press.

Rees, M. (2003) *Our Final Hour: A Scientist's Warning – How terror, error, and environmental disaster threaten humankind's future in this century – on earth and beyond*. New York, NY: Basic Books.

Regan, D. (2002) 'Why are they poor?: Helder camara in pastoral perspective'. *Theologie und Praxis*, 13. Münster: Lit Verlag.

Reischauer, E.O. (1974) *Japan: The story of a nation*. New York: Knopf.

Reisinger, W.M., Miller, A.H., Hesli, V.L. and Maher, K.H. (1994) 'Political values in Russia, Ukraine and Lithuania: Sources and implications for democracy'. *British Journal of Political Science*, 24 (2), 183–223.

Reuters (2015) 'Google lobbying spending reached new high in early 2015' by Diane Bartz, 21 April. Online. www.reuters.com/article/us-google-lobbying-idUSKBN0NC1UO20150421 (accessed 27 December 2015).

Rischard, J.F. (2002) *High Noon: 20 global issues, 20 years to solve them*. London: Perseus Books.

Rittberger, V., Zangl, B. and Kruck, A. (2012) *International Organization*, 2nd ed., Basingstoke: Palgrave.

Robins, Nick (2006) *The Corporation That Changed the World: How the East India Company shaped the modern multinational*. London: Pluto Press.

Rocha, Z. (2000) *Helder, o dom: Uma vida que marcou os rumos da Igreja no Brasil* (Helder, the Gift: A life that marked the course of the church in Brazil). Recife: Editora Vozes.

Rogers, E.M. [1962] (2003) *Diffusion of Innovations*, 5th ed., New York: Simon and Schuster.

Roosevelt, T. (1926) *Social Justice and Popular Rule: Essays, addresses, and public statements relating to the progressive movement (1910–1916)*. New York: Scribner.

Rose, C. (2010) *How to Win Campaigns: Communication for change*, 2nd ed., London: Earthscan.

Rothkopf, D. (2008) *Superclass: The Global Power Elite and the world they are making*. New York: Little, Brown.

— (2012) *Power Inc.: The epic rivalry between big business and government – and the reckoning that lies ahead*. New York: Farrar, Straus and Giroux.

Roubini, N. and Mihm, S. (2010) *Crisis Economics: A crash course in the future of finance*. London: Allen Lane.

Rushton, K. (2014) 'Google: The unelected superpower'. *The Daily Telegraph*, 16 April. Online. www.telegraph.co.uk/finance/newsbysector/mediatechnologyandtelecoms/digital-media/10773901/Google-the-unelected-superpower.html (accessed 11 August 2016).

Russell, B. (1938) *Power: A new social analysis*. New York: Norton.

Sahlberg, P. (2015) *Finnish Lessons 2.0: What can the world learn from educational change in Finland?*, 2nd revised ed., New York: Teachers' College Press.

Sampson, Anthony (2004) *Who Runs This Place? The Anatomy of Britain in the 21st Century*. London: John Murray.

Salamon, L. (2002) 'Explaining nonprofit advocacy: An exploratory analysis'. *Center for Civil Society Studies Working Paper No. 21*. Baltimore, MD: Johns Hopkins University Institute for Policy Studies. Online. http://ccss.jhu.edu/wp-content/uploads/downloads/2011/09/CCSS_WP21_2002.pdf (accessed 11 August 2016).

Salamon, L. and Lessans Geller, S. with Lorentz, S.C. (2008) 'Nonprofit America: A force for democracy?' *Center for Civil Society Studies*. Baltimore, MD: Johns Hopkins University Institute for Policy Studies. Online. http://ccss.jhu.edu/wp-content/uploads/downloads/2011/09/LP_Communique9_2008.pdf

Scammell, M. (2014) *Consumer Democracy: The marketing of politics*. New York: Cambridge University Press.

Schmidt, E. and Cohen, J. (2014) *The New Digital Age: Reshaping the future of people, nations and business*. London: John Murray.

Scholtes, P. (1998) *The Leader's Handbook*. New York: McGraw Hill.

Schumpeter, J. (1942) *Capitalism, Socialism and Democracy*. London: Routledge.

Schwab, K. (2015) 'The fourth industrial revolution: What it means and how to respond'. *Foreign Affairs*, 12 December 2015.

Seddon, J. (2008) *Systems Thinking in the Public Sector*. Axminster: Triarchy Press.

Senge, P. [1990] (2006) *Fifth Discipline: The art and practice of the learning organisation*. New York: Doubleday; Random House Business.

Sharp, G. (2010) [1993] *From Dictatorship to Democracy: A conceptual framework for liberation.* East Boston, MA: Albert Einstein Institution. Originally published in Bangkok by the Committee for the Restoration of Democracy in Burma.

Shirley D. (1997) *Community Organising for Urban School Reform.* Austin, TX: Texas University Press

Shostak, F. (2001) 'What is up with the GDP?' *Mises Institute* blog, 23 August. Online. https://mises.org/library/what-gdp (accessed 14 June 2016).

Shostak, F. (2014) 'Real world economics: An interview with Frank Shostak'. *Mises Institute*, blog, 31 July. Online. https://mises.org/library/real-world-economics-interview-frank-shostak (accessed 14 June 2016).

Simon, H.A. (2000) 'Universal basic income and the flat tax'. *Boston Review*, October–November. Online. http://bostonreview.net/forum/basic-income-all/herbert-simon-ubi-and-flat-tax (accessed 14 June 2016).

Skidmore, P., Bound, K. and Lownsbrough, H. (2006) *Community Participation: Who benefits?* York: Joseph Rowntree Foundation.

Slaughter, S. and Leslie, L. (1999) *Academic Capitalism: Politics, policies, and the entrepreneurial university.* Baltimore, MD: Johns Hopkins University Press.

Smail, D. (2005) *Power, Interest and Psychology.* Ross-on-Wye: PCCS Books.

SMCPC (Social Mobility and Child Poverty Commission) (2014) 'Elitist Britain?' chaired by Alan Milburn. London: Cabinet Office. Online. www.gov.uk/government/uploads/system/uploads/attachment_data/file/347915/Elitist_Britain_-_Final.pdf (accessed 11 August 2016).

Smith, A. [1776, 1904] (1976) *An Inquiry into the Nature and Causes of The Wealth of Nations.* University of Chicago Press. Ed. Edwin Cannan.

Smucker, B. (1999) *The Nonprofit Lobbying Guide*, 2nd ed., Washington, DC: Independent Sector. Online. www.independentsector.org/lobby_guide (accessed 11 August 2016).

Snyder, B.R. (1970) *The Hidden Curriculum.* New York: Knopf.

Solt, F. (2008) 'Economic inequality and democratic political engagement'. *American Journal of Political Science*, 52 (1), 48–60.

Stachawiak, S. (2013) *Pathways for Change: 10 theories to inform advocacy and policy change efforts.* Seattle: Organizational Research. Online. http://orsimpact.com/wp-content/uploads/2013/11/Center_Pathways_FINAL.pdf (accessed 16 April 2016).

Steenblik, R. (2008) *A Subsidy Primer.* Geneva: Global Subsidies Initiative, IISD. Online. www.iisd.org/gsi/sites/default/files/primer.pdf (accessed 11 August 2016).

Stiglitz, J. (2010) *Freefall: Free markets and the sinking of the global economy.* London: Penguin.

Stiglitz, J., Sen, A. and Fitoussi, J-P. (2010) *Mis-measuring Our Lives: Why GDP doesn't add up.* New York: The New Press.

Stiglitz, J. and Bilmes, L. (2008) *The Three Trillion Dollar War.* New York: Norton.

Stoker, G. (2006) *Why Politics Matters: Making democracy work.* Basingstoke: Palgrave Macmillan.

— (2010) 'Democratic renewal: Can political science design solutions?' In Hay, C. (ed.) *New Directions in Political Science.* Basingstoke: Palgrave Macmillan.

Stone, D. and Denham, A. (eds) (2004) *Think Tank Traditions: Policy research and the politics of ideas*. Manchester: Manchester University Press.

Taylor, A. (2014) *The People's Platform: Taking back power and culture in the digital age*. London: Fourth Estate.

Taylor, F. (1911) *Principles of Scientific Management*. New York: Harper and Brothers. Online. www.gutenberg.org/etext/6435 (accessed 11 August 2016).

Temple, J. (2009) 'Salman Khan, math master of the Internet'. SFGate. Online. www.sfgate.com/business/article/Salman-Khan-math-master-of-the-Internet-3278578.php (accessed 17 August 2015).

Tett, G. (2009) *Fool's Gold*. London: Little, Brown; Abacus.

The Guardian (2014) 'Pensions plan sparks slide in shares of annuities providers'. Online. www.theguardian.com/uk-news/2014/mar/19/budget-2014-pensions-plan-sparks-slide-shares-annuities-providers (accessed 14 April 2016).

— (2015) 'FGM affects three times more people in the US than previously thought' by Alexandra Topping. Online. www.theguardian.com/society/2015/feb/05/fgm-numbers-affected-us-women (accessed 14 April 2016).

The International Association of Political Consultants (IAPC) (2016) http://iapc.org/about/history (accessed 5 June 2016).

This is Money (2012) 'Grin and share it: Former PM Tony Blair alleged to have earned up to £80 million since 2007'. Online. www.thisismoney.co.uk/money/celebritymoney/article-2167655/Former-PM-Tony-Blair-alleged-earned-80million-2007.html (accessed 4 October 2014).

Thomson, S. and John, S. (2006) *Public Affairs in Practice: A practical guide to lobbying*. London: Institute of Public Relations; Kogan Page.

Tiffen, R. (2014) *Rupert Murdoch: A reassessment*. Sydney: University of New South Wales Press.

Tilly, C. (2003) *The Politics of Collective Violence*. Cambridge: Cambridge University Press.

Transparency International (2014) *Corruption Perceptions Index 2014*. Berlin: Transparency International. Online. www.transparency.org/whatwedo/publication/cpi2014 (accessed 11 August 2016).

Truman Commission on Higher Education for American Democracy (1948) Chair: George F. Zook. Washington, DC: US Government Print Office, 1947. New York: Harper and Brothers.

Tuchman, Barbara W. (1997) *The March of Folly: From Troy to Vietnam*. London: Abacus.

Tuovinen, J.E. (2008) 'Learning the craft of teaching and learning from world's best practice: The case of Finland'. In McInerney, D.M. and Liem, A.D. (eds) *Teaching and Learning: International best practice*. Charlotte, NC: Information Age Publishing, 51–77.

UNICEF (2013a) 'Female Genital Mutilation/Cutting: A statistical overview and exploration of the dynamics of change'. Online. http://www.data.unicef.org/corecode/uploads/document6/uploaded_pdfs/corecode/FGMC_Lo_res_Final_26.pdf (accessed 11 August 2016).

— (2013b) 'Child Labour and UNICEF in Action: Children at the centre'. Online. www.unicef.org/media/media_70610.html (accessed 11 August 2016).

United Nations Population Fund (UNFPA)-United Nations Children's Emergency Fund (UNICEF) (2013) *Joint Programme on Female Genital Mutilation/Cutting: Accelerating change.* Online. www.unfpa.org/publications/unfpa-unicef-joint-programme-female-genital-mutilationcutting-accelerating-change (accessed 11 August 2016).

US Congressional Budget Office (CBO) (2007) 'Testimony on estimated costs of US operations in Iraq and Afghanistan and of other activities related to the War on Terrorism'. Washington: Congressional Budget Office. Online. www.cbo.gov/publication/19202?index=8690 (accessed 11 August 2016).

US Department of Education (2012) *Advancing Civic Learning and Engagement in Democracy: A road map and call to action.* Washington, DC: Office of the Under Secretary and Office of Postsecondary Education. Online. www.ed.gov/sites/default/files/road-map-call-to-action.pdf (accessed 11 August 2016).

Van Parijs, P. (2000) 'A basic income for all'. *Boston Review*, 1 October. Online. http://bostonreview.net/forum/ubi-van-parijs (accessed 11 August 2016).

Verba, S., Burns, N. and Schlozman, K.L. (2003) 'Unequal at the starting line: Creating participatory inequalities across generations and among groups'. *The American Sociologist*, 34, 45–69.

Verba, S., Burns, N. and Schlozman, K.L. (2005) 'Family ties: Understanding the intergenerational transmission of political participation'. In Zuckerman, A.S. (ed.) *The Social Logic of Politics: Personal networks as contexts for political behavior.* Philadelphia, PA: Temple University Press, 95–113.

Vidyarthi, V. and Wilson, P.A. (2008) *Development from Within: Facilitating collective reflection for sustainable change.* Herndon, VA: Apex Foundation.

von Clausewitz, Carl (1832) *On War.* Princeton, NJ: Princeton University Press.

Wang, X. (2002) 'Assessing administrative accountability results from a national survey'. *The American Review of Public Administration,* doi: 10.1177/0275074002032003005.

Wang, X. and Wan Wart, M. (2007) 'When public participation in administration leads to trust: An empirical assessment of managers' perceptions'. *Public Administration Review,* 67, 265–78.

Waring, M. (1989) *If Women Counted: A new feminist economics.* London: Macmillan.

Warren, M.A. (1985) *Gendercide: The implications of sex selection.* Lanham, MD: Rowman and Littlefield.

Warren M.R., Mapp, K.L. and the Community Organizing and School Reform Project (2011) *A Match on Dry Grass.* Oxford: Oxford University Press.

Wasby, S.L. (1966) 'The impact of the family on politics: An essay and review of the literature'. *The Family Life Coordinator*, 15 (1), 3–24.

Washington Post, The (2014) 'Google, once disdainful of lobbying, now a master of Washington influence' by Tom Hamburger and Matea Gold. 12 April. Online. www.washingtonpost.com/politics/how-google-is-transforming-power-and-politicsgoogle-once-disdainful-of-lobbying-now-a-master-of-washington-influence/2014/04/12/51648b92-b4d3-11e3-8cb6-284052554d74_story.html (accessed 27 December 2015).

Watkins, M.D. (2013) [2003] *The First 90 Days: Proven strategies for getting up to speed faster and smarter.* Boston: Harvard Business Review Press.

Watson, T. and Hickman, M. (2012) *Dial M for Murdoch: News Corporation and the corruption of Britain*. London: Penguin.

Weber, M. (1922) *Wirtschaft und Gesellschaft*. Tübingen: Mohr.

Wells, H.G. (1920) *The Outline of History: Being a plain history of life and mankind*. Garden City, NY: Garden City Publishing. Online. www.pdfarchive. info/pdf/W/We/Wells_Herbert_George_-_The_Outline_of_History.pdf (accessed 11 August 2016).

White, T.J. (ed.) (2013) *Lessons from the Northern Ireland Peace Process*. Madison, WI: University of Wisconsin Press.

World Health Organization (WHO) (2004) *World report on road traffic injury prevention*. Geneva: World Health Organization.

— (2013) 'Global and regional estimates of violence against women: Prevalence and health effects of intimate partner violence and non-partner sexual violence'. Geneva: World Health Organization. Online. www.who.int/reproductivehealth/ publications/violence/9789241564625/en/ (accessed 11 August 2016).

Williams, M. (2009) 'Speech made to the UK conference of road safety partnerships, Manchester'. Online. www.brake.org.uk/what-s-happening/10-take-action/613-speech-by-brakes-ce-mary-williams-201009 (accessed 11 August 2016).

Wilks, S. (2013) *The Political Power of the Business Corporation*. Cheltenham: Edward Elgar.

Wilks-Heeg, S. and Crone, S. (2007) *Funding Political Parties in Great Britain: A pathway to reform*. London: Democratic Audit.

Williamson, E. (2012) 'Two ways to play the "Alinsky" Card'. *Wall Street Journal*, 23 January. Online. www.wsj.com/articles/SB1000142405297020462420457717 77272926154002 (accessed 12 May 2015).

Woetzel, J., Madgavkar, A., Ellingrud, K., Labaye, E., Devillard, S., Kutcher, E., Manyika, J., Dobbs, R. and Krishnan, M. (2015) *The Power Of Parity: How advancing women's equality can add $12 trillion to global growth*. McKinsey Global Institute.

Wolf, M. (2015) *The Shifts and the Shocks: What we've learned – and have still to learn – from the financial crisis*. London: Penguin.

Woodin, T. (2012) 'Co-operative education in the nineteenth and early twentieth centuries: Context, identity and learning'. In Webster A., Brown A., Stewart D., Walton J.K. and Shaw L. (eds) *The Hidden Alternative: Co-operative values past, present and future*. Manchester: Manchester University Press, 78–95.

World Bank (2000) *Higher Education in Developing Countries: Peril and promise*. Washington, DC: World Bank. Online. http://siteresources.worldbank.org/ EDUCATION/Resources/278200-1099079877269/547664-1099079956815/ peril_promise_en.pdf (accessed 11 August 2016).

— (2016) *Doing Business 2016: Going beyond efficiency*. Washington, DC: World Bank. Online. www.doingbusiness.org/

World Trade Organization (WTO) (2006) *World Trade Report 2006: Subsidies, trade and the WTO*. Geneva: World Trade Organization. Online. www.wto.org/ english/res_e/publications_e/wtr06_e.htm (accessed 11 August 2016).

Yang, K. (2005) 'Public administrators' trust in citizens: A missing link in citizen involvement efforts'. *Public Administration Review*, 65 (3), 273–85.

— (2013) 'The million-dollar question of instrumental benefits: Are participatory governments more efficient, effective and equitable?' Paper presented at the 20th Madison Research Conference, Madison, WI, June.

Yang, K. and Callahan, K. (2007) 'Citizen involvement efforts and bureaucratic responsiveness: Participatory values, stakeholder pressures, and administrative practicality'. *Public Administration Review,* 67 (2), 249–64.

Yates, M. and Youniss, J. (1996) 'A developmental perspective on community service in adolescence'. *Social Development,* 5 (1), 85–111.

Yoon, R. (2013) 'First on CNN: Bill Clinton's $106 million speech circuit windfall'. CNN Politics. Online. http://politicalticker.blogs.cnn.com/2013/05/23/first-on-cnn-bill-clintons-106-million-speech-circuit-windfall/ (accessed 4 October 2014).

Young, J.R. (2010) 'College 2.0: A self-appointed teacher runs a one-man "academy" on YouTube'. *The Chronicle of Higher Education.* Online. http://chronicle.com/article/College-20-A-Self-Appointed/65793 (accessed 11 August 2016).

Zetter, L. (2014) [2008] *Lobbying: The art of political persuasion*, 3rd revised ed., Petersfield: Harriman House.

Zimmerman, M.A., Israel, B.A., Schulz, A.J., and Checkoway, B. (1992) 'Further exploration in empowerment theory: An empirical analysis of psychological empowerment'. *American Journal of Community Psychology,* 20 (6), 707–27.

Zimmerman, M.A., Ramirez-Valles, J. and Maton, K.I. (1999) 'Resilience among urban African American male adolescents: A study of the protective effects of sociopolitical control on their mental health'. *American Journal of Community Psychology,* 27 (6), 733–51.

Index

Index